26/11

MUMBAI ATTACKED

OTHER LOTUS TITLES

FORTHCOMING TITLES

26/11

MUMBAI ATTACKED

Edited by HARINDER BAWEJA

Ashish Khetan

Bachi Karkaria

Chris Khetan

George Koshy

Harinder Baweja

Harsh Joshi

Julio Ribeiro

Rahul Shivshankar

LOTUS COLLECTION
•
ROLI BOOKS

Lotus Collection

© 2009: Authors for their respective pieces
Ashish Khetan | Bachi Karkaria | Chris Khetan | George Koshy
Harinder Baweja | Harsh Joshi | Julio Ribeiro | Rahul
Shivshankar

First published in 2009
The Lotus Collection
An imprint of
Roli Books Pvt. Ltd.
M-75, G.K. II Market, New Delhi 110 048
Phones: ++91 (011) 40682000
Fax: ++91 (011) 2921 7185
E-mail: info@rolibooks.com
Website: www.rolibooks.com
Also at Bangalore, Chennai, Jaipur, Kolkata, Mumbai 8 Varanasi

Photo credits: Front cover: Michael Rubenstein; Back Cover: AP
Photo, David Guttenfelder; Map: Ashish Naorem; page viii: Crime
Branch, Mumbai Police

Cover Design: Supriya Saran
Layout: Naresh L Mondal

ISBN: 978-81-7436-707-5

Typeset in Utopia by Roli Books Pvt. Ltd.
and printed at Saurabh Printers.

In Memoriam

National Security Guard
Major Sandeep Unnikrishnan
Havildar Gajendra Singh

Mumbai Police
Joint Commissioner (ATS) Hemant Karkare
Additional Commissioner Ashoke Kamte
Inspector Vijay Salaskar
Sub-Inspector Bapusaheb Durgude
Sub-Inspector Prakash More
Assistant Sub-Inspector Balasaheb Bhosle
Assistant Sub-Inspector Tukaram Gopal Omble
Constable Ambadas Pawar
Constable Arun Chitte
Constable Jaywant Patil
Constable Vijay Khandekar
Constable Yogesh Patil

Other Security Personnel
Inspector Shashank Shinde (Railway Police)
Head Constable M.C. Chowdhary (Railway Protection Force)
Home Guard Constable Mukesh Jadhav
Constable Rahul Shinde (State Reserve Police Force)

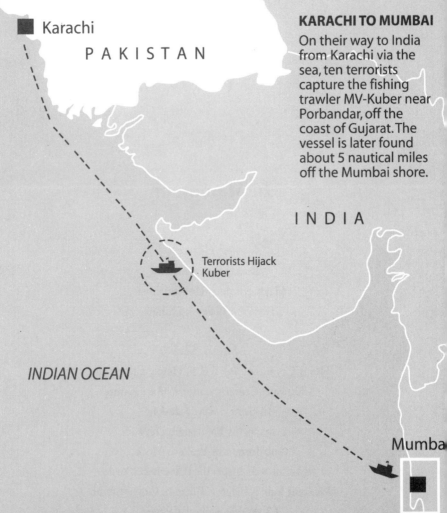

Karachi

P A K I S T A N

KARACHI TO MUMBAI
On their way to India from Karachi via the sea, ten terrorists capture the fishing trawler MV-Kuber near Porbandar, off the coast of Gujarat. The vessel is later found about 5 nautical miles off the Mumbai shore.

I N D I A

Terrorists Hijack Kuber

INDIAN OCEAN

Mumba

TERROR'S TRAIL

20:20: On 26 November, 2008, the terrorists come ashore in an inflatable speedboat at Badhwar Park jetty, Cuffe Parade, and split into five pairs.

21:40: Team-1 armed with AK-47 rifles enters the passenger hall of CST, opens fire and throws grenades, killing many people.

22:50: They flee from there into a lane, past the Times of India and BMC buildings, firing continuously, and reach Cama Hospital. They kill the guards and go up to take hostages but get into an encounter with the police for nearly an hour.

23:50: Three senior police officers reach the hospital and attack the fleeing terrorists. More firing ensues in which Joint Commissioner (ATS) Hemant Karkare, Inspector Vijay Salaskar, Addl CP Ashok Kamte and four policemen are fatally wounded. The terrorists dump their bodies and escape in the police vehicle.

23:55: More firing in front of GT Hospital and Metro Cinema.

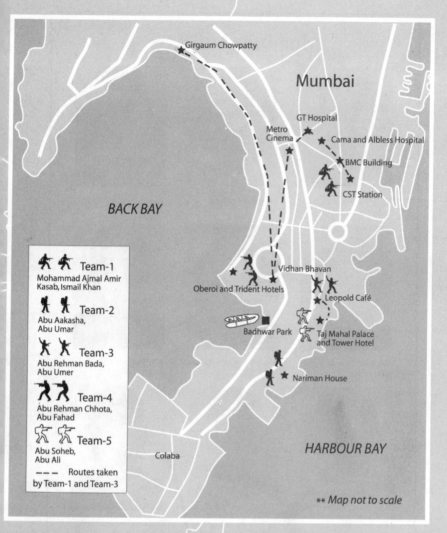

BACK BAY

Girgaum Chowpatty

Mumbai

GT Hospital

Metro
Cinema

Cama and Albless Hospital

BMC Building

CST Station

Vidhan Bhavan

Oberoi and Trident Hotels

Leopold Café

Badhwar Park

Taj Mahal Palace
and Tower Hotel

Nariman House

HARBOUR BAY

Colaba

** Map not to scale

 Team-1
Mohammad Ajmal Amir
Kasab, Ismail Khan

 Team-2
Abu Aakasha,
Abu Umar

 Team-3
Abu Rehman Bada,
Abu Umer

 Team-4
Abu Rehman Chhota,
Abu Fahad

 Team-5
Abu Soheb,
Abu Ali

— — Routes taken
by Team-1 and Team-3

00:00 – 00:15: They change their vehicle from the police SUV to a hijacked silver Skoda at Vidhan Bhavan. They then speed towards Girgaum Chowpatty.

00:30: Both terrorists are shot at by the police at Chowpatty. One of them, Ismail, dies while Kasab is captured alive.

21:40: Team-2 enters Chabad (or Nariman) House and takes the residents hostage.

21:38: Team-5 enters the new Taj hotel from the main lobby and opens fire.

21:40: Team-3 enters Leopold Café and starts firing indiscriminately.

21:43: Then Team-3 also breaks into the old Taj hotel from the south side.

21:50: Team-4 enters the Trident hotel and starts firing. Within minutes, they cross over to the Oberoi hotel and spray bullets into the restaurants.

Mumbai's Attackers

Abu Rehman Chhota alias Abdul Rehman

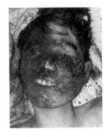

Abu Ali alias Javed

Abu Soheb alias Shoaib

Abu Rehman Bada alias Hafiz Arshad

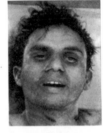

Abu Fahad alias Fahadullah

Abu Ismail alias Ismail Khan

Abu Umar alias Nasir

Abu Aakasha alias Babar Imran

Abu Umer alias Nazeer

Mohammad Ajmal Amir Kasab

Contents

Editor's Note

The book is an attempt at understanding the enormity of Mumbai 26/11. India has seen serious assaults on its democratic institutions – including on the Red Fort and its Parliament – but 26/11 was vastly different in both its intent and its intensity.

The ten-member *fidayeen* squad that sneaked in via the sea route from Karachi, all the way to Mumbai was distinctly different from any other. Mumbai's attackers had clearly been trained well; the conspiracy had been in the making for close to a year; ten of the thirty-two who had been trained were handpicked for Mission Mumbai and the planning was as detailed as it was lethal.

Several chapters in the book take a long, hard, even despairing look at how terror unfolded, step by step for over sixty long hours as India was held hostage. The chapters contain hitherto unpublished information on how the operation was planned and executed. Well-known journalists Ashish Khetan and Rahul Shivshankar have painstakingly reconstructed the horror at the three main target sites: hotels Taj and Oberoi and Nariman House and all three chapters give crucial insights into the terrorists' modus operandi, hair-raising conversations between the attackers and their handlers in Pakistan and the fight back – the almost impossible manner in which the National Security Guards got down to the task of pinning the terrorists down, even as they groped in the dark without too much help from other agencies who had begun intercepting the calls being made between Mumbai and Pakistan.

The book also details the intelligence failures, critical failures that are in urgent need of redress. Another chapter tracks the story back to Muridke, the infamous address just outside Lahore, where the Lashkar-e-Toiba is headquartered and where Ajmal Kasab, the lone surviving terrorist was trained for the Mumbai attack.

For gripping first hand accounts from hostages who survived near-death, and for insights into Mumbai's sociology and psychology, read Harsh Joshi, George Koshy and Bachi Karkaria.

The book takes a full 360 degree look at 26/11 and while Chris Khetan pays rich tribute through accounts of meetings with the wives of the slain policemen in Mumbai, it delves deep into each and every aspect of the attack – its planning, its execution and the investigation. Importantly, it casts a critical eye at the future and includes chapters on why India will be hit again and how the country ought to deal with the ever-pervading threat of terror. Julio Ribeiro, well-known police officer who has earned his spurs dealing with terror outlines the way forward.

A must read book that has been carefully put together by a very able team of editors at Roli Books – Priya Kapoor, Nandita Bhardwaj, Neelam Narula, Richa Burman and Simar Puneet.

'They kept the soldier's promise ...'

Bravehearts

Chris Khetan

Death visits everyone. It's the only certainty. Life isn't certain and therefore must be treasured and guarded, zealously. That's the basis for every decision that human beings take, for themselves and those around them. But then there are those who are dangerously deluded, thinking they are ordained by the 'will of God' to take precious life. They call themselves 'jehadis' or 'holy warriors'. On the night of 26 November 2008 Mumbai was attacked by ten such warriors of death. On their target were unarmed civilians, some waiting to catch a train back home after a long day at work, some sharing a meal with loved ones and friends at a restaurant, some tourists and some business folk. Innocent people going about their business of life. The job to stop these religious madmen, these harbingers of destruction, fell upon the Indian security personnel – initially the Mumbai police and later the NSG – sworn to protect the citizens of this country. The three-day long gun-battle saw India lose eighteen of its security personnel – sixteen policemen and two NSG commandos.

Following are the stories of four such brave men: Joint Commissioner (ATS) Hemant Karkare, Additional Commissioner Ashok Kamte, Assistant Sub-Inspector Tukaram Omble, and Constable Jaywant Patil, who died that night making good the vow they took when they were sworn in – the one they made to their team-mates and to themselves. To go down fighting like Kamte said he would, or to lead from the front like Karkare did, or rise to the occasion like Omble did, and finally, be the inspiring policeman that Patil was.

Tragically, what they left behind are families for whom the reality of their loss would stay on even after the bugles of the last farewell are sounded, after news of that night is relegated to the insides of the newspaper, the TV debates that highlight other issues and the awards begin to gather their first specks of dust.

These women, wives and mothers, will forever take their pain with a measure of pride knowing that their men died like warriors. They will cry silent tears, for the years gone by and the ones that would have followed. The following stories are of these men and their women, India's bravehearts, who lost their lives in this fight against a deadly enemy, sacrificing their future for ours.

'He was happy with himself and at peace with his surrounding.'
Kavita Karkare, wife of Joint Commissioner (ATS) Hemant Karkare

Behind every brave cop is a wife, braver still. When Hemant chucked the cushy corporate job that came with a house in breezy Juhu, among other perks, to become a public-serving policeman, she encouraged him. When the punishing routine of the police academy kept him away from his infant daughter, Jui, she doubled up as both mother and father. She had to repeat the act with her second daughter, Sayali as well as the youngest, son Akash. When the stipend of a rookie cop went solely towards the crisp khaki of his uniform, she kept her bank job to make ends meet. When serving for India's external intelligence agency – the Research and Analysis Wing (RAW) – in Austria kept him away for a period of five years, she stayed back and settled for the occasional visit so the children's education would not be disrupted. Finally, when he bucked lucrative and more importantly, safe, private sector offers and even an international mission in favour of the position of Maharashtra's Anti-Terrorism Squad chief, Kavita bit down.

She reminisces over the decision now, 'When he took the ATS job, I had a sixth sense that something would go wrong. Even then I tried to tell him to apply for a job with the UN.'

In her early fifties, Kavita is tall, well-built, her shoulder-length hair wiry and raven black. The recent stress has given her eyes a dispassionate quality, her strong face barely registering any emotion. And she's restless, flitting about as if trying to dislodge the thoughts in her head. The dust of the last few weeks is beginning to settle, the byte-hungry media is calling less often, and the stream of well-wishers has thinned gradually. She's alone with her thoughts now, her daughters have returned to the West – Jui to her husband and Sayali to her studies. The weight of her loss bears down on her with every new day, for the loss of Hemant, for the life they led together and the life she was looking forward to share with him. Thinking about the solitude awaiting her, she says, 'I am fifty-plus and at this age I really need my husband, it's not like my kids are small any more.'

Kavita met Hemant nearly thirty years ago at a personality development class he was conducting, which she was attending. At the end of the ten-day course, they realized their attraction towards each other. She rolls back the years and the associated memories but says succinctly, 'I liked the person I saw, I admired the way he dedicated himself; he was very hard-working.'

They married before long and Kavita saw Hemant quit his nine to five job, take up a police career and excel at it just like he had with everything he had done till then. He had many stints; as Kavita tries to remember them all she lists Busaawal, Nanded, Akola, Thane, Bhiwandi and Mumbai, including the Vienna spell. Wasn't it hard for her as a wife and mother to get uprooted every time and to start over? 'Not really. He was such a perfectionist that he would get everything arranged for me, from the house to where the cabinets and their contents would go,' she responds stolidly. Theirs was an uncomplicated marriage; she gave him the space he desired to do his job and be the person he wanted to be. Their lives were simple much like the backgrounds they came from.

Hemant's was a typical middle-class Maharashtrian family. The only difference was that they were relatively more cosmopolitan since the head of the family, Kamlakar Karkare was posted in the railways and his postings took the family all around Maharashtra. His mother Kumudini was a professor, and so the environment that Hemant and his three siblings grew in was largely academic. It was something Hemant, the eldest, thrived on. From an early age, he loved books. He devoured anything on economics, sciences and even mythology. His brother Shirish, younger by just two years, remembers, 'Aaji (their mother) would ask Hemant to sit next to her and recite the stories of mythology to all of us. And Hemant would do so word for word like it was in the holy texts.'

When the Karkares put Hemant in school, he came home later that day, bored – simply because he knew everything the teacher had introduced in class. And so he was given a 'double-promotion' and moved to a class ahead after passing a test. This was a matter of great pride, especially in those days. This was how Hemant fared through his entire academic career: always topping his class, standing first in the fourth standard in all of Wardha, the go-to guy for his classmates and his siblings, whenever they were stumped for an answer to a math problem. Shirish remembers an instance when he was particularly baffled over a vexing trigonometry question. He had been trying in vain to draw the attention of Hemant who was sleeping nearby. And then, quite abruptly, Hemant woke up, just long enough to solve the problem for his younger brother, and quietly went back to bed.

Hemant was good in languages and managed a smattering of Gujarati and Bengali, while being fluent in Marathi, Hindi and English. His favourite works were by the distinguished Marathi writer, P.L. Deshpande and the English playwright and novelist, Somerset Maugham. Even in recent times, he would travel around in his car with the two reading lights in the back focused on the book before him; there were always some books in the car Hemant travelled in.

With all these interests, Shirish remembers that their mother would sometimes be a bit alarmed when she didn't see Hemant plugging away before an exam. He would reassure her by saying, 'If anyone pays enough attention in class, they would have grasped all there is to know.' In school, teachers considered Hemant brilliant. He eventually graduated in mechanical engineering. But Shirish also remembers his brother's artistic disposition. If you walk into the Karkare residence, you will see corners adorned with works of wooden sculpture.

During a stint in the Chandrapur forests near Nagpur in 1991, Hemant took interest in driftwood, discovered artistic shapes in them and converted them into wooden sculptures. The carefully chosen pieces display an artistic sense generally uncommon among policemen. In fact, so fastidious was he about aesthetics that it was he who always selected the décor of the house and would come to know even if a single item had been disturbed in some remote corner of the house.

Hemant's scholarly and artistic accomplishments aside, he was extremely humble, always stressing on to his siblings, who adored him that a man's internal virtues were of far more relevance than what he projected on the outside. He was soft-spoken, believing that one never got much done by being loud and arrogant. Similarly, with his men in the force, he was gentle but firm.

On 22 January 2008, following his return to the state cadre, after serving in Vienna, Austria, Hemant was appointed the joint commissioner of police in the Maharashtra Anti-Terrorism Squad.

Being a man with an academic bent of mind, he had studied enough on terrorism and with the requisite police experience, he was the man to head a department set up to deal with it. Concerned with the well-being of his policemen, he also took on the dual responsibility of police welfare. To improve their conditions he started yoga classes for his men and even desired more family time for them. For police events, he enlisted his men to enact dramas like 'Agnishikha' and 'Mahapatra'.

And yet, even though he was happy to be back in Mumbai, this was his last and most tormenting stint. Hemant's team – the ATS – had cracked the 29 September 2008 Malegaon bomb blast case, and had arrested Hindu extremists in a breakthrough that shocked the entire nation and added a new dimension to the subject of terror and Hindutava politics in India. But the case got caught in a political circus and the ATS was accused of targeting the Hindu nationalist brigade. These were trying times for Hemant and for the family as well. But Hemant shrugged that off. As was his nature, he led by example, with discipline, honesty and from the front. That was how Kavita and her children lost the most precious person in their lives, their Chief. He suffered three bullet injuries in his chest as he charged at the terrorists outside Cama and Albless Hospital on the fateful night of 26 November 2008.

Even as the news of his death flashed on television, Kavita did not believe it. Days later, while trying to make sense of his death, she describes Hemant in the simplest of Marathi terms, 'He was *satchit anand.*' It means he didn't derive his happiness from any external factor, he was happy within himself and at peace with his surroundings. Apparently simplistic, this is an elusive quality for any individual. Even more so for the two sets of fanatics from opposite camps who Hemant had to deal with – the first who called him a traitor to his own religion and the second who invaded his city that night.

[Joint Commissioner (ATS) Hemant Karkare was honoured with the Ashok Chakra, posthumously.]

'At 11.28 p.m. when I spoke to him, Arjun wanted to remind his dad to wear his bulletproof jacket ... '
Vinita Kamte, wife of Additional Commissioner Ashok Kamte

He used to tell his wife Vinita, 'I get paid to pursue my passion.' On the night of 26 November 2008, his passion exacted its price. Ashok Kamte, the Additional Commissioner of Mumbai police for the East region, died fighting terrorists outside the Cama and Albless Hospital, in a narrow lane opposite the CST (Chhatrapati Shivaji Terminus) station. Four bullets had pierced his body, including the two bullets that went through the embroidered IPS logo of his police cap. Twenty years ago, when asked to state his preference in the Union Public Service Commission exam, he had listed IPS as his only option. Such was Ashok's love for the police force.

But it's not just the image of a tough police officer that defined Ashok. There are other images as well. The ardent suitor who proposed to Vinita only the second time they met; the loving father of their two kids, fifteen-year-old Rahul and eight-year-old Arjun; the devout man who prayed every night for his loved ones; the provider who secured his family's future by taking out life insurance policies and most importantly, the love of Vinita's life.

Despite being content and grateful, a thought would often strike Vinita. Her life with Ashok was too perfect to be true. Things were picture perfect. The Kamte house is located in a quiet neighbourhood in Pune and is surrounded by a well-tended garden. A porch opens into a small sitting area. Past that is a large drawing room where the family would spend their weekends when Ashok would come home from his posting in Chembur, Mumbai. The bar is in another corner of the drawing room, where Ashok would sip his evening drink on his off days or entertain. The furniture is practical, as there are two growing boys and four frisky dogs – two sand-coloured labradors and two prized basset hounds – in the house. Knickknacks collected over the years dot the entire room.

A mounted shelf in a corner holds books on guns, war and terrorism. It also holds two framed black and white pictures, one conspicuous for the man in the photograph, Prime Minster Jawaharlal Nehru seated at a dining table with a knowing smile on his face and next to him standing, addressing the crowd at the table is Ashok's grandfather, N.M. Kamte – the first inspector-general of police, Maharashtra. On another wall, high up, are earned medals, framed and displayed prominently. The only recent addition to the room is the carved wooden coffee table that holds a large frame with Ashok's photograph, a garland of sandalwood shavings and incense sticks are arranged around it. Massive trophies and plaques in glasscases in memorium are placed on the floor.

Vinita arrives, petite and unpretentious in her printed kurta and blue jeans teamed with a stole draped over her shoulders. Her face does not betray her loss or the trauma of the last few weeks. She apologizes for being late, having spent the last few minutes trying to console another policeman's wife over the phone. She has to keep it going for Rahul, Arjun, her in-laws – Ashok's sister in particular whom she is close to – and her own parents who loved Ashok. She says, 'If I break down, all of this is going to come crashing down; I know I just have to keep going.'

She talks about Ashok, remembering the time she shared with him, details about him that she often mulls over. His life pours out through her words. Ashok was born in Dehradun to Prem and Colonel Maruti Rao Kamte. He spent much of his school years in boarding schools in Rajkot and Kodaikanal and then in a hostel while earning a Bachelor of Arts degree from St Xavier's College, Mumbai, and post-graduation from St Stephen's College, Delhi. 'He loved history, and he had a great memory, he remembered dates and places.' Ashok was a resolute sportsman, participating in shotput, athletics and weightlifting. So ingrained was the habit of physical activity that he was billed as being one of the fittest police officers in India. He always read the newspaper back to front, sports being foremost on his mind. Vinita says, 'Even if we had guests over, if Ashok hadn't got his workout for the day, he would excuse himself and head out for an hour or more. He had to work out everyday.' Even in the force he stood out: though an average five-feet-ten, he looked taller than most with his broad forty-four inch shoulders and unlike most Indian frames, was well-built on the legs as well. 'In the house he always lounged around in shorts. He'd fool around with the boys and ask them if they had ever seen anyone with calves like his,' Vinita smiles at the memory.

Her mother and Ashok's father were their matchmakers. So when the couple headed out on their first date, Ashok asked her if she wanted to get married. Unsure if the question was generic or personal, she answered vaguely that she would like to sometime in the future. The matter was soon sorted out because four days later the couple was engaged and married within six months. What followed were years of postings in communally sensitive places, with Vinita following him, staying back only when she was pregnant or more recently to avoid disrupting the boys' schooling. Yet Vinita didn't have any complaints, maintaining that Ashok had struck a perfect balance between family and work. 'He was there whenever we needed him; he was a wonderful son, husband and father. He wasn't very active socially, work and family were all he ever wanted.' Ashok was very conscious of the home that Vinita had made for him and the boys, often marvelling at the love and care that she heaped upon Rahul and Arjun. Vinita looks wistful when asked about Ashok the police officer. Even though he expressed his intention that his sons join the army or the foreign service, she believes he would have been secretly pleased if either one was to opt for the police force.

She explains that he never had any political affiliations. She calls him 'every citizen's policeman – brave, professional, fair and just'. She talks of the time in Solapur when his beating up of a goon MLA aroused the passions of the citizens to such an extent that they put up hoardings of him and threatened to immolate themselves if he were transferred by any political party. Among these people he was accorded idol status, with people reaching out to touch him like he was some dashing film star. She makes a special mention of his human management skills, describing his fantastic leadership qualities. He encouraged his men to take exams to improve their professional standing or even told them off if he got wind that any of his men had been rough with their wives.

He liked to stand shoulder to shoulder with his deputies and constables. Vinita narrates an incident when Ashok had just been posted to Solapur, he was faced with a huge mob of 5,000 people who were armed with rudimentary weapons like chilli powder and knives. With just fifteen policemen he knew he had to do something drastic to stop them from progressing and wrecking havoc. So he told his men that he would attack the man who was leading the charge. Ashok dealt the mob's leader a blow with his lathi. The moment the leader was down, the rest of the crowd fled and Ashok's men took care of the rest. Vinita believes his take on people who were breaking the law was simple, 'act first, question later'; he didn't care to be easy with lawbreakers, he felt a policeman's job was simply to police. This was particularly helpful when dealing with mobs, which was why he was always called on to handle situations like these.

On the fateful day the last time Vinita spoke to her husband was at 11.28 p.m. when he was in the Cama Hospital lane. She had called because Arjun wanted to remind his father to wear a bulletproof vest. The next time she tried, that is, at 1 a.m., the phone just kept ringing. And minutes later when she turned on the TV and saw the 'breaking news scroll' list Ashok among the dead, she refused to believe it. She fought the sickening dread as it spread inside her and threatened to engulf her, knowing that something had gone terribly wrong. She didn't want to call anyone; that would only confirm the sickening truth. It also saddens her that the police misled her about the circumstances of her husband's death. It was Ashok who had shot Mohammad Ajmal Kasab but the Mumbai police never gave him credit for his heroic act.

Holding back her tears, Vinita says, 'I knew in my heart what had happened, one, from the determination of the terrorists and Ashok's own way of taking challenges head-on. He always used to say he'd go down fighting.' That was Ashok, who kept his soldier's promise.

[Additional Commissioner Ashok Kamte was honoured with the Ashok Chakra, posthumously.]

'Amongst us four sisters, he always said he was a brother we never had.'
Vaishali Omble, daughter of ASI Tukaram Omble

His one selfless, unflinching act on the witching hour of 26 November has forever immortalized Assistant Sub-Inspector Tukaram Omble. After dutifully serving Mumbai police for the last thirty-one years, Omble had just been promoted to the rank of assistant sub-inspector and was to retire from the same position in four years. While his brothers never rose above being contract labourers, he was grateful for the life he had with a police job, loving wife, four daughters and government accommodation. He had reached the pinnacle of his police career. Now he was entitled to ride pillion on the police patrol bike, with a walky-talky in one hand and a lathi in the other. If he wanted, he could order around the other constables but his new status did not bring about any change in him. If a head constable had taken the motorbike, he would still patrol his assigned area on foot. If other police constables worked twelve hours a day, he would clock fourteen. When his colleague wanted to catch a nap at night, he would willingly stay up, and if asked to sweep the station house, he would pick up a broom and unflinchingly do the job. He never offended anyone, never picked a fight and never grumbled; whatever the task, he would do it without questioning or complaining.

On 26 November, a constable on beat number 4 which covers Girgaum Chowpatty, was on leave. Omble was told to fill in and he promptly did. Even as Omble and the others were carrying out orders to evacuate the beach, they could clearly hear gunshots and grenade explosions coming from the Trident-Oberoi hotels, hardly a few kilometres down the road. It wasn't until a couple of hours later that the cops saw a silver Skoda car speeding towards them. In the midst of the firing that ensued, Omble with a lathi in his hand walked up to the car while the other policemen hesitated, staying a few paces behind. Omble had never shirked any responsibility. If others were too tired to count the rounds of fire while making the inventory at the end of the day, he would do it. With the same spirit, fifty-four-year old Omble; dutiful and compliant cop, sole breadwinner of his family and loving father, went ahead and opened the car door. A remarkable act of courage.

An ordinary man, some would say, and yet Omble's life was extraordinary in its own way even before the attacks, as his family will tell anyone who cares to know.

Upfront in the Omble home, is a tiny living room that now resembles a sanctum sanctorum with numerous trophies and plaques that honour the man who once lived here. A massive picture frame of Tukaram Omble, garlanded and surrounded by incense sticks, sits atop a makeshift altar which has been fashioned out of a coffee table.

Omble was father to four daughters, the elder two – Pavitra and Vandana – are married while the younger two – Vaishali and Bharti

– are still studying. Vaishali, twenty-two, who also tutors children at home, has taken over the role of interacting with well wishers and journalists, dispensing precious details about her father. She even took it upon herself to find out the circumstances behind Omble's death. 'Why was my father the only person to reach Kasab and stop him, why didn't the others pitch in,' she queries pointing to colour printouts of CCTV grabs that have been spirally bound into a book. She has other data on the subject, including newspaper articles that have been laminated and stapled together and elaborate media reports on the final minutes preceding Omble's death at Girgaum Chowpatty. She intends writing a book on her father.

Omble's wife, Tara, sari pallu drawn over her shoulders, is a typical Maharashtrian woman, grieving for her husband in the time-honoured ways of her community, discreetly and reverentially. She entrusts the job of interacting with people to her daughter Vaishali and Omble's closest friend, another cop, Ashok Pathak before retreating into her solitary bedroom. Vaishali and Pathak both take turns, sketching different facets of Omble that depict the hero in the husband, father and friend.

Tukaram Omble came to Bombay in 1976 from a village called Kedambe in the Satara district of Maharashtra. The son of a farmer, Omble had intended to go back to his three brothers in the village after his retirement. He had never lost touch with them; visiting them three, sometimes four times a year. Ashok Pathak and Omble had been close friends since the time they got acquainted while signing up for the police force in 1978.

Omble would confide in him while the two stood outside Pathak's house, sipping tea. Pathak recalls how Omble would stop to help anyone in need – from children needing coins for their bus fare, to the accident victims that he brought to the local hospital. Once, Omble had averted the suspension of another cop by catching a runaway criminal. Amazingly, he never lost his temper – a trait that a lot of cops imbibe while working the beat in Mumbai. Whatever hour he turned in at night, he would always rise at 5.30 a.m. to do yoga.

His only aspirations for his daughter were that they get a good education and stay happy. He indulged them, bringing home treats that the girls never asked for. Indeed, he was a resolute family man, calling home every two hours to check on his family; having late night conversations with Vaishali and Bharti after returning home from a day shift. Vaishali murmurs, 'We were closer to him than we were to our mother, he used to say that he would be the brother that we didn't have.'

With alternating day and night shifts every week, Omble performed his duties like a model cop. 'He got to work early and left late, never missed a day,' remembers Vaishali. Even a mild heart attack was ignored in favour of his duty at Lalbaugcha Raja, one of the most popular Ganesh pandals during Ganesh Utsav, in Mumbai. He simply stood his ground, popping pills, his only remedy for a heart ailment. Still, his family never feared for him knowing that he would return home at the end of the day.

On 26 November Omble had the night shift and had told his family he was on marshalling duty at Girgaum Chowpatty. He promised Tara he would be back soon the next morning to take her to the jeweller to get her mangalsutra fixed. Before leaving home at 6.30 p.m., he indulgently fed his two daughters cream cake with his own hands, and stopped to say hello to the neighbours on his way out.

As news of the terrorist attack spread, Omble called on his family for information being broadcast on television. He assured them that all was clear at his end, stressing that all the trouble seemed to be at the Taj, Trident-Oberoi and CST areas. The last time the family spoke to Omble was at 12.30 a.m.; he maintained in his conversation that all was okay and advised them to turn in for the night. Ten minutes later, Assistant Sub-Inspector Tukaram Gopal Omble armed with just a lathi, saved his colleagues and secured a gunman in one of the most audacious terrorist attacks to take place on Indian soil. Even as six AK-47-vicious bullets entered Omble's body ripping apart his chest on the right side, he held onto the gunman and his gun. He died a hero's death. Significantly, Omble has also provided his country with the most crucial evidence in Mohammad Ajmal Kasab, the only terrorist who survived and was captured.

Weeks later, on a hot afternoon, Omble's widow Tara; eyes vacant, whispers that for her, her husband's death will forever be marked by an uneasy mix of pain, as well as pride.

[Assistant Sub-Inspector Tukaram Omble was honoured with the Ashok Chakra, posthumously.]

'Don't call me Shreemati … call me Veer Patni Pratibha Patil.'

Pratibha Patil, wife of Constable Jaywant Patil

Pratibha hasn't shed a single tear since she discovered that her husband is no more and she is now the lone parent to their two children. However, Pratibha's bottled up grief manifests itself in more worrying and disturbing ways. When she speaks, one sees a stoic face, emotions in check, but a closer look reveals her upper body heaving and shaking uncontrollably. The symptom gets triggered every time her husband, Jaywant, is discussed. Pratibha seems oblivious to this bodily reaction; as if her mind and body were detached, each functioning independently.

Constable Jaywant Patil lived with his family at S.M. Dubey Chawl in crowded Bhandup West, Mumbai. The *chawl* is atop a hill and in the evening, looks like a carpet of bulbs draped on a land rise. To reach their home one has to snake through a labyrinth of homes, asking for directions to the way up. Don't expect squalour because there isn't any; the tiled path between and leading to each home here, is narrow but clean.

Everybody who has met the couple has been enchanted by them. They were quite the vision of marital bliss. Their friends even awarded them a 'best couple' award at one of their social gatherings. Whenever any marital problems had to be sorted out amongst other couples, they always approached Jaywant and Pratibha for a resolution or counselling.

Thirty-eight-year-old Jaywant was well built. At a statuesque five-feet-eight, Pratibha nearly matched his height and is fair with full lips, her face outlined by thick eyebrows. She recalls how he liked to dress and would spend time checking himself in front of the mirror. Pratibha would often tease him, 'Don't be so proud of yourself, because as you get older, you might find that the shine on your face will diminish.' Jaywant would shoot back, 'Don't you worry … I'll take my shine with me to my death.' On the night of 26 November, Constable Jaywant was travelling with his boss Additional Commissioner Ashok Kamte when their vehicle was ambushed by two of the terrorists. Like Kamte, Jaywant too, died on the spot.

The days following Jaywant's death, Pratibha refused to attend events held in honour of 26/11 heroes, even closing the door on media reporters. But now, she is seeing a psychiatrist who's encouraging her to talk and vent her feelings. As a result, she has slowly begun to open up and express her pain and anguish. Deliverance, though, seems to be a long way off. When Pratibha heard that the Ashok Chakra was being awarded to all those who lost their lives fighting the terrorists, it was the first time she saw a glimmer of happiness that made her feel better. After all, they had all died heroic deaths including her husband. But the news that Jaywant was to be excluded from this honour, nobody knows on what grounds, has left Pratibha angry. She feels the government has chosen to distinguish on the basis of rank, placing a value on each policeman's death, in a way undermining their sacrifice. She slipped back into depression over this debate for the Ashok Chakra.

She breaks into an impassioned monologue, 'Don't call me Shreemati … call me Veer Patni Pratibha Patil. Honour all the wives whose husbands have laid down their lives for the country. That will be a constant reminder of the sacrifice made by our husbands and the country's and the government's acknowledgement of these men. This will allow us pride in their death; after all we are not just ordinary widows who lost their spouses to illnesses or accidents. We've given up a loved one so that this country could be safe. Who will look after our homes once our men are gone? I'm twenty-nine, I know of women who are so much younger and more vulnerable. These men died fighting for their country. At least honour those who made this supreme sacrifice. If you don't, who will want to fight for the country in the future?'

As these thoughts tumble out of Pratibha in a rush, the other family members stare helplessly at her, completely immersed in her rage. She's hurt, angry and wants to be heard. She's lost so much; a lifetime with the man she adored, the father to her kids -- six-month-old Shaurya, who'll never know his father and six-year-old Esha, who still oblivious to her father's death, plays happily undisturbed.

She's exhausted, but her face wears the innocence that Jaywant always strived to protect. When she asked him about the events of his routine day, he would tell her that he didn't want to corrupt her by describing the violent world he encountered. For the most part, Pratibha didn't know much about Jaywant's work. Not having even seen him in full police uniform, she says, 'It's only now that I'm beginning to get a sense of the person he was outside, as people from his workplace come to visit and tell me more about the person he was.'

Pratibha claims that in all the years of their marriage, the couple seldom fought. If an argument broke out, both would break down and make up. She remarks that he never did anything wrong, he was the perfect husband. The first time she saw him was when their parents set up a meeting at her house in her native village. That same evening she told her friends that he was the man she wanted to marry. Looking back at their years together, she says with fervour, '*Saat janm ka rishta, saat saal me nibhaya.* (In seven years we lived out the relationship of seven lives.)'

Jaywant was the kind of man who always got a second look. Childhood friend, Madan Deshmukh describes that quality by saying, '*usme* personality *tha*'. He was the eldest and only son to the Patil's. A couple who left their fields and came to the city; his father drove a taxi while his mother rolled *papads*. He came up the hard way, studying through night school, while picking up odd jobs during the day. He took an interest in things like drama, art and literature and after he became a family man he strived to better things for Pratibha and the kids. Early in his career, he graduated in commerce even while he did police *bandobast*. He studied computers and took a typing course in Marathi. He had flunked the Police Sub-Inspector Examination twice, but had recently made it on the third try. Such was his dedication to his work and his family, he never stopped trying.

Similar to the role played by Shivaji's bodyguards during his infamous meeting with Afzal Khan, and then again when Governor Inayet Khan conspired to kill him by sending an assassin, Constable Jaywant Patil was a bodyguard in modern times. He covered Ashok Kamte, for three years before both he and his boss died in the encounter with Ismail Khan and Mohammad Ajmal Kasab. The AK-47s fired by the terrorists left Jaywant's body riddled with eighteen bullets.

Yet his face remained untouched, just the way Pratibha knew it to be. And so will remain his memory, for his Veer Patni and their kids.

[Constable Jaywant Patil was honoured with the President's Police Medal for Gallantry, posthumously.]

'His pants were starched with coagulated blood ...'
The Fight for Nariman House

RAHUL SHIVSHANKAR

Rivka Holtzberg was cradling her world, her *malach* or angel as she called him, in an attempt to goad him to sleep. As is with most two year olds who have stayed up a wee bit longer than they should have, Moshe was cranky and it was proving to be a bit of a chore. But Rivka, twenty-nine, six months pregnant and tiring fast after a long and busy day, was patient almost to a fault. This ritual was after all her favourite little activity of the day, a palliative if you like for the mind which was coming to terms with a devastating personal situation. Moshe was Rivka's third child, her first-born Manchem Mendel succumbed to a debilitating genetic disorder, which was now tragically ravaging her second child too. (Dov, Rivka and Gavriel Holtzberg's second child also lost his battle to the genetic disorder, Tay-Sachs in December 2008.)

On another floor of the Chabad-Lubavitch House in Colaba market, South Mumbai's labyrinthine nerve centre, her husband, thirty-year-old Rabbi Gavriel Holtzberg, was preparing for the third and last *minyanim* (prayer ceremony) of the day. After that, as was the custom in most Chabad houses around the world, the *shliach* (the rabbi) would serve kosher food to the guests in the house. Rivka and Gavriel were known to create, as was often remarked 'a tremendous atmosphere'. At the Shabbat table, visitors to the house will tell you, Rabbi Gavriel gave each person in the congregation an option to say something about the *parashah* (the holy text), teach or lead a song, share an inspiring story or announce some *mitzvah* (religious ceremony) they were committing to undertake.

Ever since the couple had set up the Chabad-Lubavitch House in Mumbai in 2003, hundreds of Israelis, many of them involved in business in India, a fair number of Americans and scattered Jews from other countries had passed through its gates. Many of them, traumatized by the ugly scabs of heart wrenching poverty that pockmark the time-worn cheeks of Mumbai, returned to seek out as frequent visitor Joseph Telushkin puts it, 'a lighthouse in the middle of a dark ocean'.

On that balmy Wednesday night Rabbi Gavriel was showing Marc Shwalb, a diamond trader from Antwerp around the five-storey building. 'Have a look at the rooms,' Gavriel proudly told Shwalb, 'it's not a five-star hotel but it is nice.'

Shwalb wasn't standing in judgement, he was obligated to Gavriel and Rivka for hosting him on Shabbat the previous week and before leaving for his native Belgium later that night only thought it decent to thank them in person for their generous hospitality.

Shwalb had no way of knowing that he was to be one of the last few people to have left the Chabad House alive.

The Kuber was approaching Mumbai. Its eleven occupants had been on the high seas for almost three days. The Gujarati fisherman at the wheel of the trawler, the well-built Amar Sinh Solanki, must have been a nervous wreck. The unshakeable grip of death had taken hold of the trawler and was slowly choking his will to live. He had been witness to the brutal killing of four of his mates. Their eviscerated bodies had been tossed out to sea. It all happened in a flash, off the coast of Porbandar, after the Kuber was taken over by ten pirates. They had waved a white flag from aboard their boat and as was the custom on the high seas he responded to their distress signal. Now, duped and at the mercy of his captors who didn't kill him because only he could get them past the Coast Guard, Solanki must have been convinced he was next.

But when would his captors slash his neck?

From his vantage point on the bow of the Kuber, twenty-one-year-old Mohammad Ajmal Amir Kasab could pick out the faint outline of the vertiginous temples erected in the honour of Midas –

Nariman Point's resident deity. Unlike the others who had been lucky enough to scout the fabled Manhattan of the East, he had only seen glimpses of Mumbai's shimmering gilt-edged public visage in Bollywood movies.

But where was the time to take it all in?

As the Kuber with its engines silent bobbed up and down in the water marking time, Kasab began to cut the emotional chords connecting him to his target. He was here on a mission with divine sanction – a soldier of the 'Army of the Pure' or the Lashkar-e-Toiba – to avenge as he believed the humiliation Muslims have had to endure at the hands of the *kafir* oppressor. There could be no ambivalence now.

For months his handler, the inspirational Mujahid and Lashkar commander Zaki-ur-Rehman Lakhvi or Chacha as they lovingly called him, had drilled into his head that it was his sacred duty as an honourable Muslim to fight those who had sworn themselves to subjugate Islam. He now focused on that message, the tight embrace and Lakhvi's hot breath as it brushed his ear when he whispered the talismanic words, 'May Allah be with you', just as they parted company in the dark of the humid Karachi night.

But Kasab's meditations were rudely interrupted by the sickening gurgle of a man choking on his own blood. The Gujarati fisherman lay dying on the blood-smeared deck of the Kuber. His throat was slit open after the call came from Pakistan ordering the execution. Babar Imran and Fahadullah were quite literally washing the blood off their hands even as the herald of death, the Thuraya satellite phone, was lying by their side.

Babar Imran and his partner Nasir, members of Team 2, were tasked with the most critical mission of them all. They were under orders to take over the Chabad House (or Nariman House) and round up the Israelis before making their way back. Kasab was to later tell his interrogators that he didn't know the duo's exact plans as the teams were not encouraged to get familiar with each other but from what he'd heard through the grapevine at the Muridke (40 Km from Lahore) camp they were, like him, from Punjab and in particular from the towns of Faisalabad and Multan. Crucially, he'd also learnt that the duo had even been to Mumbai before.

Much after the attacks, the Mumbai crime branch said as much after they began probing the activities of five local recruits who constituted a local sleeper cell. Crime branch concluded that sometime last year, the cell helped a group of six Lashkar operatives who had travelled from Karachi to Mumbai by sea on fake Indian voter identity cards. There is a high probability that at least two of the six terrorists were Imran and Nasir.

In late 2007 or early 2008 the module apparently gathered operational details from the sleeper cell while they stayed in the area around Nariman House in a rented accommodation passing themselves off as students.

But on that Wednesday evening, aboard the rudderless Kuber, the ten sat down for that one last time as a group to go over the plan to kick into motion the siege of Mumbai. Imran and Nasir were being particularly given to detail as they went over a hand-drawn map of the reticulum of lanes that were going to take them from their port of call to Chabad House.

As the Mumbai crime branch was to later discover, the rough map was supposedly the handiwork of Faheem Ahmed Ansari, a Mumbai-based Lashkar operative who had been arrested in February 2008 by the Uttar Pradesh special task force. Ansari had, among other things, been charged for secretly filming more than a dozen potential targets in Mumbai. According to the police, Ansari handed over his spy fact-book to the sleeper cell that eventually passed it on to some of the men, maybe even Imran and Nasir.

As dusk turned to night the conference aboard Kuber ended. The ten men had their minds set on disembarking on the newly constructed jetty at Badhwar Park, Cuffe Parade. Each of the men had been handed a rucksack just as they were boarding the mother ship, the *Al-Husseini*. Each rucksack contained an AK-47, eight grenades, two magazines, hundreds of rounds of cartridges and one cellphone with an Indian SIM card. But the cellphones came with strict instructions from their trainers – under no circumstances were they to be switched on before the group landed in Mumbai.

There was more. Aside from what was in the rucksack the group was entrusted with a plastic bag that contained an IED (improvised explosive device) rigged with 4-5 kg of RDX, 4 kg of steel ball bearings and a programmable timing delay switch. Each of the bombs was to serve a distinct purpose and each person in the group had been thoroughly briefed on what that was. They were also given packets of mostly dry fruits. This, after all was not going to be a long-drawn operation.

But on the Kuber nobody was thinking that far. An inflatable rubber dinghy had been cast into the water and the ten men gingerly stepped overboard taking care not to wet their gear and took their place on the wooden slats that served as seating.

Once they were all on board someone in the group revved up the 40 horse power (hp) Yamaha engine and with a splutter the dinghy lurched away from the bobbing Kuber. The terrorists were cruising noisily in the direction of the Badhwar Park jetty off Cuffe Parade.

At Nariman House, an unarmed private security officer sat in his chair guarding the entrance to the building. It was an unusually warm and sticky night for late November in Mumbai and he was longingly eyeing the men's saloon a few doors away in the hope that one of the four barbers would be free to give him a shave before closing time. There wasn't much for him to do in any case. No one was expected to visit the building at half-past eight and especially when the guests and the rabbi and his wife Rivka were sitting down to dinner and prayers.

Earlier in the day five Jewish travellers had dropped in for afternoon prayers and stayed on for a kosher meal and a bed for the night. Among the guests was Yocheved Orpaz, a sixty-year-old Israeli who was en route to join her family on an Indian vacation. Also in the house that night was Rabbi Aryeh Leibish Tietelbaum, a thirty-seven-year-old American resident of Israel and his twenty-eight-year-old friend, and Rabbi Bentzion Chroman a dual US-Israeli citizen. Both were apparently in India on Chabad-related business.

The three were joined by two others – David Bialka, a fifty-two-year-old diamond trader and a frequent guest at the centre on his business travels and Norma Shvarzblat Rabinovich, a fifty-year-old Mexican Jew visiting India and said to be on her way to start a new life in Israel.

As the quorum broke up after dinner and prayers they made their way to their respective rooms on the fourth and fifth floors to retire for the night. For Chroman, however, there was still much to do. He had conditioned himself to stay awake long into the night to pore over the book of Torah studies.

On the second floor, Rabbi Gavriel Holtzberg and his wife Rivka were also awake discussing preparations for Shabbat and going over a checklist of supplies needed to cook kosher meals for at least fifty people. None of them had an inkling that death was lurking in the shadows of the dimly lit lane that lead to the Chabad House.

The rubber dinghy was aligned to the Badhwar Park jetty. The Yamaha engine fell silent and the eight merchants of death with murder on their minds hoisted themselves out of the dinghy. Standing on Indian soil, on enemy territory, each of them turned to the two left behind in the dinghy and flashed a thumbs-up sign. Barely twenty feet away Hemant Shankar Dhanu, a local fisherman who was sailing in the placid water looked on understandably baffled.

Who were these well-dressed boys? What were they doing disembarking on a jetty reserved for fishermen? Where were they going? Where were they from? Dhanu couldn't contain his curiosity; he paddled closer to the dinghy to put the questions to them in person. The dinghy and the sudden emergence of eight boys also caught the attention of another group of fishermen. Suspicious, they approached the group cautiously.

One of them, a scrap dealer called Anita Rajendra Uraiyar confronted the boys and tried to block their way to prevent them from getting off the jetty. 'Who are you and why do you come here?' Uraiyar asked. One of the boys spoke up for the group. He first pulled out the ID card of a Hyderabad college and then explained that they were on an excursion trip. The fisherman couldn't quite pick out the last part of the answer drowned out as it was by the Yamaha engine as it roared to life at the instance of the two figures in the dinghy. Within seconds they pulled out and away from the jetty.

As the fisherman turned to watch the dinghy speed away towards Nariman Point the eight intruders filed past making their way through the barricades and on to Cuffe Parade. Fahadullah and Imran were leading the pack. They were looking for an obscure hole in the wall that served as the mouth to a narrow alley that connected the end of the railway colony at Badhwar Park to the 4th Pasta Lane which leads on to the main Colaba market road.

Faheem's hand-charted map served the duo well. Armed with it the group had no problems finding their way about, briskly walking past the listed landmarks – Kismet building, the Shiv Sena *shc':ha* office, the graceful Namdar Manzil, and the colonial Pipewallah building that housed the Bootlegger Bar.

It was getting on to 9 p.m., the group was nearly two hours behind schedule. The shadowy Lashkar commander Abu Kahfa had told Kasab and Ismail that they needed to strike at the CST by 7.30 p.m., because at that time the terminus would be packed to the rafters and the bullets would cause the greatest damage.

Upon reaching the Colaba market road, the terrorists embraced for the last time before melting away into the night. Some catching taxis, others on foot. Now, alone for the first time on enemy territory and a little overwhelmed, Nasir and Imran drew a little closer to one another. So far it was looking good. They hadn't attracted any attention to themselves and there was no police around.

They could, even from where they stood at the mouth of the 4th Pasta Lane, pick out the facade of the Jewish centre. It had always stood out dwarfing the old colonial structures around it.

They made their way across the Colaba main road, to the petrol station. The staff at Express Petroleum car servicing and petrol station, led by the outlet manager Ram Bhuwal Yadav were far too busy tending to the last rush of customers to notice the sinister shape of two youths as they slipped behind a row of cars parked along the far wall of the compound. There, crouching behind a boxy sedan, Imran and Nasir set the timer on the RDX-laced IED for 10.45 p.m. They then surreptitiously ducked out of the station and headed towards Rajwadkar Street which would lead them to the Chabad House.

The security guard outside the Nariman House abandoned his vigil at 9.30 p.m. He had missed out on a shave but he was lapping up the refreshing masala tea and the little nuggets of gossip coming his way at a little stall behind the adjoining Abdul Karim building. He was lucky to be where he was because if he had delayed by barely five minutes, he would have had to face the two unforgiving youngsters, Imran and Nasir, who with their AK-47s cocked had slinked into the Chabad House.

A lane away on Pestonji Street in their squat, dank, three-room tenement with a brick-washed façade, the Harawalas had just finished dinner when a rapid volley of shots rang out. Salim Harawala, the master of the house, pushed away his plate, sprang to his feet and hurried towards the front door to bolt it. As Salim approached the door he heard a blood-curdling scream from somewhere straight ahead, beyond Pestonji Street, from the direction of the towering Chabad House. He stuck his head out and stole a glimpse but as a hail of bullets and the sound of shattering windowpanes enveloped their home, he staggered back and ducked under the dining table. His wife and his twenty-eight-year-old son Mohammad cowered behind a couch.

Outside on the crowded Rajwadkar Street in the two buildings – Merchant House and Abdul Karim building – that flank the Jewish centre terrified residents lay flat on the ground as a hail of bullets shattered windowpanes and ricocheted off the wall. Death and danger danced all around, one false step, one panicky reaction, could spell the end.

In the Chabad House there was horror. A Muslim youth employed by the Rabbi, Zakir, and Moshe's nanny Sandra Samuels were in the kitchen stowing away leftovers in the fridge when they came face to face with one of the terrorists. Later, much later, Zakir recounted that encounter. 'We didn't see the face, just the big gun. We knew something was wrong. We had barely entered the library on the first floor and turned to quickly lock the door shut. We rushed to the balcony and started shouting for help. But as the firing continued we ran towards the store room (on the first floor).'

No sooner had Zakir and Sandra entered the store room that a huge explosion tore through the first floor. The door, just bolted by the terrified Zakir and Sandra, was torn off its hinges, acrid smoke, and a film of soot and dust covered everything. The plaster coating the walls and ceiling was stripped away to expose the masonry. Shards of glass and splinters of wood were sticking out of the sofa as if it was a giant pincushion. It was a miracle that Zakir and Sandra were still alive. Zakir said later, 'Even the terrorists thought we died in that explosion, but we hid between two steel fridges, praying.'

The shooting and grenade explosion on the second floor made a startled David Bialka sit up bolt upright in bed. The blood-curdling wail that followed a while later sent a tremor down his spine. Bialka crept out of his fourth floor room and edged to the balustrade that ringed the stairwell. As he peeked over he was almost immediately accosted by plumes of thick smoke, so acrid that it hit the back of his throat and stung his eyes. Choking back tears and cupping his hand over his mouth, Bialka slipped back into his room making sure that he locked the door behind him. He needed to do something, and fast, if he was going to escape this hell. He glanced across the room but found that all the windows were grilled; the only way out was through the bathroom window. Bialka forced it open and reached for the drain pipe. Clinging to it for dear life, he slid down slowly till he reached the motor component of a newly installed air-conditioning unit. His arms were tiring and his hands were chaffing and he was happy for a foothold. Standing on the air-conditioning unit as it groaned and creaked under his weight he looked down nervously and became aware of the dozens of people who were gathered around the Nariman House.

There was smoke billowing out of a room in the neighbouring Merchant house and someone on the second floor was crying for help. Bialka was scared that the person's cries may attract the terrorists who might open fire or may spot him. Left to choose between the prospect of losing his life to a bullet and a fatal fall, Bialka chose the latter. There was no time to lose and he decided to hop on to another air-conditioning unit slightly below. Now as he was down to the second floor he decided to jump. But his ordeal was not over. The residents turned on him thinking he was a terrorist. 'They almost lynched me, before realizing I wasn't a terrorist. Twice I freed myself off them and tried to get near the building, wanting to go back and help, but they put me in a cab and took me to the police.'

Meanwhile, on the second floor of the Chabad House Rabbi Gavriel and Rivka, who had swept Moshe up into her arms, were bracing for the worst. They had heard the gunshots and moments later had felt the building tremble when the big explosion rumbled through it. They had heard Zakir and Sandra scream for help. They knew instantly that some great evil was out there and was now waiting for them on the other side of the door.

―――

At around the time the terrorists were making their way up to the second floor a phone rang at the Israeli consulate. Ehud Raz, a twenty-nine-year-old security officer was on duty. He answered it. It was a call from the Chabad House. The calm voice at the other end of the line identified itself as Rabbi Gavriel. Raz could hear a lot of commotion in the background and only just heard the Rabbi say, 'This is not a good situation,' before the line went dead.

Raz wasted no time. He along with another armed Israeli security official made their way to Nariman House. But the crowd was so agitated after Bialka had rappelled down the building that they turned on the Israelis too, thinking they were terrorists. Both were chased to the local police station where they were detained. Precious time was lost.

Imran and Nasir's first priority was to take the Israeli hostages and then secure the building. It is believed that they accomplished the first of their tasks within half an hour of entering the building. Now they focused on the second mission. The duo split up. An eyewitness recalls seeing one of them atop the water tank on the sixth floor and lobbing a grenade in the direction of Merchant House in a murderous attempt at pushing back the crowds. The blast caused a lot of damage. The façade of the Rex Bakery and Mehta building bore the brunt. Windowpanes of apartments right up till the fourth floor were blown out of their sills. Most window grills were mangled and dozens of two-inch wide craters appeared like a rash across the buildings exposed to Nariman House. The grenades achieved the objective as the crowds dispersed quickly. The area around Nariman House went deathly quiet.

Thinking it was all over, Salim Harawala, his wife Maria and son Mohammad crawled out from under their hiding places. Despite the earth-shaking blasts their home was intact. 'My father and mother were very curious to see what was happening. They decided to go to the terrace to have a better look at the area around their home. I followed them too. But as soon as they stepped out on the roof the terrorists opened fire. The shots appeared to have been fired from the third floor of the Nariman House. My parents were killed on the spot. A bullet grazed my head and I fell to the ground knocked out of my senses.'

At about the same time, closer to Nariman House on Pestonji Street, Harish used the lull in the firing as an opportunity to run from his exposed hiding place to a safer position in the building opposite. As he stepped out of the shadows into the arc of light cast by a street lamp the terrorists picked him out. Harish died on the spot from a bullet injury to his head.

The area around Nariman House was now potentially a killing field. The residents knew that the terrorists were now selecting their targets before killing them. Who would be next?

An hour had elapsed since Imran and Nasir had entered the building. Ram Bhuwal Yadav, the petrol pump manager had heard the gunshots and the deafening blast. He asked his team to immediately disband and go home. Since he couldn't leave the pump, he locked himself up in the main office.

Then as he says, 'I drew the blinds, and hid behind the solid steel desk. I just had this feeling that the worst was yet to come. And I wasn't wrong. At around 10.45 p.m., roughly half an hour after I took cover there was a massive explosion. Such was the force that I was thrown on to my back. Due to the impact of the blast the metal frame of the desk was bent out of shape. The office window was shattered. Thankfully, the blinds prevented the shards of glass from flying back into the office or I would have been a bloody mess. Nothing remained of the canopy that covered the petrol station. Nothing was left of the five or so cars parked on the far side. Nothing in fact was left of the compound wall. Fearing a fire I immediately ran out. Several people were running helter-skelter on the main street of Colaba outside Collabawallah House. It was a miracle that no one was injured.'

A kilometre away ACP Isaque Bagwan was sitting down to dinner at his home in Colaba when the phone call came informing him that two people were shooting at guests at the busy Leopold Café in Colaba. Bagwan didn't waste a second. He grabbed his service revolver and rushed out. On his way to Leopold Café he heard a deafening explosion, 'It was so loud that I could instantly make out it was a time bomb. Within seconds I got a call from my superior. He ordered me to rush to Nariman House.'

Bagwan made a quick stop at the police station to collect half a dozen constables all armed with standard issue .303 calibre rifles and took off for Nariman House. The group didn't know it then but they had crossed a taxi that was ferrying David Bialka and his captors (the suspecting local residents) to the Colaba police station. It was the slain encounter specialist Vijay Salaskar who allegedly questioned Bialka at the police station and immediately released him after being convinced of his identity.

On reaching Rajwadkar Street, Bagwan and his team had to thread their way through a sea of onlookers and residents who had completely choked the entrance. Once Bagwan led his men past them they hid in the narrow porches that framed the entrance to the buildings around Nariman House.

At 11.15 p.m. an additional force of six commandos from the State Reserve Police Force (SRPF), armed with SLR guns, was sent to Nariman House to assist Bagwan and his team.

Bagwan, who was part of the team that was involved in Mumbai police's first encounter in 1983, was later to say, 'Even as the terrorists were firing indiscriminately and had lobbed a hand grenade, I knew with limited manpower and ammunition we would be no match for the terrorists in an open encounter. I instead asked the men to encircle the building and respond. But I also told them to only fire one after the other so that the terrorists were fooled into thinking that there was a huge police contingent surrounding the area.'

But as the police began to make their way through the maze of dark, wet, cobbled passageways they stumbled upon cowering residents and three dead bodies. 'I realized then,' recalls Bagwan, 'our first objective was to evacuate people from the buildings that stood in the direct line of fire.'

News of the encounter at Nariman House came in last at around 11.45 p.m. on most television news channels. I was in the studio (Times Now), anchoring, when our reporter Kashif Khusro reached the spot. I remember him standing outside the petrol pump describing the grim scenes of devastation. It was a war zone. Several police jeeps with their beacons flashing and sirens wailing were either parked or riffling past. Several ambulances were at the site and the purple-blue glow from their beacons was bathing people and buildings in a ghostly hue. Men with gauze masks and oversize white jump suits with green shower caps milled amongst the crowd. Another group, resembling aliens from Mars, in padded black overalls, huge oven-baking gloves, oversize shoes, and giant helmets moved around with zombie like deliberation. This was the bomb disposal unit.

From the petrol station, Khusro made his way to Rajwadkar Street that was now off limits to a restive crowd that was straining at a thick jute rope hastily slung between two poles.

'I can hear heavy gunfire and loud explosions Rahul!' shouted Khusro into the mike as he was being jostled by the crowd. 'I am being told that the Nariman House, a centre for Jews, has been taken over by terrorists. Apparently these are from the same terrorist module that has entered the Trident, the Taj and CST. A policeman has told me that some people, Jews included, may be being held at gunpoint. I can't confirm this just as yet but there might be some casualties too.'

The broadcast was caught by Marc Schwalb, the diamond industry professional who was at the Nariman House earlier in the day talking to Rabbi Gavriel Holtzberg. At the time I was relaying the news from the studios of our TV station, Schwalb was barricading himself in his room on the nineteenthth floor of the Oberoi hotel after he heard, as he describes it, 'A terrible noise, horrible shooting'. The nerve-jangling bursts of machine gun fire had led Schwalb to walk across the hall and peer down at the atrium below, where he saw gunmen with backpacks firing AK-47 assault rifles randomly into groups of guests and diners at the hotel's restaurant. 'They were shooting at everything,' he recalled, 'the coffee shop, the lobby, afterwards they took hostages. I locked myself into the room and turned on the TV to watch the news. But there was nothing on the attack. In fact, for quite a few hours there was nothing and then suddenly I saw pictures of the Taj hotel, the CST and Café Leopold. And then I thought what about us? Doesn't anyone know that there are terrorists in this hotel too?'

It was at that point, sometime around 11.00, that Marc Schwalb called the Nariman House to inform the Holtzbergs of his plight. Though the ring went through, no one took his call.

He was to later reveal that when TV channels finally did broadcast pictures of Nariman House he broke down thinking, 'I didn't know when I said goodbye to Rabbi Gavriel, that it would be for ever.'

Post-midnight, as the action at the Taj hotel and the Trident-Oberoi complex peaked the guns fell silent at Nariman House for a while. Or to put it a little differently, the intensity of the encounter waned a touch. Inside the building, Imran and Nasir had taken complete control. The rabbi and his wife Rivka were confined to a sitting room on the second floor. They were the prize catch. Rivka was cradling Moshe and the rabbi was reciting from the book of Torah studies. The others didn't matter. They were dead.

Coroners in Israel were to reveal later that the three others, Orpaz, Tietelbaum and Chroman were most probably slain by the terrorists on the first night itself. This they deduced from the fact that their bodies had decomposed to a greater extent.

From time to time, just to make sure, Imran and Nasir would take turns at one of the windows on the second floor, surveying the neighbourhood. Sometimes they would fire aimlessly into the inky blackness of the night to warn their enemies that they were still around lest they were planning any misadventure.

Nasir and Imran had also switched on the computer in the library of the Chabad House a little after turning on their mobile phones to get in touch with their principal handler in Pakistan. The crime branch of the Mumbai police confirmed after the Mumbai carnage ended that they had traced an international company that was providing Voice-over Internet Protocol (VoIP) service used by the terrorists.

The handler was relaying a wealth of information over the mobile phones to all the terrorists involved in the Mumbai operation. In particular, he focused on the deployment of police and commando movements by following the news on Indian television channels.

Meanwhile, as the extent of the conspiracy became known and it became clear that the police were totally out of their depth and rattled by the killing of three of their biggest stars, a panicky Maharashtra government began sending out SOS messages. The then home minister Shivraj Patil, a Maharashtrian himself, was petitioned for help.

At around 11.40 p.m., the home secretary, Madhukar Gupta, finally called up the one man who could be counted upon to deliver the goods – National Security Guard (NSG) Director General J.K. Dutt. The message was short but urgent: 'Get your team down to Mumbai in the shortest possible time and clean up this mess.'

Moments later calls went out to several commandos living on the sprawling NSG complex in Manesar, Haryana, to report to the office immediately.

Dutt recalls the haste with which the NSG moved, 'Most of my men had to be roused from their sleep and they slipped on t heir uniforms, strapped on the safety gear, collected ammunition and firearms and boarded an IL-76 plane at 3.00 a.m. on Thursday morning.'

As the NSG prepared to take off for Mumbai, at 2 a.m. a detachment of marine commandos or MARCOS had also joined Bagwan and his police posse outside Nariman House. The MARCOS, were flown in from the *INS Abhimanyu* after a desperate Maharashtra government put a call to Vice-Admiral J.S. Bedi of the Western Naval Command. But the MARCOS were ordered to be very careful lest they endanger the lives of the Israelis held hostage by the terrorists.

Privately, one of the MARCOS told me that the delays in getting them down there and then asking them to limit themselves to a containing job proved to be critical in the final analysis. 'Unless counter-action is initiated within thirty to forty-five minutes of the attack the enemy can take up defensive positions,' he said.

With their offensive capability reigned in, the police and MARCOS began to conduct house-to-house evacuations. Thanks to the MARCOS and the police, a lot of innocent people got saved that night. Had more time been lost evacuating the trapped residents Mumbai would have been witness to a grizzly bloodbath as the terrorists had received orders to 'teach the Indian swines a lesson they would never forget' if they found themselves losing the battle.

Inside Nariman House, Nasir and Imran were preparing to do just that now that they were aware they had been encircled. They also realized that in a perverse way the roles had reversed. It was they who were hostage to the situation now.

At 9 a.m. on Thursday morning the NSG commandos under the leadership of the stoic J.K. Dutt took over operations at the Nariman House.

The NSG is the elite of the elite and Dutt's intentions left no one in doubt as he spelt them out with chilling sanguinity, 'My commandos are here to neutralize these cowards who are waging an underhand, dirty war against our nation. We will make them pay heavily.'

The 51-SAG (NSG battalion) were certainly equipped to make the terrorists pay. They were clad in intimidating black jump suits and balaclavas with built-in body armour. Strapped to their waist were bow knives, Glock pistols, ammunition pouches and several grenades. In their hands they carried Heckler and Koch MP-5 submachine guns. Besides the obvious accoutrements these men were physically and mentally conditioned to fight at close quarters.

I was in the studio during the deployment and remember very clearly asking our in-house strategic affairs analyst Mahroof Raza how the NSG could make a difference. Raza, a proud former army man himself, with palpable incredulity if not a hint of contempt for my naivety said, '... that Rahul, is a question that needn't even be posed, these men are the finest the country has to offer, the terrorists have no hope in hell, they are specialists in building intervention operations, highly decorated, don't even know the word fear exists.'

Within minutes the SAG took up positions in the buildings around Nariman House. Several trooped into Abdul Karim and Merchant House that flank Nariman House, barely ten metres away. They had a direct view of the stairway and snipers, and made sure they had a view of the landing too.

Imran and Nasir had no idea that they were being tracked by HHTIs (hand-held thermal imagers). But luckily for them the imagers weren't as effective as they normally are due to the odd angles within Nariman House.

At around 10.30 a.m. Rabbi Gavriel Holtzberg's cellphone started ringing. It was Rabbi Levi Shemtov, a Chabad emissary in Washington; he wanted to ensure the safety of Jews taken hostage and find out if the terrorists had any demands. But the call didn't amount to anything as the person on the other side, Imran, spoke in Urdu.

Shemtov then began to hunt for an interpreter and tracked down P.V. Viswanath, professor at Pace University New York. Viswanath was the prefect candidate. Besides being an orthodox Jew he was familiar with Urdu as he had spent the initial twenty years of his life in Mumbai. Viswanath had also met the 'kindly and generous' rabbi and his wife Rivka at the Chabad House.

It was midnight in New York, Viswanath recalled, 'When I got on a conference line to the Chabad House. I heard a low male voice. The person identified himself as Babar Imran. At first there was a little difficulty understanding Imran's Urdu but gradually I got accustomed to it.'

Imran was calm and was tutored not to say too much. He had been in fact given a few lines to speak and in a measured voice he delivered the message, '*Hum Bharat sarkaar se baat karna chahte hain. Hamara ek banda aapke kabze mein hia, hamare saamne use pesh kar do.* (We wish to negotiate with the Indian government. One of our men is in your custody, bring him to us).'

When Viswanath translated the demand back to Rabbi Shemtov, the Chabad emissary said he wanted to know if the hostages were alive. Chillingly Imran answered, '*Humne unko thappad bhi nahin mara hai.* (We haven't even slapped them around as of now).'

But Viswanath persisted and Imran still calm but more menacing growled into the phone, '*Yeh batein zaroori nahin hain* (It isn't important).'

Over the next few hours the rabbi and Viswanath kept talking to Imran. In an attempt to prolong the negotiations and try and win over the terrorists, the rabbi asked Imran if they were safe and had eaten any food. The unyielding terrorist shot back, with a curt, '*Hum yahaan khana khaney nahin aaye hain.* (We haven't come here to wine and dine).'

At one point Shemtov managed to put through an Indian police official to Imran but the connection was bad and no one could hear anything. After that, later in the afternoon on Thursday, no one answered Rabbi Gavriel Holtzberg's phone. But Shemtov's phone call was godsent for three people inside Nariman House.

While the terrorists were busy speaking to the rabbi in Washington, they had no idea that Sandra and Zakir had crept out of their hiding place between two oversized refrigerators on the second floor. Zakir described the scene, 'We came out of the store room at around 11 a.m. on Thursday and we saw the destruction, slowly making our way through the broken glass and pieces of concrete. We were near the stairs when we heard baby Moshe's cries. Sandra and I then stole up the stairs to the second floor. While I waited by the stairs she went in and picked up the baby. Both of us then ran out of the building.'

Sandra later said that Moshe was lying in a pool of blood in the midst of four motionless bodies, including those of his parents. His pants were starched from coagulated blood.

Sadly that was to prove to be the lone high point of the day.

Outside, the SAG had set the stage for the final assault. Methodically, the windows to the entire Nariman House were blown away. Every now and then a gust of wind would sweep back the curtains on the fifth and fourth floors and reveal glimpses of the closely guarded secrets of the Jewish centre but never long enough for anyone to form a solid impression.

A MI-17 helicopter made tight circles over the house, building up the expectation. Apart from its whirring rotor blades there wasn't a sound to be heard. It wasn't a tranquil silence, but an uneasy one of the type that suffuses cavernous MRI rooms in large hospitals, or shrouds towns that have been evacuated in the anticipation of some great natural calamity.

A SAG commando said that the team was deliberately holding back for a while. 'There were important people being held hostage, any hastily thought-up move could've endangered the hostages, the media, especially the international media would not have let us forget it.'

To be sure, the odds were stacked against the SAG from the word go. I asked a commando what he made of the operation as we sat shoulder-to-shoulder on the squalid rooftop of Divine Mansion fifty metres across Nariman House. He kept it simple, 'These boys have not just been picked up from some madrasa and handed a gun. We are up against a highly trained, motivated and desperate enemy. And apart from all of this they are entrenched in a tactically superior position. The Nariman House has limited entry points. To use any of them to access the house means exposing oneself completely to hostile fire. We need to wait it out, keep them guessing, tire them out and then move for the kill.'

So all through Thursday the cat-and-mouse game continued. The NSG snipers watched. Their fingers on the trigger, eyes glued to the telescopic gun sights. Motionless. Pensive. Calculating.

All the while their wily quarry, also on to the game, kept changing positions and firing intermittently to throw the commandos off their scent.

Every new position was mapped by the NSG commandos and relayed back over RT sets to the tactical command centre that had been set up just off Pestonji Street. 'Every time these cowards move we have to reassess the situation and rethink our tactics,' said an NSG commando who had been involved in countless similar operations.

Suddenly at around midnight, the stillness was shattered by wild cheering and much congratulatory chatter on Rajwadkar Street about sixty feet from the Nariman House. A dozen or so residents, mistaken for rescued hostages from the Jewish centre made their way out under NSG escort.

One of them was known to Violet Fernandes, a mother of two who lived in Kasturi building, barely two doors away from the Jewish centre. 'I recognized my neighbour immediately, I went to her and wanted to know if my building was intact. But she couldn't even talk, she was so traumatized and scared that I thought she would collapse on me. She just kept constantly mumbling Ram, Ram, Ram ...'

Several residents who were caught in the crossfire were to later suffer post-trauma stress syndrome and needed to be counselled, but not the Israeli hostages of Nariman House. They were all dead.

By Friday morning, the NSG had determined from the intercepts of the terrorist communication that the hostages had been killed and now there was now only one thing to do – storm Nariman House.

There was only one way in and that was from the top. So a little after sunrise, at 7.15 a.m. or so, a MI-17 IAF helicopter appeared over the building. Suddenly, about twenty NSG commandos slithered down a rope on to the roof of the building. The militants tried to shoot at the helicopter but couldn't take aim because NSG snipers were providing covering fire.

When I asked him what prompted the commanders to take the decision to para-drop the commandos, DG J.K. Dutt, the NSG head told me rather cryptically, 'By that point we had nothing to lose and everything to gain.'

The NSG commandos, employing as they were a top-down approach, started to move down floor by floor.

From my vantage point atop Divine House it was clear that a

methodical clean-up operation was being undertaken in what was the endgame at Nariman House.

But Nasir and Imran weren't about to surrender. They had just tasted their first success in killing Havildar Gajendra Singh during the gun-battle.

Triumphant, they wasted no time in relaying the information to their jubilant handler.

At around five in the afternoon, just as the rooftops around Nariman House teeming with an assortment of celebrities, politicians and curious expats began to resemble boxes in some Victorian opera hall, the SAG fired a succession of rockets into the fourth floor. They knew the terrorists were trapped there.

Then there was a lull. But soon I could see the NSG commandos walking around the first floor and slowly creeping up the stairwell to the second floor. They had also begun moving down on to the fifth floor. Some leaned over the roof and started shooting downwards into the windows of the fourth floor. A huge hole had been blown open on the far side of the building and smoke was billowing out of the fifth floor.

As I watched on I couldn't help but spare a thought for the hostages. It was a horrific way to die. And what of the families who were being compelled to watch on TV the macabre dance of death as it consumed their flesh and blood.

But even before the mind could comprehend the brutality of the moment it was jolted by a deafening explosion – a shockwave so strong that it threw me off my feet. Seconds later through the haze of dust and smoke we saw the creaking shell of Nariman House – a giant smouldering sarcophagus.

The building was crawling with NSG commandos. They were sifting through the rubble, torch in hand, looking for God alone knows what. There was nothing, absolutely nothing left to salvage. The dark ocean of bigotry had risen up and swallowed the Lighthouse – that once was the Nariman House.

'Men, women and children ... Kasab's AK-47 did not discriminate.'

The Carnage at CST

GEORGE KOSHY

As twenty-seven-year-old Bharat Navadia reached Chhatrapati Shivaji Terminus (CST) with his wife and two young children he couldn't help but secretly pride himself at being able to afford a trip for the family to Kolkata for a wedding. His income from being a door-to-door clothes salesman hardly afforded them luxuries such as holidays, so this trip was special. His wife Poonam held their two-and-a-half-year-old daughter Anjali and one-year-old son Viraat close to her while Bharat went to check their reservation status. As Bharat walked towards the reservation chart display he heard the sound of crackers and before he could turn around to reach his family he was hit hard by something on his right shoulder. As he fell he could hear Poonam's scream – this was the last sound he heard before he blacked out.

Mohammad Ajmal Amir Kasab and Abu Ismail alighted from the taxi (MH 01 G 779) they had taken from Badhwar Park and entered CST station from the side entrance near platform number 18. They had left behind a parcel under the front seat of the taxi, which was to seal the fate of fifty-five-year-old Laxminarayan Goyal, a resident of Hyderabad who was in Mumbai on business. Goyal had missed his train, the Hussainsagar Express, to Hyderabad and decided to take the same train the next day. He was still on the phone with his family when the parcel under his seat exploded near Vile Parle, killing him and the taxi driver, Umer Abdul Khalid at 10.40 p.m.

The narrow passage past platform numbers 14 to 18 was bustling with people. No one paid any attention to two young men who made their way past the waiting room and the parcel room into the men's toilets. Seventy-two-year-old Babulal Sahu, who was the restroom attendant allowed the two men in with their bags. After all it was not an unusual request – no one wanted to leave their bags unattended and these two had two large rucksacks, which he did not want to take responsibility of. It is now widely believed that the terrorists used these toilets to load their arms and prepare for the attack.

It was a busy night for Riyaz Rashid Khan, the man in charge of Re-Fresh, the food plaza on the first floor in the main hall of CST. He was making sure that no customer overstayed after finishing his meal – the tables were few and therefore precious for business. At around 10 p.m. he heard a loud explosion near platform number 12. The next sight left Riyaz Khan astounded. A young man in his twenties was standing near platform 13 and firing indiscriminately at the helpless passengers waiting in the hall.

There was instant panic as people ran helter-skelter. One eyewitness described it as 'mayhem personified'. There were at least 300 people in the hall – men, women and children. A spray of bullets met them as Kasab's AK-47 did not discriminate between anyone. Babulal Sahu still thought they were sounds of celebrations (there was an India-England ODI earlier that day) until he saw an injured man rushing into the toilet. Instinctively, he ran inside the toilets and hid there for the next hour and a half with thirty other scared bystanders.

As Riyaz watched the entire episode from his vantage point, a few bullets whizzed past and shattered the glass windows of the restaurant. He did not know that a bullet had injured a colleague Mukesh Aggarwal on the ground floor. Riyaz quickly led all the customers in the restaurant into the kitchen that was secured with brick walls. Downstairs the shooter was still spraying the hall with bullets. A witness noticed a pattern in the shooting. Kasab was firing in the direction of the main hall but made sure no shots were fired towards the passage leading to platforms 14 to 18. Intelligence agencies say this could be because he was providing cover to Ismail who had gone in that direction to reach the parcel depot to plant a bomb among the boxes (discovered a week later).

Riyaz saw the gunman reloading his gun at least thrice (there were three empty magazines and an unexploded grenade that was later found near the platform 12 entrance). He kept re-loading from his half-open rucksack that was now slung sideways. He then moved towards the mail-train ticket counters and fired at the people running to save themselves.

Assistant chief ticket inspector, S.K. Sharma, hearing the commotion, walked outside his office but couldn't miss the volley of bullets that came his way. He died on the spot. A bullet also hit one of the newspaper vendors who was trying to flee. The piercing sound of glass shattering filled the hall as bullets hit the glass panels of the ticket counters. A grenade was hurled towards counters 14 to 17. By this time several policemen had also fallen victim to the shooting.

Meanwhile Vishnu Zende, the railway announcer on duty, received a call from his officer informing him of the firing. While others thought it best to run, he decided to use his office to alert passengers. There was a train approaching platform 4 so he had to act quickly. '*Kripaya dhyaan dijiye, yaatriyon se nivedan hai ke weh* train *ke baahar nahi nikle aur saavdhaani baratein,* (Your attention please, kindly stay inside the train and be alert),' he announced in a calm and stern voice. 'Walk to the back and leave the station through Gate No. 1,' he directed in both Marathi and Hindi. Passengers alighting from the train were caught off guard by the strange announcement. Many on the other end of the train quickly got out and fled to safety.

Sitting in the announcer's booth on the first floor, Zende was at a vantage point and used his unique spot to inform the police of the terrorist's movements. The gunmen soon located his announcement booth and fired at him. Zende escaped unhurt as the bullets punctured the window. 'Deep down inside I feared for my life,' he later admitted.

Railway Protection Force (RPF) head constable Jillu Yadav, (one of the few policemen who were armed), was manning platforms 3 and 4 when suddenly he heard screams as passengers ran towards him. 'Firing *ho rahi hai.* (There is firing)!' they yelled at him. He ran towards the sound of the firing to find empty platforms. He quickly closed the exit gates and saw a person carrying heavy bags in a corner loading his weapons. Another man was standing guard.

Yadav, who by now had run out of ammunition (six rounds in his pistols) asked an armed constable who was standing by to fire at them. But he didn't respond – he stood frozen and stunned. Yadav, in service for thirty years, snatched the .303 calibre rifle from the constable and confronted the terrorists. However, his weapon was no match for their guns as the two terrorists surrounded him from both ends and started firing at him. Yadav took cover behind a wall.

Inspector Sandeep Khiratkar and Sub-Inspector Kiran Bhonsale of the RPF soon joined him. The two terrorists quickly made their way down the platform and took the stairs out of the station.

As the firing subsided Riyaz left his hiding place in the kitchen. He noticed a few ragpickers and homeless people who usually used the main hall of CST as their resting place for the night, rushing in with handcarts and picking up the bodies. Some were lifeless while some showed signs of life. Seeing them Riyaz was encouraged and mustered the courage to help the injured. Those in the adjoining parcel office too ran out to help.

Soon help arrived for Bharat and his family and they were taken to JJ Hospital. Unfortunately, Poonam was declared 'dead on arrival' – a bullet had pierced through her head. Bharat had injuries on his right shoulder. His left shoulder was rendered useless by an earlier fracture. The only shoulder that bore the weight of his bundle of clothes that he 'marketed' in shops and homes was now gone. His son misses Poonam desperately and stares blankly at him while Anjali thinks her mother went to Kolkata without the rest of the family.

FBI investigators who later saw the bodies of the deceased along with Indian intelligence agencies observed how this had signs of a typical commando operation. All bodies bore bullet injuries on the upper torso; many on the head and neck – indicators of militant training by the army.

As Riyaz and the helpers continued to load the bodies on to carts, he noticed that three women who had died did not have any bullet wounds or injuries – they had died of shock. A young man was staring at the lifeless body of his sister – they were to travel to Chennai for her wedding in four days. Riyaz gently picked her up and loaded her on to a handcart – her brother remembered his kindness and came back to thank Riyaz a few days later.

By now more police and a few journalists had arrived. There was luggage, food and footwear strewn everywhere. The railway authorities took control – the city had to move on. Almost immediately cleaners sprayed the floor with water and disinfectant as workers put up temporary ply boards to hide the bullet marks on the walls.

CST had never been this quiet. It was probably the first time in many years that the public address system was silent (unlike the suburban lines where the trains halt for a few hours in the night; the long-distance trains at CST continue to ply through late night). The cleaners worked noiselessly – only the swooshing sound of their brooms meeting the floor filled the hall. Another group collected the luggage found in the hall and stored it in the parcel room.

The two terrorists had walked out of the station on to the over-bridge at the end of platform towards the adjoining Times of India (TOI) building. A photographer on the third floor of the building saw them walking with their guns drawn and managed to take a picture. The sudden flash startled the duo and they fired in the direction of the window.

They were now looking to get inside another building. The TOI CCTV cameras show them walking along the parking lot of the building. The quick thinking of an alert security officer, P.A. Varghese saved the lives of nearly 300 staff members inside the building. As he heard the news of the first gunshots at CST he instructed his team to pull down all the shutters and ordered everyone to stay inside.

Kasab and Ismail continued on foot past Azad Maidan police station. Police personnel at the Azad Maidan station had already been alerted of the approaching terrorists. A journalist present at the station recounts how most of the constables on duty were scared and were not ready to leave. They quickly shut off the lights and secured the doors. By now the terrorists had reached the rear entrance of the Cama and Albless Hospital for Women and Children.

Ismail spotted someone sitting outside a shanty near the Laxmi Refreshment Centre at the entrance of the hospital. Thakur Wagela, despite his mother's warning, had taken his dinner plate outside his shanty when two men approached him asking for water. It was when one man finished drinking the water that Wagela noticed the gun in the other man's hand. Before he could react, a bullet had gone through his upper torso as his six-year-old son looked on. They also fired at Bhagam Shinde who looked out of his building hearing the commotion. He later succumbed to his injuries.

The two terrorists then jumped over a closed entrance at the back of the hospital. They spotted a guard who had his back turned towards them. Kasab's gun found another target. Another unarmed guard who rushed in to investigate the sounds of gunfire too had the same end.

All floors in Cama Hospital have grills and doors protecting each ward. As news poured in of the attack the hospital staff switched off the lights and locked the grills on each floor. Wherever they couldn't find locks they used bed-sheets to secure the doors tightly. The terrorists kept moving up the six floors of the hospital as they tried to find people to hold hostage. On the fourth floor they spotted a relative of a patient and stabbed him.

Addl CP Sadanand Date first checked on the US Consulate and then the Breach Candy Hospital. As he proceeded towards CST, a message on the wireless alerted him of the terrorists being spotted at Cama Hospital. Date and his team of seven immediately made their way to the hospital. Eyewitnesses warned him that there was a chance the terrorists were holding hostages on the fourth floor.

Date posted a constable on the ground floor to monitor and report updates on the wireless while he led the rest of the team checking each floor. They did not spot anyone on the first six floors. There was a terrace on the seventh floor. To check if anyone was hiding in the shadows Date threw a metal piece on to the terrace and this was responded to by a burst of AK-47 firing.

The team was carrying two carbines and was armed with service revolvers and pistols. There were only three bulletproof vests – Date and two members put them on and moved the remaining members of the team to a floor below and away from the firing. They were to fire carbines in response. Suddenly a grenade landed on their floor severely injuring two constables including Date. His right eye was injured. What had seemed like a skirmish between two gangs had now taken on a different light. This was war! And he was facing highly trained operatives.

He instructed the constable manning the wireless to ask for backup. By now the firing had intensified. The two injured constables were in no position to fight back. Date quickly took the carbine from one of the constables and started firing. The terrorists lobbed another grenade. The 'area weapon' used by the terrorists was making it difficult for them to remain on that floor. He asked his remaining team members to carry the injured constables to a floor below.

The standoff continued for a while until the terrorists released a hostage from the terrace. The police personnel spoke to the hostage to ascertain his identity. Date noticed that the gunmen were following the freed hostage at a safe distance and fired over his head. The gunmen retreated back into the darkness and lobbed another grenade. Date provided cover to the released hostage and led him down to the fifth floor.

The terrorists had also reached the fifth floor landing. Date fired at them and in response a grenade landed near him seriously injuring his leg. A constable received shrapnel injuries on his neck. As the terrorists rushed down the stairs they left behind a backpack with AK-47 magazines and a satellite phone among other things.

Date radioed the escape route of the terrorists who had left through the hospital's main gate adjoining St Xavier's College. The time was now 11.50 p.m. It had been almost an hour since the terrorists had entered the hospital. As Date lay in excruciating pain nearly blinded by the shrapnel in his right eye he called his wife and informed her of his condition and asked her to let his batchmate know of his situation. It would be another fifty-five minutes before help arrived and shifted Date to KEM Hospital.

While Date and his team were fighting the terrorists inside Cama Hospital, three top cops from the Maharashtra police – ATS chief Hemant Karkare, Additional Commissioner Ashok Kamte and Inspector Vijay Salaskar were near the rear gate, chalking out a plan of action. Hemant Karkare had earlier gone to CST but found it deserted. Policemen on the spot had informed him that the terrorists had gone towards Cama Hospital.

Karkare had also received a wireless message informing him of Date's injuries and the constable's death at the hospital. Karkare, accompanied by four constables, immediately left for Cama while his personal Z-security guards were ordered to take positions near the TOI building. The team was moving cautiously towards Cama to gauge the situation. No one really seemed to know what was happening.

Inspector Salaskar and Additional Commissioner Kamte, who had met up at CST, also arrived near Cama Hospital shortly after. Salaskar was accompanied by five subordinates of ATS. As this team headed towards the rear entrance of the hospital, they heard gunshots. An injured constable rushed out of the entrance informing them that six police personnel including Date were battling the terrorists inside the hospital and they were seriously injured. At that moment, a grenade came flying out of the building which landed within the hospital premises itself. Kamte quickly responded with a burst of AK-47 firing. As investigations would later reveal, the fear of backup arriving and this time, armed with more sophisticated weapons, had prompted the terrorists to exit the building quickly.

Karkare, Kamte and Salaskar quickly discussed their next move. Kamte suggested they enter the hospital from the main gate. They got into a police SUV stationed there, and later, as they approached the special branch (the more common name for the CID Verification Office – where all foreign nations have to report for passport verification), Salaskar volunteered to take the driver's seat.

Oblivious to all this, the two terrorists had meanwhile come out of the hospital. A constable stationed outside the hospital called out to them to identify themselves. Ismail took out a revolver from his bag and opened fire at the constable killing him instantly. Not knowing that the lane next to Xavier's actually led to where they came from; they took a right turn. They saw a Honda City approaching them and shot at it. The car belonged to an IAS officer and the driver played dead while the terrorists quickly moved in to break into the car. Twenty-six-year-old Prashant Koshti found himself in the terrorist's line of fire. A bullet hit him on his shoulder but he mustered the strength to climb up the adjoining GT Hospital wall and escaped to safety.

The terrorists heard the sound of an vehicle coming behind them. It was the SUV with the police officers. The gunmen quickly took cover behind nearby trees opposite an ATM kiosk. Someone in the adjoining building had called the control room and informed them of two terrorists in that area. But this information (it was later known) was not passed onto the approaching officers who kept advancing.

In fact most eyewitnesses in the area who saw the police vehicle thought it had been sent by the control room. Kamte saw someone hiding in the bushes and fired at him with his AK-47 injuring the terrorist. He opened the door to alight the vehicle when the second terrorist stepped out of the shadows with a burst of fire from his AK-47. The officers had not seen him.

Everyone, except for constable Arun Jadhav who was sitting at the back, was killed. (Salaskar was seriously injured and later succumbed to his injuries.) Jadhav had been hit by three bullets on his right elbow and two others had scratched his left shoulder. The terrorists dragged the bodies of the officers out of the vehicle and threw them on the street while driving away in the police jeep.

No one knew that a police vehicle had been hijacked. They were driving toward Metro Junction. A fire truck, two police vans and an ambulance had blocked one side of the road at the Metro Junction. The waiting police and media personnel saw the police SUV slowly approaching the barricade. No one had an inkling of the occupants of the vehicle until a burst of fire from the car shattered the silence. One police constable was hit fatally and a bystander on a bike fell flat on the ground as bullets pierced through his hands.

News channels simultaneously started flashing the news of a police jeep being hijacked. Things were getting out of control. No one had a clue that these were the same terrorists who had fired at people at CST. Now each vehicle and person on the road was stopped and frisked. Policemen with guns drawn were pointing at people on the road asking them to move slowly and raise their hands. It was a war zone.

Unknown to the two terrorists, Arun Jadhav lay silently in the vehicle under two dead constables. He could barely move his shoulder to reach up to the AK-47 that was lying between two seats. When one of the dead constable's phone rang an injured Kasab opened fire in the direction of the sound. Jadhav ducked and missed the burst. With Ismail on the wheel they proceeded to Vidhan Bhavan. A message had been flashed on the wireless by then to look out for a police SUV with the number MH 01-BA 5179.

The SUV criss-crossed South Mumbai until one of its rear tyres was shot at near Mantralaya. The vehicle swerved as Ismail tried to turn it around. They spotted another car moving towards them. Sharan R. Arasa had come to the Oberoi to check on a friend who was dining there and had escaped the attack. He now found himself face to face with two armed gunmen asking him to get out of his car.

Sharan threw the keys of his silver Skoda Laura under the car and walked away when one of the assailants called him back, asked him for the keys and threatened to shoot. He quietly pointed under the car. Ismail then asked him on gunpoint to retrieve it. It still remains a mystery why the terrorists let Sharan go unharmed.

Arun Jadhav, still in the abandoned SUV, put out a message on the wireless about the carjacking of the Skoda and the direction in which it had sped. About twenty personnel of the D.B. Marg police station had already stationed themselves near Girgaum Chowpatty and set up a barricade there. They were armed with just two .303 rifles and two bulletproof jackets, which were given to those using the guns. The rest were only armed with lathis. They were screening every vehicle passing them.

They suddenly noticed a Skoda speeding towards them. The driver was warned to lower his lights but not only did the driver turned his headlights to high beam blinding the waiting policemen, but had also switched on his wiper and windshield cleaner making it difficult to see the occupants.

The driver then opened fire. The two armed constables fired back killing the driver Ismail instantly. Kasab slid down pretending to be dead. But as Assistant Sub-Inspector Tukaram Gopal Omble reached closer he noticed him moving. Kasab was also holding an AK-47. Omble sprang at Kasab who managed to fire multiple rounds; most of them hitting Omble. But the grip that Omble had gained remained while the other police personnel sprung in with their lathis beating Kasab. The police recovered bags with several magazines, 9mm pistols and grenades besides two AK-47s.

The police thought both terrorists had died even as they transferred them to a hospital. The lone terrorist to be captured alive, Mohammad Ajmal Amir Kasab was to later become the most valuable asset in the investigations.

'Assemble bed-sheets, carpets, mattresses, set them on fire.'

60 Dark Hours at Hotel Taj

Ashish Khetan

Scene 1

Deputy Commissioner of Police Vishwas Nangre Patil had hardly slipped into a light slumber when his phone rang. Patil, an officer in his early thirties, with a broad forehead, firm jaw, dark black hair parted to the side and a pencilled moustache, was in charge of Zone 1 of Mumbai. For policing purpose, the city has been divided into twelve zones; Zone 1 covers a major portion of South Mumbai with localities like Colaba, Nariman Point and Marine Drive falling under its jurisdiction. Only an hour earlier Patil had returned from a security review meeting at the Trident hotel, situated in the Oberoi hotel complex, a looming skyscraper located at the famous Queen's Necklace, an arch shaped stretch along the shore of the majestic Arabian Sea. Prime Minister Manmohan Singh was scheduled to attend an award function at the Trident hotel on the evening of 28 November. Though providing security to the Indian prime minister is the job of an elite force called the special protection group (SPG), the local police provides the fringe security like cordoning off and barricading the areas that include the PM's movements.

After meeting the members of the SPG team at around 8.30 p. m., Patil returned home – a fifteen-minute drive from Nariman Point to the Stone Building, near Metro Cinema, where he lived in a modest government flat. After dinner with his wife and two children, as Patil was settling down to take a nap – before a meeting at 11 p.m. – when Addl CP South region, K. Venkatesham called. It was 9.40 p.m. 'There are reports of firing outside the Leopold Café at Colaba. One of our police constables has been injured. Please rush to the spot immediately,' said Venkatesham in a hurried voice. In a flash Patil put on his khaki uniform and tucked a Glock pistol and two magazines in his holster. Accompanied by his personal bodyguard Amit Kheple, Patil rushed to Leopold Café, a joint located in the crowded Colaba market, which is a strip popular with Western tourists.

As the orange-beaconed car sped towards Colaba, Patil's head was reeling with possibilities. Was it gang war related firing? Maybe an unrelated personal vendetta? Before he could enquire from his officers at the Colaba police station, situated opposite Leopold Café, Patil received another phone call. This time it was the director general of Maharashtra police, A.N. Roy. The time was 9.45 p.m. 'Rush to the Taj Mahal Palace hotel. I can hear gunshots and sounds of blasts coming from the Taj,' the panic was evident in Roy's voice. Additional chief secretary of the Maharashtra government, the second-most senior bureaucrat in the state, Chitkula Zutshi was attending a party in the Taj when the terror attack began. Zutshi had called up Roy to inform him that some unidentified gunmen had struck at the hotel. It was Patil's worst nightmare coming true.

Barely two months before Patil had received an intelligence input from the IB (Intelligence Bureau) about a possible terrorist attack on the Taj hotel. On 29 September, Patil, with a team of police inspectors, carried out a detailed survey of the hotel's layout and security measures put in place by the hotel management. On 30 September, in a meeting with senior hotel officials, he laid down a set of stringent security instructions – the minutes of the meeting were duly prepared and given to the Colaba police station for follow-up action with the hotel management – that the hotel needed to implement:

- Only the main entrance of the new Taj hotel, known as Taj Tower, would be used and the gates of the old Taj (six-storeyed Taj Mahal Palace hotel) would be kept closed.
- Automatic doors for all vulnerable entrances, which could be

closed in the split of a second sensing any danger, would be installed.

- All guests will pass through door-framed metal detectors (DFMD), then be frisked with handheld metal detectors.
- All baggage will be scanned through X-ray machines.
- A wooden panelled glass door on the southern side of the hotel would be closed permanently with iron meshing.
- CCTV footage would be monitored round the clock from the CCTV control room.
- Armed guards will be deployed at the entrance of the new Taj hotel.

In fact Patil had recommended a security apparatus on the lines of the Bombay Stock Exchange, which after being bombed in 1993 had put in place an elaborate, multi-layered security structure. Four armed Mumbai policemen were also deployed at the hotel only to be withdrawn on 14 October after riots broke out in Dhule, a remote district in Maharashtra, necessitating police deployment in communally sensitive areas of Mumbai. The Taj hotel did install door metal detectors only to withdraw them two weeks prior to the attack citing inconvenience to its guests. Other security measures, though, were never implemented. First reports of firing at the Leopold Café and now at the Taj hotel – Patil knew this was not just an underworld related shootout.

Scene 2

The Taj Mahal Palace and Tower – two buildings, the first done in an eastern style and over a hundred years old, and the second, a looming tower constructed in the '70s – stand on little less than three acres of reclaimed land on the seafront at Apollo Bunder, facing an awesomely endless expanse of the Arabian Sea. On the evening of 26 November, like any other evening, the hotel was shimmering with lights, capped with its central dome that shone like the moon, and the smaller domes glistened like stars flanking the two ends of the hotel. Inside was an oasis of opulence and bustling revelry, with soft music in the lobby and corridors, a celebratory buzz in the ballroom, and animated chatter at the tables with the accompanying clatter of crockery. Outside, the sea was calm, the last of the tourists at the Gateway of India were filing out, a few vehicles were plying the roads. Just 500 metres to the west of the Taj hotel, the Colaba market was cacophonic, packed with tourists and late night revellers jostling through narrow alleys, stores filled with discerning shoppers, pavements lined with hawkers selling everything from fruits to bric-a-brac, and on the narrow roads, cars, taxis and buses were wrestling for every possible inch, honking frequently, their engines rattling and humming in an accompanying symphony to the human chaos. At the end of a lane adjacent to the Taj, stood Leopold Café, packed with a motley crowd, more noticeably the Western backpackers, sipping on chilled beer.

At the front entrance of the restaurant, two young men stood waiting, as if expecting a friend to join, before going in. They had swollen rucksacks on their backs and two equally stuffed bags were placed on the pavement. They stared at the crowd in the restaurant, soaking in the blissful hustle-bustle. Then the two bodies reclined over each other, hugged and patted each other's backs. A hawker even saw that one of them had tears in his eyes; it was an emotional parting like two dear friends splitting, not knowing when they would meet again. Then the two bent over their bags, like they were ready to leave. But no. They opened the bags and pulled out two menacing guns, assault rifles to be precise, the black of the barrel matching the dark of their clothes. Then the two stepped into Leopold Café using two different doors, one on the left and another on the right. One tossed a small round object towards the cash counter. It was a grenade. An ear-splitting explosion. Smoke and fire. The nightly sounds of Colaba market were abruptly interrupted by foreign, alien sounds. A succession of rifle shots followed. The guests dining and drinking inside the restaurant were showered with bullets. The place went blue, and then red: the colour of blood and flesh swamped the other colours – the brown of furniture, the white of the floor, the yellow of the walls.

The duo then came out on the pavement, took aim and sprayed bullets like Holi colour. They then took a right and entered the lane leading to the Taj. On the way they fired randomly as if to clear the passage to the hotel. And yes. The gun-toting men did, in fact, have friends. Two of them were lurking around somewhere. The two colleagues, who were not more than 100 feet away, made their own movements, getting ready to partake in their share of the bloodbath.

They also entered the lane, but instead of going straight took the first left, stopped at Gokul restaurant on the way, placed a bulging bag on the pavement, proceeded ahead and took the first right, and kept walking till they reached the vast open space facing the Gateway of India. After placing another bag 100 feet off the main porch of the new Taj, the duo turned around, walked through the porch and entered the new Taj hotel. The time was 9.38 p.m.

There was nobody to stop the two who first went to the reception and stood there for five minutes, admiring the luxury and grandeur of the place. Then one man went towards Shamiana restaurant, stopped in front of it, the beautiful glass doors catching his fancy, pulled his assault rifle out of the bag and aimed at the glass doors. Half a minute later, the second man left the reception and walked through the corridor linking the new Taj to the old, passing by Harbour Bar, showrooms of Mont Blanc, Ravissant and Dia on his right, and Masala Kraft restaurant on his left, and reached the small lobby facing the swimming pool. In the meantime, the two gunmen who had opened fire at Leopold, reached the southern side of the old Taj. They smashed a wooden-framed glass door with the butt of their rifles and entered the hotel. It was now 9.43 p.m. They then made their way to the swimming pool and on reaching opened fire. Meanwhile, the man standing in the small lobby opposite the pool, kept his bag down, pulled out an assault rifle and showered the place with bullets. A sniffer dog and its attendant came running towards the lobby only to be killed by the trigger-happy gunman. Then all four assembled in the small lobby and took an elevator for the sixth floor, the topmost floor of the old Taj.

Scene 3

DCP Patil asked his driver to get on the wrong lane and speed towards the Taj hotel. As his car approached the Prince of Wales Museum, Patil heard gunshots coming from the Gateway of India. The roads were almost deserted, a few curious bystanders were rooted to their spots on the pavements. Foregoing the front entrance of the Taj hotel, Patil's car headed for the rear. An eerie silence engulfed the hotel, the road leading to it was starkly empty. After parking his car in the lane adjacent to the rear compound of the old Taj, Patil walked towards the swimming pool and saw the chief security officer of the Taj hotel, Sunil Kudiadi, along with three security guards waiting for the first police enforcement to arrive. Sunil Kudiadi came forward to receive Patil. 'Terrorists have barged into the hotel and they are killing people,' he stuttered. Patil, his bodyguard Amit, Kudiadi and another Taj security guard rushed to the first floor. The time was 9.53 p.m.

The scene on the first floor was surreal. On the sparkling Italian marble floor were two bodies on top of each other in a pool of blood. A young girl was crawling in another corner with one of her hands partially blown off. She was howling in pain, begging for help. Before Patil could rush her to medical aid he heard more gunshots coming from above. Patil and the others rushed to the second floor. The corridor on the second floor was completely deserted. Tiptoeing around the aisle, Patil, followed by his bodyguard and two Taj employees, came upon a bend when Kudiadi spotted three men armed with assault rifles on the staircase. Kudiadi pointed out the gunmen to Patil and retreated.

Patil took cover behind a pillar and fired three rounds from his Glock pistol. The gunmen responded with a volley of bullets. No one was injured on either side. For a few minutes there was a complete lull. Patil emerged from behind the pillar and stole a look up the corridor. The terrorists had vanished. It was not clear in which direction. The time was 10.02 p.m. Patil asked Kudiadi to guide him to the sixth floor thinking that the topmost floor of the old Taj hotel would give him strategic advantage over the terrorists. Kudiadi escorted Patil and his bodyguard to the sixth floor through a narrow staircase at the back. It was now 10.15 p.m. On reaching, Patil proceeded to the south wing and scanned every corner but there was no trace of the three terrorists. Working his way down, Patil reached the fifth floor and went around a corridor, kicking open a few doors that were ajar, peeping inside the rooms, peering down the banister of the corridor. But the search was futile.

More than twenty minutes had passed since the crossfiring between Patil and the terrorists. A deafening silence had enveloped the imposing U-shaped structure – a place otherwise alive with music, soft tinkling of glasses and buoyant chatter. There were dozens of rooms on each floor, most of them occupied. But as Patil went round the aisle, there wasn't any sign of life. Suddenly there was a succession of thuds, like the hard kicking on a door, that echoed through the hotel. Soon the sound faded out. The terrorists were kicking hard on the door of room no. 384 A on the third floor. It was the liquor room of the Taj situated in the north wing. Hundreds of expensive liquor bottles were stored in the room. For several minutes the terrorists kicked at the door trying to break into the room. But the door did not give way. Possibly, the terrorists wanted to set the liquor room on fire. The time was 10.27 p.m. In the meantime Patil came down to the fourth floor and continued his search as he could not trace the source of the sound.

Scene 4

While Patil and his men were going around the galleries of each floor of the old Taj hotel looking for the gunmen, another team of policemen led by Special IG Hemant Nagrale stormed into the Taj Tower. At around 9 p.m. Sub-Inspector Nitin Kakade had come to a small post just across the Gateway of India and switched on the computer to make entries of the hawkers in the area. Around 9.35-9.40 p.m. Kakade heard loud cracker-like sounds. He thought since it was wedding season and the Radio Club situated at the bend of the road hosted wedding parties almost every day, the loud sound must be of the crackers. But after a few moments there was again a loud thud. This time Kakade stepped out of the post to check and saw people running amok. He stopped one man who informed him that someone had fired inside the Taj hotel. Kakade ran across the street towards the porch of the new Taj hotel. On reaching the entrance he saw that there was nobody, either at the gate or in the porch. Kakade then ran towards the Colaba police station. He collected his service revolver and six rounds of fire.

As Kakade, along with four police constables, was leaving the police station, Special IG Nagrale who was posted as director (vigilance) at Maharashtra State Electricity Board, and was staying above the Colaba police station, joined him. Nagrale saw three dead bodies lying on the side of the road closer to Leopold Café. Nagrale and Kakade crossed the road and reached the entrance of the restaurant. Two bodies were lying on the pavement. At the entrance three foreigners were lying in a pool of blood. The policemen saw that some guests were hiding under the chairs and tables and on the loft inside the restaurant. Nagrale ordered all those who were there to come out with their hands up in the air. A wireless van and an ambulance had also reached. After shifting the injured and the dead to the waiting ambulance, Nagrale and

Kakade, along with two police constables, walked towards the old Taj hotel.

When they reached the Diplomat hotel situated on the lane leading to the Taj, a few eyewitnesses informed them that about half an hour before they had seen two heavily armed terrorists making their way towards the Taj hotel. Nagrale, Kakade and the two constables saw that a glass door at a corner of the south wing of the old Taj was broken. Nagrale decided to go towards the main entrance of the new Taj hotel and told his men to follow him. When they reached the front entrance, a taxi driver told them that he had seen two terrorists entering the hotel through the main entrance. He had also seen them placing a bag across the road in the open space near the Gateway. Nagrale and Kakade went to the spot and saw a big black luggage bag with its flap slightly open lying in a corner. Though it was pitch-dark the cops figured that the bag must be containing a bomb. Nagrale immediately used the wireless to ask for the bomb disposal squad. Kakade then suggested moving towards the north side of the Taj Tower and see if they could peep through the glass wall on that side.

A portion of the lobby – visible through the glass when seen from outside – was empty. Nagrale and Kakade then decided to enter the hotel through the main gate. Along with two constables, they shuffled along the wall towards the main entrance. On reaching the main glass door, Kakade first went inside and Nagrale gave him cover. Nagrale and the two constables then followed Kakade inside the hotel. The lobby was completely deserted. Another few steps into the lobby they saw a hand grenade on the carpet close to a settee. The sight of a live grenade stopped them in their tracks. They waited a few moments but when the grenade did not go off, they realized it was faulty. Then Kakade and Nagrale went towards the passage leading to the old Taj and saw the body of a bellboy lying near the restroom. A glance towards the passage on the left side of the main reception leading to Shamiana restaurant revealed two bodies lying at the door of the restaurant. As Nagrale and others walked towards the restaurant they saw an elderly white couple with bullet injuries, crouching in a corner. In the meantime a police wireless van had arrived at the porch of the hotel. Kakade went out and took a stretcher from the wireless van. After shifting the couple on to the stretcher, Nagrale sent a wireless message to the control room asking for additional force.

The bomb disposal squad van had also reached. Kakade led the squad to the black bag filled with explosives. After two hours of perusing and snipping of many wires, the squad successfully diffused the bomb (its timer was set at four hours fifty-seven minutes from the time it had been switched on, and was expected to go off at around 2.30 a.m.) that could have killed many media persons and security personnel standing on the periphery. Leaving the squad to its task, Kakade and Nagrale took out bulletproof jackets from the wireless van and went back into the hotel. The owners and employees of several shops, situated on the ground floor inside the new Taj, were hiding in their shops all this while. Nagrale and Kakade asked them to immediately rush outside. After evacuating more than two dozen people, Nagrale led his men through the corridor leading to the old Taj. There were guests hiding in two restaurants – Harbour Bar and Masala Kraft – along the corridor. Nagrale asked those inside the restaurant to vacate the premises. More than fifty people were evacuated to safety through the main door of Taj Tower.

Scene 5

While Nagrale and Kakade were evacuating people from the shops and restaurants, Patil and his men were scanning the corridors of the south wing of the old Taj. Having found no trace of the terrorists there, Patil came out of the hotel and went towards the front entrance. There he saw two SRPF constables – Rahul Shinde and Sadanath More – who were visibly shaken and scared. He took them, his bodyguard Amit Kheple and one Taj security guard to a smaller lift at the back, and this time went straight up to the sixth floor, and then headed towards the north wing. Again, assisted by the other police personnel, Patil launched a hunt for the terrorists on the sixth floor. Determined but cautious, Patil and his men covered the entire aisle around the hotel rooms on the floor but the terrorists were nowhere to be found. Suddenly (as the CCTV footage later revealed), three terrorists with rucksacks on their backs and assault rifles in their hands appeared on the fifth floor. One was wearing tight black trousers and shirt and had a red-and-blue coloured rucksack on his back. Another was in a red T-shirt, red cap and black trousers. The third was in a light yellow coloured T-shirt and brown trousers. While Patil and his men were looking for them on the sixth floor of the north wing, the terrorists were prowling on the fifth floor of the south wing. The time was 10.47 p.m. For the next ten minutes both the policemen and the terrorists kept looking for each other. By now terrorists were sure that the policemen present in the hotel were not well-armed or in large number. With AK-47 rifles in their hands and backpacks full of hand grenades, the terrorists were surer of themselves and strutting around the fifth gallery looking for the kill. Patil, having failed to find any terrorist, took the lift and came back to the ground floor.

In the meantime DCP Rajvardhan, in charge of the special branch of the Mumbai police and entrusted with the responsibility of registering all the foreigners coming to Mumbai, reached the old Taj. Though law enforcement did not fall under his purview, Rajvardhan, after watching the news of the terrorist attack breaking on television, left his house. But in the hurry he forgot to carry his service pistol. As Rajvardhan's car pulled up at the front entrance of the hotel he saw Patil herding a few policemen. Patil briefed Rajvardhan about the happenings of the last one hour. For Rajvardhan it was like reliving his old days. During his tenure as superintendent of police in the Naxal affected district of Gadchiroli for over four years, Rajvardhan had been at the centre of guerrilla warfare and ambushes. Five years later Rajvardhan found himself in the middle of a similar battle. Only this time, instead of jungles, the action was inside one of the most luxurious hotels of the world located in the posh business district of cosmopolitan Mumbai.

By now Nagrale and Kakade had also come to the front door of the old Taj. As Patil, Rajvardhan and Nagrale made frantic calls to the control room for additional reinforcements, Kakade, along with two constables and the Taj security guard Puru, went to the first floor of the old Taj using a lift at the rear. Kakade saw people holed up in a tennis court size kitchen and in ballrooms. He persuaded them to leave the hotel using the rear exit. While many agreed, a few were so petrified that despite Kakade's repeated requests they refused to leave. After trying his best, Kakade came back to the front door of the hotel. In the meantime, a platoon of SRPF pulled up near the hotel. As Patil was strategically deploying over fifty SRPF personnel at different points at the periphery of the hotel, Sunil Kudiadi informed him that some civilians were stranded at the reception of the old Taj. Kakade, along with two SRPF personnel, and Kudiadi, went to the reception and safely evacuated about a dozen people, half of them women. By now Inspector Deepak Dhole of Colaba police station had also arrived. At this time, Rajvardhan and Patil decided to take control of the CCTV command room that was on the second floor in the south wing and trooped back inside the hotel. The time was 12.10 a.m.

Until now the cops had no clue of how many terrorists in all were present inside the hotel. Patil had seen three on the second floor. Eyewitnesses and a taxi driver had told them about four terrorists going towards and entering the Taj hotel. In the midst of the confusion and chaos, Patil, Rajvardhan, Kakade, Nagrale, Dhole, four police constables and two SRPF constables accompanied by the Taj security officer Puru took a corner lift and went to the CCTV control room. CCTV footage from the sixth floor first showed two terrorists. To know the exact number of terrorists in the hotel Patil went out of the room, pointed his Glock pistol towards the hotel roof, fired one round, and scampered back inside the CCTV room. The trick worked. Soon the CCTV footage showed three terrorists coming to the banister on the sixth floor hurling grenades and firing indiscriminately with guns pointed down towards the second floor. Immediately, Patil relayed messages on the wireless to the police control room that there were at least three terrorists and more could be hiding inside the rooms. Commissioner of police Hasan Gafoor replied: 'King to Zone 1. The MARCOS should be there in a few minutes. Keep them pinned down.'

As Patil and his men helplessly watched the drama unravelling, the terrorists took five people hostage and after kicking them with their boots and hitting them with their rifle butts, they locked the hostages in rooms 631 and 632. They then started to break open other rooms. As Patil's agonizing wait for the MARCOS continued, he saw on the CCTV that the terrorists were constantly talking to somebody on the mobile phone. After making a few calls the terrorists then started setting the sixth floor on fire. They first set the carpet of the gallery on fire. Then they pulled out bed-sheets and blankets from a few rooms and set them ablaze. Patil again relayed a message to the control room and informed his seniors about this new development. More platoons of SRPF and RAF (Rapid Action Force) arrived and cordoned off the hotel. Quick Response Teams (QRT) – a special force dressed in military fatigues and armed with AK-47 rifles and Glock pistols, under the control of the ATS – and later army personnel also surrounded the hotel.

As flames started ravaging the sixth floor, the terrorists came down to the fifth floor. They also brought the hostages along. In between, the terrorists continued throwing hand grenades and kept firing randomly from the top. In the midst of the raining grenades, bullets and fire, Rajvardhan, and Patil and his team, armed with .303 rifles and pistols, held out in the CCTV control room. Every now and then the cops came out on the corridor and fired a few rounds in the air in a bid to keep the terrorists from coming down, creating an impression that police was present in a large number.

The fire was spreading rapidly. Balls of fire were also dropping down on the floor of the second floor. (The hollow created by the staircase in the north and south wings of the old Taj hotel ends at the second floor. There is a slab on the second floor because when the hotel was first constructed it had only two floors. Others floors were added later.) A few CCTV cameras went off due to the fire. The fire continued to spread through the hotel and after a few hours all the CCTV cameras throughout the hotel stopped working. At about 3 a.m. the terrorists blasted an IED containing RDX on the sixth floor. The explosion was of such magnitude that it also partially damaged the fifth floor while triggering off a wild fire on the sixth floor.

The second floor too began to fill up with smoke which started choking the men in the CCTV room. Patil and Rajvardhan finally decided to leave the place. Puru told the cops about the fire exit door on the rear side, from where they could leave. Patil suggested that all of them would walk quietly in a line giving each other cover. The group pushed the door of the CCTV room open and started making their way in the dark towards the fire exit door. Halfway into the gallery the cops were showered with a volley of bullets. In the dark they could only see the fire of the bullets. It seemed they were coming from above. Two bullets brushing past the leg and belly of Amit Kheple, Patil's personal bodyguard, hit SRPF constable Rahul in his stomach and leg. The sudden assault split the group into two. While Patil and Rajvardhan managed to escape, Kakade, Dhole, and Puru, along with the constables were forced to retreat into the CCTV room. They also dragged Rahul, who was felled by the bullets, back with them. Smoke continued to fill inside the room. Kakade and Puru then decided they would try to escape through another door on the left side of the corridor. Dragging the injured Rahul along, the four came out and started groping for the door in darkness. Puru found the door and they all managed to escape. They survived with burn injuries. But in the fracas they could not rescue Rahul whose body and a .303 rifle were retrieved by the NSG from the second floor two days later.

Scene 6

Deven Bharti, Addl CP crime branch – a specialized force of the Mumbai police for tackling organized crime – was at Vile Parle, in the middle of an important operation, when he received a phone call from his supervisor and the chief of the Mumbai crime branch, Joint Commissioner Rakesh Maria, telling him about the indiscriminate firing at Leopold Café. A quiet, self-effacing man, standing just under five-feet-seven, Bharti had been leading arduous and tortuous anti-terror operations against a shadowy Muslim terrorist organization called Indian Mujahideen – responsible for almost all the major terror strikes across Indian cities since 2005 – for the last several months. But for Bharti, the news of firing at Leopold was confounding. Then poured in reports of firing at the Taj hotel, the Oberoi hotel and the CST station as well. It was getting from bad to worse.

Bharti placed calls to all the twelve units of crime branch – spread across the length and the breadth of the city – under his command, and told them to be ready for any eventuality. The officers posted at Unit numbers one, two and three – all of which were closer to South Mumbai – were told to rush to the police headquarters. After collecting enough arms and ammunition and bulletproof jackets, they were instructed to move to the different spots where firing had taken place. By the time Bharti reached the police headquarters located in Crawford Market, the terrorists at the Taj, the Oberoi and the Nariman House had already taken strategic positions inside the buildings. Two terrorists at the CST, after the railway police opened fire, had stormed into Cama Hospital, a vast complex situated across the road from the CST. After arming themselves with AK-47 rifles, Glock pistols and ample rounds of fire, Bharti, along with seven best officers of the crime branch and some armed constables, rushed towards the hospital. Bharti and his men entered the compound of the Azad Maidan police station and through its back opening on to the lane leading to Cama Hospital, reached the Anjuman-e-Islam school building, a six-storeyed building across the hospital and used the lift to go to the terrace of the building, which gave them a clear view of the hospital. In the dark of the night, Bharti and his team precariously waited for the terrorists, in the hope of spotting them on the terrace of the hospital, without much luck. The time was 12.30 a.m.

At around 1.10 a.m., Bharti received a call from Maria. He told Bharti that the IB had managed to intercept a telephonic communication between the terrorists and it seemed someone was constantly guiding and instructing the terrorists holed up inside the Taj: 'What can you see from the hotel windows?' 'Assemble bed-sheets, carpets, mattresses, set them on fire.' 'Throw grenades from the window, this would deter the police.' Like a football team coach, the man was guiding his team, giving tips, strategizing, showing the next move. The IB suspected the instructor to be in the vicinity of the Taj hotel, possibly in one of the many small hotels that dot Colaba. For the next two hours the crime branch team did a massive combing operation in over half a dozen rickety hotels. After body-frisking and rummaging through the baggage – clothes, laptop, mobile phones – of more than three dozen foreign nationals, most of whom were Iranians, Palestinians and Lebanese, the crime branch concluded the man instructing the terrorists was not present in the area. 'The instructor of terrorists is not here in any of the hotels, possibly he is not in Mumbai or the country itself,' Bharti informed his seniors by 3.30 a.m.

Scene 7

Bespectacled, balding, with hair on the temple and at the back, sixty-nine-year-old K.R. Ramamoorthy, the non-executive chairman of ING-Vyasa Bank (the profile of his job and that of his face would shortly land him in trouble), was, on the night of 26 November, staying on the sixth floor of the heritage wing of the old Taj in room no. 632. After having dinner in his room at around 9.15 p.m., Ramamoorthy readied himself to go to the Business Centre on the fifth floor. But as he stepped onto the corridor outside his room he encountered Taj security guards who told him to get back in and lock the door as there was some kind of trouble in the hotel. He did as he was told, turning on the television set in his room to learn more. TV channels flashed the news that the Taj hotel had been attacked by heavily armed terrorists. At around 11 p.m. there was a loud knock on his door by a person identifying himself as a waiter. Ramamoorthy refused to open the door.

A few moments later two gunmen – one tall and another of average height – stormed into the room, the door lock giving way to gunshots. They caught hold of Ramamoorthy, who was trying to hide, and tied him up. Soon, two more terrorists joined them. For the next two hours, Ramamoorthy's room was used by the terrorists as a command centre, the four gunmen making several phone calls to their handlers in Pakistan, speaking in Urdu with a heavy Punjabi accent – a dialect Ramamoorthy hardly understood. The four armed men were busy chatting among themselves and on the phone, fleshing out their strategy, discussing the manoeuvres and the use of hostages.

Time: 01. 04 a.m.
[The timings are from the phone intercepts later shared by the ATS, Mumbai.]

[The cellphone held by one terrorist started to ring.]
    Terrorist: Hello.
    Handler: *Salaam ailekum.*
    Terrorist: *Wailekum as-salaam.*
    Handler: See, the media is saying that you guys are now in room no. 360 or 361. How did they come to know the room you guys are in? ... Is there a camera installed there? Switch off all the lights ... If you spot a camera, fire on it ... see, they should not know at any cost how many of you are in the hotel, what condition you are in, where you are, things like that ... these details will compromise your security and also our operation. [The man showed sternness and elderly concern in his advice.]
    Terrorist: I don't know how it happened ... I can't see a camera anywhere,' the terrorist replied, embarrassed at his failure to figure out the location of the CCTV cameras [the setup of the five-star Taj was so different from the terror camps – mobile tents in the middle of jungles – where the terrorists been trained].
    Handler: Why can't you see the camera?
    Terrorist: There are many switches and lights. ... I can't figure this out.

Handler: Okay … Start setting the place on fire.
[The phone call ended with the instruction of mayhem.]

Time: 01.15 a.m.

[The cellphone used by the terrorist rang again.]
Terrorist: *Salaam ailekum.*
Handler: *Wailekum as-salaam.*
Handler: Have you set the room on fire or not?
Terrorist: *Bas kapde ikatthe kar rahe hain.* (We are just collecting the clothes).
Handler: *Jaldi laga do.* (Start the fire fast). And look for a suitable stronghold.

[After munching on some eatables stored in the minibar, two of the gunmen go out looking for suitable hideaway or 'stronghold' – the word terrorists repeatedly dropped in their discussions, preferring it for its militaristic connotation.]

Time: 01.25 a.m.

Terrorist*: Salaam ailekum … Salaam ailekum.*
Handler*: Wailekum as-salaam. Aag lagi ki nahi lagi.* (Has the fire started or not?)
Terrorist: *Nahi aag nahi lagi.* (No the fire has not started.) *Woh gadde-shadde … parde-warde … ikatthe kar raha hun aag lagane waaste.* (I am making a heap of the mattresses and curtains for the fire.) I am just waiting for the two to return.
Handler: Where have they gone?
Terrorist: They are checking the other rooms.
Handler: *Kaun kaun gaya hai?* (Who all have gone?)
Terrorist: Ali and Umer. *Woh neeche kaam shuru ho gaya hai.* (The operation has started downstairs.)
[The terrorist updated the man pointing out to the gunshots being fired by Patil and other cops from downstairs.]
Handler: Is somebody firing downstairs?
Terrorist: *Haan ji.*

There was some more discussion on how to set the hotel on fire and to prolong the attack after the caller disconnected.
A little later, the two gunmen returned, hauling four more

hostages along with them. All the five including Ramamoorthy were then undressed, their hands tied at the back, and were told to lie flat on the floor, head facing down. The terrorists then planted a nine-kilogramme on the sixth floor following which they dragged the hostages to the fifth floor of the heritage wing, in a room identified as a 'stronghold' by the two terrorists. The hostages were the bargaining chip for the terrorists. Their handlers in Pakistan were constantly instructing them to use them for placing demands before the Indian government and if that did not work, as human shields.

Time: 02.02 a.m.

[The phone rings.]
  Terrorist: *Salaam Ailekum.*
  Handler: *Wailekum as-salaam … Kya haal hai.* (How are you doing)?
  Terrorist: *Rahmatullah.* (All is fine with Allah's grace).
  Handler: *Aur kitne murge hai ab?* (So how many hostages do you have now)?
  Terrorist: We have five hostages now. One of them is speaking in some Kannad language.
  Handler: What is his name?
  Terrorist: What's your name (posing the question to the hostage)? … Ramamoorthy … He is saying his name is Ramamoorthy.
  Handler: Ask him what he does.
  Terrorist: What do you do? … Teacher *hai … kah raha hai teacher hai.* (He says he is a teacher) … [Then speaking to the hostage] You would not be getting more than 20,000 rupees salary … Smuggler *to nahi hai tu?* (Are you a smuggler?) You are staying in the Taj hotel … teacher *to khwab mein bhi nahi aata idhar.* (A teacher will not come here even in his dreams.)
  Handler: Ask him which university he is from.
  Terrorist: Which university are you from? … Karnataka University he is saying. [The three-way dialogue continues.]
  Handler: Remove his purse, check his full name. What is his first name? What is his father's name? Ask him.
  Terrorist: He is saying his full name is K.R. Ramamoorthy.
  Handler: K.R. Ramamoorthy. Who is he? … A designer … A professor … Yes, yes, I got it … [The caller was doing an internet

search on the name, and the results showed up a picture of Ramamoorthy] ... Okay, is he wearing glasses? [The caller wanted to match the image on his computer with the man before the terrorists.]

Terrorist: He is not wearing glasses. Hey, *chashma kidhar hai tumhara?* (Where are your glasses?)

Handler: *Saamne se ganja hai?* (Is he bald from the front?)

Terrorist: Yes, he is bald from the front ... he is fat and he says he has got blood pressure problems. [The terrorist confirms the appearance to his instructor.]

Handler: *Sar ganja hai?* (Is he bald?)

Terrorist: *Aey sar idhar kar.* (Hey, show me your head.) ... *Haan, ganja hai.* (Yes, he is bald.) [The terrorist confirms.]

Handler: Ask him if he is from Madras? [The instructor wanted to match the profile showing up on the search page.]

Terrorist: Are you from Madras? [Asks Ramamoorthy.] He says he is from Bangalore.

Handler: Okay. On which floor are you guys now?

Terrorist: We are on the fifth. We have set three-four rooms on the sixth floor on fire. The rooms were facing the sea, they were very opulent.

Handler: Okay, in case of any eventuality no hostage should remain alive.

After some chatter on the guerrilla tactics to be employed, the phone was disconnected. At around 3 a.m., there was a huge explosion. The bomb planted on the sixth floor had gone off, starting a wild fire on the entire floor. The lights of the heritage wing went off and the place starting filling up with smoke. Soon the fire spread to the fifth floor as well. Balls of fire were raining from the top. The terrorists and their hostages were choking up. The explosion was so huge that it shook the place. It seemed like the building would collapse.

For the first time, death was staring at both the captors and the captives in equal measure. Forgetting the standing instructions of not leaving behind any hostage alive, the terrorists ran for their own lives. In the dark, the terrorists dropped their phones and disappeared. The five captives now had to contend with fire and smoke. Four of the hostages somehow managed to find their way out of the hotel on their own but

Ramamoorthy was rescued the next morning by security and fire brigade personnel.

Soon after the big explosion, dozens of MARCOS, dressed in menacing black and armed with sophisticated assault rifles, reached the Taj. They were first briefed by the police on the last known location of the terrorists which was the fifth floor as seen on the CCTV footage. The Taj security personnel then apprised them of the complex layout of the hotel with the help of maps. Now it was the turn of these commandos to storm the hotel.

Scene 8

Bhisham Mansukhani dislikes attending weddings. He never goes to any of them. 'Only at gunpoint,' he says. The irony of this flippant admission doesn't escape him now. A journalist by profession, Mansukhani was a wedding guest at the Taj hotel's Crystal Ballroom – a popular venue on the first floor of the old Taj for weddings. Accompanied by his mother, Bhisham climbed the hotel's front steps into the lobby. The time was 9.30 p.m. After a brief stop at the washroom adjacent to the lobby, they proceeded to join the wedding party, narrowly missing the gunmen who made their entry just a few minutes later. Guests were yet to arrive and even the groom's parents were not there. Bhisham mingled fleetingly, then stopped to exchange information with a friend who worked the stock markets. That's when the first shots rang out. At first no one identified the sounds. Only when shards of shattered glass from the ballroom windows hit the guests did the sick dread of what-could-be set in. People dove for the floor and crouched under tables. It didn't take long for the Taj staff to act: they locked the doors in a flash. Held inside were roughly thirty people, a vulnerable set consisting mainly of elderly folk, a few of them aided by crutches.

A while earlier that day, four members of Parliament – Lal Mani Prasad of BSP, Jaisingh Gaikwad of NCP, N.N. Krishna Das of CPM and Bhupendra Singh Solanki of BJP – had checked into the old Taj hotel as members of a parliamentary committee on subordinate legislation. Gaikwad had taken room no. 319 and Krishna Das, 367; Lal Mani had taken room no. 228; and Solanki was in room no. 477. Besides the four MPs there were officers and staff of the committee who were also staying at the Taj. Solanki went to have dinner at the

Shamiana restaurant at around 9.30 p.m. As he walked in he saw Lal Mani emerging out of the restaurant and going towards his room. The chairman Krishna Das and the other members of the group were still having dinner in the restaurant. As the gunshots and explosions rang out, Solanki crouched there.

A few minutes after the shooting stopped, the staff members escorted the frightened bunch from the wedding party in the ballroom on the first floor through service corridors on the eastern side of the hotel. They went through the mezzanine floor, past the banquet kitchen and using the service corridor entered a members-only area of the hotel called the 'Chambers' on the first floor of the new Taj – wood-panelled rooms with an exclusive purpose of catering to the select from the select. The Chambers provides a fantastic view of the bay out front, with a large verandah that overlooks the Gateway of India, a fine dining restaurant and five function rooms. The Chambers also consists of a few corridors and waiting spaces, besides ladies' and gents' restrooms. It can only be accessed by elevators from the new Taj (there is a separate button marked CHAMBERS in all the elevators installed in the new Taj) or by the service corridor known only to the hotel staff that links the Chambers to the first floor of the old Taj. By virtue of this isolation, Bhisham saw why the Taj staff thought this was the safest place to shelter the guests. The Taj employees soon escorted in more guests and diners and the place started to resemble the waiting terminal of an airport, with 250-300 people at least.

Mineral water was circulated and tins of potato chips were passed around. Tray after tray of chutney and cheese sandwiches and canapés, even paté and smoked salmon kept coming, followed by cans of aerated drinks. The hotel staff didn't stop at that: towels and crisp white sheets were brought in to be used as wraps to keep warm. It almost became like one big party. After the first half an hour of gunshots that rang through the air a lull had descended upon the hotel. 'No one knew what was going on in terms of the attack and the rescue operation. As for me, I wasn't afraid; I knew the Chambers was inaccessible. I thought we would be rescued at any time.' Hours flew by. Mansukhani and others at the Chambers watched TV until about 10.30 p.m. and then it went on the blink. At about 12 a.m., the Chambers was shaken out of its reverie with a loud blast that went off in another part of the hotel. Anger and impatience began to bubble over as Bhisham overheard people hatching plans to make a run from the place. But no one dared to sneak out of the room. Gunshots and explosions kept ringing intermittently. The TV was not working but that didn't stop the information from coming in – there were 200-300 mobile phones in the rooms.

In the meantime, Solanki had left the restaurant and had been hiding near the swimming pool for nearly two hours. He constantly kept in touch with his three colleagues through their cellphones. He knew that both Lal Mani and Gaikwad were in their respective rooms, and Krishna Das had been taken to a big hall with around 200 other people. Das had also given a telephonic interview to a Malyalam news channel telling them about his situation, although he did not know the name of his hiding place, which was Chambers. Solanki finally escaped around 11.30 p.m. through the rear entrance beside the swimming pool, and went straight to Colaba police station. After coming out he gave interviews to leading regional and national news channels, letting them know that his colleagues were inside the Taj. By 1 a.m. his interview had been telecast on many channels. Lal Mani and Gaikwad too had been giving telephonic interviews to major news channels from their rooms.

Subsequently, police investigation revealed that handlers in Pakistan were monitoring TV coverage of the event and after coming to know about the MPs they told the terrorists inside the Taj to go for them and take them as hostages or better still kill them. After the explosion on the sixth floor the terrorists set out in search of the MPs and landed up near the Chambers. However, timely arrival of the MARCOS prevented them from capturing any hostages.

⁓⊷⊶⁓

After detailed discussion with the Taj security staff the MARCOS decided to first go to the CCTV room on the second floor in the old Taj. They reasoned that they might get to know the current location of terrorists from the CCTV cameras. But the CCTV control room had already caught fire and the cameras had stopped functioning. This vital information was not communicated to them by the Mumbai police. As they entered the hotel they heard gunshots and grenade explosions coming from the fourth or fifth floor. The MARCOS stealthily moved to the second floor where they found that the CCTV room was full of smoke and entering the room was not possible. Just at that time, the commandos heard gunshots somewhere on that floor and rushed in that direction. While taking cover they saw twelve to fifteen bodies scattered on the marble floor. A few injured were also lying there. Soon the MARCOS came under fire and retaliated with a fusillade of bullets. Terrorists now hurled grenades at them. Fortunately, the commandos could take cover and remain unhurt. After the grenade explosions there was a lull. The terrorists had moved elsewhere. The bodies and the injured were shifted to the ground floor from where they were whisked away in ambulances.

As the gunfire kept ringing, the hotel staff on their own, around 3.30 a.m., attempted an evacuation. Everyone was asked to silently gather at the service door. Recalling the assembly, Bhisham complains about mobile phones going off and the constant chatter even as the evacuation was in progress. The idea was to lead people in threes and fours through a narrow corridor. Barely five minutes into the evacuation (by this time fifty-odd people had already reached the lobby through the narrow staircase), all hell broke loose as shots rang out nearby. After a gun-battle with MARCOS on the second floor of the old Taj, the terrorists had come down to the first floor and entered the kitchen and killed over half a dozen Taj employees. They then proceeded towards the service corridor connecting to the Chambers, looking for the MPs. A stampede took place as people scrambled to return to the safety of the Chambers.

After locking themselves inside the rooms, the guests barricaded the doors by piling up furniture and then turned off the lights. Bhisham saw a Taj personnel take a bullet in the stomach while trying to shield a couple – the Mangishkars. In the stampede, an eighty-year-old woman on crutches fell down even as bullets were going off in front of her. She was saved when two people pulled her into the 'Lavender Room' – one of the five function rooms of the Chambers – where Bhisham and his mother had fled.

The MARCOS, who were on the second floor of the old Taj, on hearing fresh gunfire – this time from the side of the new Taj – came running to the first floor of the old Taj and tried to enter the new Taj building through the connecting service corridor. But the terrorists hurled grenades and fired indiscriminately preventing the commandos from reaching the Chambers. It was absolutely dark and while the terrorists were accustomed to the darkness by then, the MARCOS found it difficult to manoeuvre their way around. In this exchange of fire two commandos were injured. The firing outside the Chambers lasted for several hours after which the terrorists managed to escape. The commandos had blocked the exit, which was towards the terrace, to prevent the terrorists from escaping. But it was too late. The terrorists had already vanished. Upon entering the service corridor, the commandos found a rucksack that contained dry fruits, a large amount of ammunition and some plastic explosives. They also found seven fully filled AK-47 magazines and approximately 400 spare rounds and grenades lying in the corridor. There was blood and dead bodies all over. Around fifteen bodies from the kitchen were removed and five-six injured were rescued.

While the MARCOS were fighting a pitched battle against the terrorists with bullets zinging back and forth in the service corridor, Bhisham and his mother along with other guests were fast losing hope. Rajan, the Taj personnel who was shot when they had tried to escape at 3.30 a.m., was writhing in pain. The Mangishkars bandaged his stomach to keep the blood and guts from spilling out. Bhisham remembers that despite the immense pain Rajan did not cry out, afraid to give away the group's location.

He recalls the bravery of the Taj staffers who were sitting and taking phone calls by the door all through the night because that's where the mobiles and the chargers were plugged. They did this knowing full well that at any time the terrorists could blast open the door with a grenade. At 8 a.m. Bhisham finally lay down on the floor next to his mother. He dozed off and woke up at 9.30 a.m. to a forceful knocking on the door. Somebody said it was the police, but another piped up cautioning against opening the door. What if it was the gunmen? Bemused, Bhisham offered that the gunmen wouldn't need to knock if they wanted to get in. The knocking was followed by a reassuring female voice that was recognized by the staff as one of their own. The door was then opened. It was the MARCOS. The bleeding Taj staffer was placed on a stretcher while the rest were asked to raise their hands as a precautionary measure. Around 200 people from the Chambers were saved by the MARCOS.

Walking out, the scene was enveloped in a smoky haze, blood on the marble floor and bullet casings everywhere, with the commandos securing the place. The gunpowder air stung Bhisham's eyes and they began to tear. Struggling to keep his eyes open, Bhisham grasped the extent of destruction that had taken place through the night. As he walked down the service corridors he saw pools and smears of blood and broken glass everywhere. The gory tour finished at the lobby of the new Taj where it had all begun; large glass panels were shattered, furniture was overturned, tiles were cracked. Outside was freedom, as three buses, two police vans and one BEST bus were parked in the driveway, waiting for the unlikely passengers.

Passengers onboard, the first bus pulled out, and as the second van started to drive off, the firing began. The gunshots seemed to be reverberating from somewhere in the old Taj. Bhisham and a few others were caught cold on the entrance steps. Even before the scene could escalate into further chaos the hotel staff made a ring around the guests. Finally when the firing abated, the group was ushered into a BEST bus, and they rode to Azad Maidan police station. A quick debriefing session ensued, where the cops got phone numbers and addresses of the guests for future reference. Bhisham and his mother got home at 11.15 a.m., nearly fourteen hours after his drive to the Taj to attend his friend's wedding.

Scene 9

At around 4.30 a.m., on the morning of 27 November, the IL-76 aircraft – a Russian manufactured medium range military transport aircraft used to carry troop forces and combat material – carrying over 160 NSG commandos touched down on the tarmac of Mumbai airport. On the plane was the former home minister, Shivraj Patil, along with NSG DG J.K. Dutta, NSG DIG (operations) Brigadier G.S. Sisodia, Deputy Force Commander Colonel B.S. Rathi and Group Commander of NSG Squadron 51, Colonel Sunil Sheoran – the four senior NSG officers who were soon going to launch a most difficult and complex operation of neutralizing terrorists in two five-star hotels and the Chabad House. After deplaning, the three officers, along with Colonel R.K. Sharma, Major Sanjay Kandwal, Major A.S. Jasrotia and Captain Varun Dalal, headed straight to crime branch chief, Rakesh Maria's office for the latest update. While Major Sandeep Unnikrishnan led the 160 odd commandos to the Mantralaya (Maharashtra Secretariat) situated in South Mumbai,

Maria gave a detailed briefing of the developments so far. Maria informed that while in his interrogation, Ajmal Kasab had said that only four terrorists were inside the Taj and two inside the Oberoi, he might be misleading the investigators and thus his claims could not be taken on their face value. But based on eyewitness accounts of civilians and police officers it appeared that there were at least four terrorists inside the Taj while two or more were hiding inside the Oberoi. He added that the terrorists in the Taj were probably operating in pairs. From what he had surmised till then, he also gave a physical description of the terrorists inside the Taj – one terrorist was in a blue shirt, one in a red shirt while two were in green colour outfits. One terrorist wearing green, he said, was stout and was balding. He was possibly the leader of the Taj gang. Maria further said that at least three terrorists were spotted first on the sixth floor and later on the fifth floor of the Taj at around 3 a.m. Maria also revealed that currently the MARCOS were in the middle of a gun-battle with the terrorists at the Chambers in the new Taj. After the briefing Brigadier Sisodia, Colonel Sheoran and Major Kandwal headed to the Taj for a reconnaissance. They went around the hotel complex, trying to understand the hotel layout and the vulnerable points that needed to be manned so the terrorists could not escape.

By 9.30 a.m. Sandeep Unnikrishnan along with 100 NSG commandos – also known as Black Cats because of the black Nomex coveralls and assault helmets they wear – arrived at the Taj hotel, their black outfits gleaming from the bus windows, in a striking contrast to the cherry red of BEST buses in which they were being transported. The NSG officers went inside the central lobby of the new Taj and met Addl CP Deven Bharti and joint commissioner (law and order), K.L. Prasad – the two senior Mumbai police officers who were camping at the Taj (DCP Rajvardhan and IG Nagrale had returned home, while DCP Patil was monitoring the cordon). Bharti told the NSG that electricity in most parts of the old Taj had gone off. Sunil Kudiadi and another Taj security personnel, Rodrigues, also joined the meeting and spread the floor plans of the hotel before the NSG. Kudiadi told them that the U-shaped old Taj building had a difficult layout as each floor was different from the other. He informed that besides the connecting corridor between the ground floor lobbies of the old and the new Taj, the two buildings were also interconnected on the first floor through the kitchens.

Col Sheoran divided the commandos into fifteen House Intervention Teams (HIT) comprising five commandos each (the remaining commandos who were not part of HIT were in ancillary roles like with the bomb disposal squad, while the others were snipers). Each team was headed by a HIT commander, a junior commissioned officer (JCO). Every commando was armed with Heckler & Koch family of 9mm submachine guns or the 7.62 mm PSG-1 sniper weapon, Glock 17 or Sig Sauer pistols, hi-tech day-and-night surveillance gadgets, searchlights, grenades, poison-tipped daggers, bulletproof jackets and hundreds of rounds of live ammunition. The commandos were told about the total number of terrorists present inside the hotel and the guerrilla tactics being used by them.

When the MARCOS had entered the hotel the terrorists were moving between the first and the second floors of the north wing in the old Taj. It increasingly appeared that the terrorists were very familiar with the complex layout of the hotel and were constantly shifting from one room to another, one floor to another, firing from different angles at a time, hurling hand grenades whenever the security personnel came close to them. After a briefing, as detailed as it could be in the given circumstances, Col Sheoran rounded up with a pep talk. The NSG commandos were entrusted with the job of both rescuing the stranded civilians and neutralizing the terrorists in a five-star hotel complex. It had dozens of rooms on each floor, a number of restaurants with kitchens and service areas, long corridors, ballrooms, conference rooms, a seemingly endless service area meant for Taj staff more sprawling than the visible ones – the labyrinth was impossible to comprehend by just looking at the maps. But the NSG did not have the luxury of time. The operation had to begin in right earnest.

Col Sheoran overall divided all the HIT teams into two groups. One group of four teams was placed under the control of Major Kandwal, while the other group, with the remaining number of teams, was put under the charge of Major Sandeep Unnikrishnan. Kandwal was ordered to storm the new Taj while Unnikrishnan led his teams into the old. Two teams of snipers under the command of Major Jasrotia and Captain Dalal were positioned strategically outside the hotel. And thus began one of the most arduous commando operations in the history of the NSG – Operation Black Tornado. Operation Black Thunder I and II in the Golden Temple complex in 1986 and 1988, Operation Ashwamedh in 1994 and Akshardham Temple in 2004, were the other anti-terrorist operations carried out by the NSG.

Major Kandwal's teams accompanied by Taj security personnel Rodrigues made their way to the first floor of the new Taj. By now the MARCOS had evacuated over 200 guests from the Chambers. The MARCOS briefed Major Kandwal and then the NSG took over. Many men and women were still hiding inside the two bathrooms in the Chambers. There were also two dead bodies lying there. Kandwal's teams evacuated those hiding in the bathrooms, the adjoining kitchen and the Taj staff inside a bakery on the same floor. Before moving to the upper levels, the NSG deployed commandos in the connecting passage leading to the old Taj. Along with the NSG four ATS officers – Shailesh Gaikwad, Shashank Shelke, Nitin Thakre and Vijay Shinde – were manning the connecting passage. Also QRT commandos of Mumbai police and the SRPF personnel were positioned at various entry and exit points inside the new Taj. After consulting Col Sheoran, Major Kandwal decided to adopt the top to bottom approach for the new Taj operation. Col Sheoran positioned himself in the CCTV command room on the fourth floor of the new Taj, which was still operational. As Kandwal led his HIT teams to the uppermost floor, the twenty-first floor of the Taj Tower, three ATS officers – Bhimdev Rathod, Vivekanand Wakhare and Basit Sayeed – also went with him. This floor had only banquet halls and kitchens. A few guests hiding in there were frisked and after verification of their identities (with the help of any kind of I-card the guests were carrying on them), they were handed over to the ATS officers whose job was to take them down to the lobby and release them only after further verification. The NSG did not want to leave anything to chance and they wanted to ensure that no terrorists escaped from the hotel in the garb of a civilian.

After sanitizing the twenty-first floor, the NSG commandos moved to the twentieth floor. There are 306 guest rooms in Taj Tower and 85 per cent of them were occupied. Each floor had seventeen rooms and the gallery around the rooms was L-shaped. All the rooms were locked and the hotel's guest lists showed that 95 per cent of the occupants were foreigners. Rodrigues was carrying the master key. After taking positions, the NSG would knock on each room, identify themselves and ask guests to open the room and come out with their hands up in the air. Most guests responded;

however, the few who didn't – their rooms were opened with the master key. But there were some guests who had put a double lock inside making the master key ineffective. For such rooms the NSG blasted down the doors with the help of explosives. In a few instances the NSG found that the person inside had placed sofas, chairs and other furniture at the door. So even after blasting open the doors the NSG could not enter inside. They would then again shout that they were the police and the person inside should immediately come out. But these occupants refused to move out. A few NSG commandos would then take positions on either side of the room while others removed the furniture blocking the entry. On entering they found just terrified civilians. In one instance a person had, after hiding inside a cupboard, covered herself with blankets and sheets. When the NSG saw the mound of blankets and sheets moving inside the cupboard for a moment they thought it was a terrorist. With their hearts in their mouth the commandos peeled off all the covers and there emerged a Thai woman. After entering a room, the NSG would first check the bathroom, then the cupboards and then finally the room.

After sanitizing a couple of floors, the NSG received an input from the ATS that there were some suspicious phone conversations being made from room no. 1201. (The technical section of the ATS was monitoring all the telephone calls being made from the Taj and in the adjoining areas.) The NSG was told that there were three to four persons present in the room who were talking in Arabic with someone in Saudi Arabia. The NSG team checked the guest list and found that the room was booked in the name of just one person named Mohammad Al-Esa, a Saudi Arabian national. The team rushed to the room and dutifully first knocked on the door and asked the occupants to move out. But there was no response. The commandos then placed low intensity explosives on the door and blasted it down. But the entry to the room was blocked with chairs and a vertically placed settee. The suspicion grew further. The commandos again shouted that they were the police and whoever was inside should immediately come out. Again there was no reply. The NSG threw a few hand grenades inside. Fortunately the guests were hiding behind the bed which was placed vertically and so none of them was injured by the splinters. The four finally emerged from behind the bed with their hands in the air. The NSG feared that they might be wearing explosives on their body. The commandos told all four to stop at a distance and take off their clothes. The four undressed themselves to their underwear. They were then frisked and their belongings were rummaged. The Saudi national was a businessman who had come to Mumbai on business and the other three were his clients who were visiting him when the terrorists struck. The NSG then moved to other rooms and the process of clearing every room in the new Taj continued till next morning. Finally at around 5 a.m. on the morning of 28 November, Major Kandwal declared that the new Taj was clear and handed it over to the Mumbai police.

Scene 10

After the gunfight with the MARCOS in the new Taj, the terrorists had slipped away. The NSG suspected them to be hiding somewhere in the old Taj. Major Unnikrishnan had about ten HIT teams at his disposal. Like Major Kandwal, he also adopted the top-bottom approach so the terrorists could be pinned down at a lower level or be forced to move towards the exit of the hotel. The entire hotel from outside – and every road and lane leading to the hotel complex – was already cordoned off by the Army, SRPF and RAF personnel. Major Unnikrishnan decided to start the combing operation from the sixth floor, the topmost floor of the old Taj. Now the moot question was how to approach the sixth floor. The lifts had been blocked by then and he did not want to restart them as using them would be a giveaway. Also, Sunil Kudiadi had informed him that entering through the central staircase was fraught with risks as the wide staircase, which ran from the ground to the sixth floor forming an atrium, would give the terrorists a very clear view of the approaching commandos. Major Unnikrishnan finally decided to take the narrow staircase at the back, the one used by Patil the previous night.

He divided his teams into two groups – one group entered the north wing and the other, the south wing. Both the groups after having scanned all the rooms in their respective wings were supposed to meet near the central staircase on that particular floor, where after positioning a few commandos they would again go back to the rear staircase and proceed to the next floor. Both the north and south wing groups were accompanied by one Taj security employee, whose task was to guide the commandos through the maze of the hotel and assist them in rescuing the guests locked up in the rooms and halls on the different floors. By now the fire on the fifth and the sixth floors had already been doused by the fire brigades. The central portion and the south wing of the sixth floor were badly charred while the north wing was less affected by the fire. The lights in most parts of the old Taj had gone off after the powerful explosion and the resultant fire the previous night. Most of the hotel was plunged in darkness. Major Unnikrishnan led his teams to the sixth floor and saw charred bodies lying in different rooms. Among the dead was Taj General Manager Karambir Kang's family – his wife and two minor sons were found in a suite.

The total number of rooms to clear was 336, not counting the service areas – 52 on each floor. The Taj security staff went from one room to another with the NSG giving them cover. They followed the same procedure for getting the guests to open the door and were able to evacuate around a dozen guests who were locked in their rooms. After having completely sanitized and secured the sixth floor the NSG teams came down to the fifth. Again they went from one room to another, keeping an eye on the bends in the corridor and the spiral staircase. Some of the suspecting guests refused to open the doors. The NSG team found one guest who was so scared since the terror attack had begun over twelve hours ago, he had remained hidden under a small table in his room. Around ten guests stranded in different rooms on the fifth floor were evacuated. After each evacuation, a room was thoroughly searched for any hidden explosives or any other suspicious object. When the fifth floor was completely sanitized, the NSG moved to the fourth floor.

On the fourth floor, after having combed around half a dozen rooms in the south wing, one NSG HIT team came under fire. This happened when one HIT team led by JCO Subedar Fair Chand was approaching room no. 472. The bullets came from two different directions. But it was completely dark and the commandos could not make out exactly which two sides the fire was coming from. All they could see were flashes of blue. Though the NSG was wearing night-vision goggles, they were of the passive variety. Passive goggles need at least some light that can then be magnified to give a clear view. Active night vision goggles do not need a light source and enable one to see even in complete darkness. This handicap of the NSG was going to cost them dear. All the five NSG commandos, one of whom was Rajbir Singh Lamba, took positions and fired in the direction of room no. 472, whose doors were flung open. The terrorists retaliated with more fire and also hurled a few grenades. Three NSG commandos – Lamba, Sunil Kumar and Fair Chand – got injured. While Sunil and Fair Chand suffered bullet injuries, Lamba was struck by splinters. The NSG commandos then crept up and took position outside the room and shouted that whoever was inside should immediately move out. But there was no response. The NSG then hurled grenades inside the room and as a result the room caught fire. The fire soon started spreading to other rooms and the floor started filling up with smoke. (After the operation was over the charred body of a civilian was found in that room. The terrorists had used the guest as a human shield. When the NSG attacked, the terrorists, taking advantage of the darkness, managed to escape – leaving the guest in the line of fire.)

While the NSG and terrorists were exchanging fire Major Unnikrishnan was combing the north wing of the fourth floor. By that time he had evacuated and secured the entire north wing of the fourth floor. After the fire-exchange, the HIT team led by Fair Chand called him on the wireless and briefed him about the episode. Major Unnikrishnan met Fair Chand and his team near the central stairwell. Fair Chand's team told him that after the room caught fire no one had tried to escape or move out. The commandos were of the opinion that the terrorists must have escaped to a lower level, since the sixth and fifth floors had been secured and were being manned by NSG commandos. The fourth floor was by now almost completely engulfed in smoke. The commandos were choking. The fire exit on the floor also became inaccessible, as room no. 472 was closer to it. Major Unnikrishnan called Col Sheoran who was camping in the main lobby. He told him to come down through the central staircase to chalk out a fresh strategy. Major Unnikrishnan complied and, with the HIT teams, reached the main lobby that Brigadier Sisodia and Col Sheoran were using as the command centre. By the time he reached the lobby the time was around 4.30 p.m.

Scene 11

Until now Major Unnikrishnan had adopted the top-down approach, accessing each floor through the fire exit, securing the top floors before proceeding to the lower levels. But due to thick black smoke gushing down the fire exit, the latter was now no longer accessible. As Col Sheoran and Major Unnikrishnan were busy chalking out a fresh strategy, at around 5 p.m. on 27 November, a Taj employee approached Addl CP Deven Bharti. The employee told Bharti that a colleague of his, a woman in her early twenties, named Florence Martis – employed with the computer section of the hotel – was held-up in a computer data centre room on the second floor of the north wing. The room was not attached with a toilet and Florence had not eaten or drank since the previous night when she had locked herself in after hearing the gunshots. Bharti, who at the time was in the main lobby, went to the reception counter, took the receiver off a board telephone (PBAX) and dialled the number of the data centre room. Martis answered the phone and on learning it was a police officer, she broke down and narrated her ordeal. In the meantime, Colonel Sheoran and Major Unnikrishnan reached the reception and Bharti briefed them about the situation of the woman. To ensure that it was not a trap being laid by the terrorists using the distraught woman as bait, Major Unnikrishnan decided to speak to Florence himself. She came on the line and reiterated her situation. She begged him to rescue her. After much deliberation, Major Unnikrishnan finally decided to do it.

It was decided that a NSG team would go through the kitchen route on the first floor and then make it to the second floor. Another two teams, of five commandos each, went to the third floor to give cover to the team on the second. A Taj security officer was persuaded to show the NSG team the way to the computer data room. The employee wore a bulletproof jacket and walked behind the NSG team, trying to guide them to the correct room. The NSG team reached the second floor of the north wing but failed to find the computer room and came back. The two teams sent to the third floor continued to man their respective positions. By this time it was almost nine in the evening. Major Unnikrishnan and Col Sheoran again went into a huddle and decided that the NSG would now go through the central staircase. As NSG commandos were climbing up the steps leading to the first floor, they were ambushed. The terrorists opened heavy gunfire and threw grenades. When the firing started Major Unnikrishnan and Sunil Kumar Jodha had reached the first floor while other commandos were still on the steps. The NSG fired back but the terrorists seemed to have taken different vantage positions and attacked the commandos from many directions simultaneously. A bullet went through Jodha's bulletproof jacket and nearly pierced his abdomen. As the duo got stuck on the first floor, other commandos were forced to retreat. Jodha was hit by more bullets and splinters. Major Unnikrishnan dragged Jodha to the right side and kept on firing.

It was pitch-dark but it appeared that the terrorists were firing from the end of the corridor and from the left door of a room named the Palm Lounge situated in front of the central stairwell. Heavy retaliatory fire by Major Unnikrishnan forced the terrorists to duck for cover. For a few moments the firing from their side stopped. The momentary lull allowed one NSG commando to clamber up the staircase. Major Unnikrishnan and the commando hauled up Jodha, who was bleeding profusely, towards the stairwell and started climbing down. The NSG commando and Jodha went ahead as Unnikrishnan gave them cover. Hardly had Jodha and the other commando climbed down a few steps that the terrorists opened fire once again. Major Unnikrishnan turned around, climbed back the stairwell, turned to the right side of the corridor and, after positioning himself behind a wall, opened fire in the direction from which the fire was coming. 'Don't come behind me,' he shouted at Jodha and the other commando. Both accelerated down the stairwell and managed to reach the ground floor lobby. Jodha was immediately shifted to hospital where he survived with eight gunshot wounds and serious injuries from grenade blasts.

Meanwhile, Major Unnikrishnan kept firing from his MP-5. The terrorists were firing from the extreme left of the corridor and from the left door of the Palm Lounge. The major took a few paces down the corridor and took cover near the right door of Palm Lounge and continued to fire. At some point he decided to enter the Palm Lounge through the right door and shoot the terrorist who was positioned at the left door. What he did not anticipate was that there was one more terrorist hiding inside the Palm Lounge who had positioned himself along the front wall. As he stepped into the lounge the second terrorist opened fire. Major Unnikrishnan retaliated but he had lost the initiative. After heavy firing from both sides Unnikrishnan was killed. The remaining team members, because of relentless heavy shelling and grenade explosions, couldn't make it to the first floor. The NSG kept trying to reach him on his walky-talky but there was no response. Col Sheoran and others thought that Major Unnikrishnan might have been deliberately not taking calls as he did not want to create any sound. They thought he might be hiding somewhere and waiting for reinforcement to arrive.

Scene 12

Throughout the night the terrorists kept firing from the first floor thwarting any attempt by the NSG to make it to the first floor. Now they were firing from at least three different directions. The NSG kept firing in retaliation but it was more to keep the terrorists from moving down than to get them. As it neared dawn, the firing from the terrorists lessened. By the break of day the terrorists stopped firing completely. Major Kandwal, who was until now evacuating the new Taj, reported to Col Sheoran in the lobby at around 5 a.m. on 28 November. It was now clear that all the terrorists were inside the old Taj. Col Sheoran asked Kandwal to lead the operation in the old Taj. At around 6 a.m. Major Kandwal moved towards the first floor with a few HIT teams under his command. The terrorists had stopped firing and it appeared they had moved to a different location. Kandwal entered the first floor taking the route of the kitchen of the Chambers. The commandos first moved into the Crystal Room on the first floor and scanned ever inch of it. After an hour-long combing process, they secured the hall. Nothing was recovered from the Crystal Room – no arms or ammunition nor any sign of the terrorists. Major Unnikrishnan was still missing.

While Major Kandwal was securing the Crystal Room, Col Sheoran went to the second floor to look for the room where Florence was hiding. Col Sheoran finally located the room and entered it. But to his surprise there was nobody in there. Col Sheoran came back to the main lobby and dialled the intercom number of the computer room. The girl picked up the phone. Col Sheoran asked her why she did not come out when he came there looking for her. She said she was hiding in the loft and feared that the terrorists had entered the room. Col Sheoran said he was coming again and this time he would say 'Police' three times which was to be the cue. Florence was finally rescued. But she told him she had another colleague who was hiding in one of the rooms on the same floor. Florence called up her colleague on his cellphone (throughout the night they had kept in touch over the phone) and said that the police was coming to rescue him. The man had been hiding behind a false wall for more than thirty hours. He too was rescued. Col Sheoran evacuated about a dozen more guests from the second floor and finally secured it.

After having secured the Crystal Room on the first floor, Major Kandwal now moved into the adjoining Sunrise Room and launched a thorough search. But here too they found nothing. Once the Sunrise Room was secured Major Kandwal led the NSG commandos into the Palm Lounge on the first floor facing the central stairwell. Major Kandwal entered the lounge through the door on the right. He would have hardly taken a few steps when he saw a body lying there. It was his friend and colleague, Major Unnikrishnan lying prone with his right hand on his stomach. His body was riddled with bullets. A few feet away from his body were lying a sock and a shoe, drenched in blood. Everything on his body – his uniform, belt, holster, shoes – was intact. The shoe and the sock were not the major's. They belonged to one of the terrorists. Major Unnikrishnan's body was carried down by the NSG to the main lobby. One of their most brilliant officers had died a heroic death. But there was no time to mourn. It had been more than thirty-eight hours since the terrorists had stormed into the hotel and were still going strong. After having secured the Palm Lounge Major Kandwal now moved into the ballroom. It was around noon.

The NSG commandos later recalled that as they entered the ballroom, they felt they had come into a theatre – there were no windows, no sunlight and with the electricity off, the darkness was blinding. There was a strong possibility that the terrorists could be hiding there. The pitch-dark of the ballroom made for a perfect hideout. As the NSG was combing the ballroom the terrorists again opened fire. The air rang with bullets but no one was sure which direction the fire was coming from. Outside the hotel, two grenades came and landed on the promenade, not far from where NSG snipers and crime branch officers were positioned. One grenade exploded while the other just rolled down to a corner. Three officers of a crime branch team were hit by splinters. It appeared that the grenades were thrown from Wasabi restaurant on the first floor. It became clear that a few terrorists were hiding inside that restaurant.

Col Sheoran came out and positioned half a dozen snipers at different vantage points outside the hotel; a few were perched on top of a fire brigade vehicle to shoot at the terrorists if they could be sighted through the windows. Every now and then the terrorists would lob a grenade from the windows on to the road. The snipers fired a few rounds but they failed to get them. Three crime branch officers – Dinesh Kadam, Sachin Kadam and Arun Chavan – also positioned themselves behind a few parked police vehicles and tried to take a shot at the terrorists. Dinesh Kadam fired a few rounds but in vain. The glass windows were very thick and tinted, thus not allowing the NSG and crime branch officers a view of the terrorists inside. Col Sheoran then borrowed an automatic grenade launcher (AGL) from the Army and one NSG team tried to lob grenades inside the restaurant through the broken windows. But the grenades failed to stop the terrorists. It was unclear how many terrorists were inside the restaurant and how many were hiding elsewhere. There was a connecting door from the ballroom to Wasabi. There was one more door to Wasabi along the corridor. The ballroom was still not cleared and it was important to secure it before storming into Wasabi.

It took the NSG more than five hours to comb the sprawling ballroom; on every step they feared they were going to be greeted with a fusillade of bullets. But there was no one. By 5.30 p.m. the ballroom was cleared. After having secured it, the NSG came out into the corridor that led to Wasabi restaurant. The NSG commandos moved down to the end of the corridor and found a GPS (Global Positioning System), an empty AK-47 magazine and few 9-volt Duracell batteries lying on the floor close to the piano that was there. The 9-volt batteries are often used to trigger IEDs. It was now almost certain that the terrorists were hiding inside the Wasabi restaurant. Instead of entering the restaurant through the door, the NSG decided to go in through the kitchen. There were two doors from the kitchen into Wasabi – one was the serving door and another door was to the right, which was bolted and a fridge blocked it. There was a possibility that the service door was booby-trapped by the terrorists. The time was around 6 p.m.

The NSG decided to remove the fridge and blast open the door. Low intensity explosives were laid at the door and a blast triggered. As the door gave away bullets came zipping across from the dark inside of the restaurant. The terrorists announced their presence inside the restaurant loud and clear. Just below Wasabi restaurant was the Harbour Bar. From the inside of Harbour Bar there was a spiral staircase to Wasabi restaurant. Major Kandwal communicated to Col Sheoran and asked him to position commandos at the entrance of Harbour Bar in the main lobby. Immediately, over half a dozen commandos were positioned at two small entry doors of

Harbour Bar, which opened into the gallery on the ground floor, leading from the new Taj to the old. Major Kandwal and Major Jasrotia, along with two HIT teams, now tried to storm inside the restaurant through the blasted door. The terrorists opened fire from two directions thwarting the NSG attempt. The NSG too opened heavy fire aimed at the restaurant and hurled grenades inside it. But despite their best efforts the terrorists remained unhurt, as they had chosen a corner in the restaurant where the structure of the walls and pillars gave them protection.

Every now and then, using the spiral staircase, the terrorists would come down to Harbour Bar and open fire and throw grenades in the direction of the two entry points where the commandos were positioned. Splinters of one of the grenades thrown by them hit one NSG commando called Surinder Singh Dalal. He survived with splinter injuries on his legs and torso and the sides of his face (but lost hearing in one ear). Heavy firing and grenade explosions from either side continued into the late night. Around midnight the hotel staff informed Col Sheoran that there were two more doors from the kitchen side of the bar that opened into the corridor near Masala Kraft restaurant. Col Sheoran and Bharti entered the bar through these doors and while groping in the dark they found keys to the doors. Col Sheoran locked both the doors. All the exit routes from Wasabi and Harbour Bar were now sealed. The terrorists were finally trapped.

The NSG now decided to opt for synchronized grenade explosions. Two or more grenades were tied together and thrown inside to blast in a synchronized manner intensifying the impact. As a result Harbour Bar and Wasabi restaurant were soon on fire. The place was full of smoke and fire. All four terrorists now descended to Harbour Bar and two of them sat near the windows. They soon stopped firing but the NSG kept the onslaught on. The commandos kept shelling the bar and firing through the doors. At around 4.30 a.m. on 29 November, the commandos heard the terrorists crying and begging for mercy. The place started ringing with their cries: '*Rabba raham kar. Ab aur bardasht nahi hota.* (For God's sake, please stop this. We can't take it any more.)' At the break of dawn one terrorist jumped out of one of the windows of the Harbour Bar. Col Sheoran and a few NSG commandos had already positioned themselves outside the windows in anticipation of terrorists trying to flee. He fired two rounds at him and the terrorist was killed. After the fire brigades doused the fire inside Harbour Bar the commandos found the bodies of the remaining three terrorists. While two, half-burnt, were lying in the centre, one was lying in a heap, near a window, his body burnt beyond recognition.

The four were later identified as Abu Soheb, Abu Ali, Abu Rehman Bada and Abu Umer. Umer, the eldest, was the leader of the Taj group. The bomb disposal section of the NSG now once again combed the entire old Taj to ensure that the terrorists had not planted explosives in any part of the hotel. By 6 p.m. on 29 November, the hotel was cleared and handed over to the Mumbai police.

'We decided we would not leave anyone behind'
A survivor's tale

Faisul Nagel and his colleagues from Nicholls Steyn Associates, a South Africa-based close protection service company had just finished dinner at The Souk, the Lebanese restaurant on the twenty-first floor of the new Taj hotel. The team, led by the director of the company Bob Nicholls, was in Mumbai for the Champion's League matches. The Taj was a place recommended to them and The Souk was the only restaurant in the hotel that had a table for seven available. The group was soaking in the breathtaking view of the famous Mumbai skyline when Bob's phone rang. It was a friend warning him about the gunshots heard inside the hotel.

They ran to the window and peeked below to see the streets surrounding the Taj crowded with people, fire trucks and police personnel. Suddenly there was a loud bang. Bob found the restaurant manager who was initially hesitant to share any information. When they pressed him he disclosed what he knew at the point – armed men had entered the hotel from the main lobby and were shooting indiscriminately.

The team huddled together to come up with an escape strategy. They realized that terrorists could easily reach the twenty-first floor through the elevators situated in the lobby. So, they first barricaded all the access points with chairs and tables and even the heavy serving counters. The all-glass interiors suddenly did not look so appealing. They scanned the floor for the exits – apart from a conference room opposite the restaurant there was not much else. From where they were standing, they could see the elevators. There seemed to be a pattern in the manner in which the elevators were moving – it would reach a floor, stay there for a while, move to the next floor, stay there for a while, go all the way down and then get to the next corresponding floor and the pattern would continue.

Bob instructed his team to switch off all the lights in the restaurant. Anyone coming up would think the restaurant was closed and if that failed at least the barricades would hold them off for a while. The sixty people present in the restaurant were shifted to the conference room via the kitchen to avoid going past the elevators.

But people had begun to panic. Bob's team split the group into two and asked them all to remain calm as they were in it together.

The group had armed themselves with knives and whatever else they could find to defend themselves. One person from the team was sent to see where the fire exit led. He reported back that the fire exit led all the way down but there was no guarantee it would come out at the back of the hotel. Nagel felt this would be the safest way out.

In the meantime they also kept trying to reach the hotel authorities. Although it was difficult initially as almost the entire hotel staff was involved in evacuating as many guests as it could, the security manager, Sunil Kudiadi was finally contacted, who put them in touch with the police team outside the Taj. After being assured by the security manager that the fire exit did indeed lead to a secured exit outside the hotel, the group proceeded down the staircase. By now the police had taken positions outside the exit points and around the buildings.

Sunil Kudiadi had meanwhile reached the twentieth floor. He had kept in touch with Bob and the group of people waiting on the twenty-first floor. Sunil assured Bob that he was reaching them in thirty seconds. There was a knock on the door of the restaurant. Bob went ahead, opened the door just an inch and after he was convinced, he let Sunil in. The next fifteen minutes entailed an intense briefing of what was really going on inside the hotel. It was much worse than any of them had expected – how were they going to get sixty people out of the hotel safely?

Bob's team decided to divide into two groups of men and women. They reasoned that in case of an eventuality the husbands would try to reach out to their wives and this could jeopardize their operation. There was another worry – a seventy-eight-year-old lady who could barely walk was also among the diners. But it was clear – the group would not leave anyone behind. They sat her on a chair and decided to carry her. Bob Nicholls decided to lead with Sunil's help.

The descent was not smooth. They had to enter the main hotel building, walk through the service corridors, come down a flight of the main stairway, and then walk past the elevators in the lobby. Everyone in the group was asked to take off their footwear to avoid making any noise. The operation was further compounded by the fear of fire. So the group carried fire extinguishers along.

The thirty-minute rescue seemed to be stretching to eternity when they walked into the glare of the waiting television cameras outside the Taj.

George Koshy

'At the Tiffin restaurant there was blood, blown-out bits of flesh ... splattered on the floor.'

How Hotel Oberoi was Secured

ASHISH KHETAN

Scene 1

The darban, an imposing Sikh in a white *sherwani* and black turban, was graciously welcoming guests in the typical Indian style – hands clasped, a gentle smile, and a 'namaste' on the lips – when he saw a beat-up black and yellow taxi, one of a million that dot the roads of Mumbai, pulling into the porch. Two youngsters in their early twenties, clean shaven, with a rucksack each on their backs and one in their hands, emerged from the backseat of the taxi and quietly paid the fare. In the assemblage of gleaming expensive cars moving under the porch of the thirty-four storey Trident hotel the taxi did stand out, though it was not uncommon for guests to arrive at the hotel in the city's taxis. The darban was about to bow his head in greeting, when the two boys, instead of walking in through the high glass doors, whipped out two black assault rifles from their bags, turned around and aimed at the Gucci showroom, across the glass entrance door. A spray of bullets shattered the clear glass walls and doors of the showroom, piercing the glass counters and the mannequins. The staff and customers took cover behind anything that afforded protection. An employee manning a counter was hit by bullets. The strapping darban fled down the driveway. The bellboy standing next to the darban followed, but while the darban chose to hit the road, he ran inside, took a right and hid under the high counter of the baggage section. Outside, the gunmen took a few steps down the porch; one placed a swollen white carry-bag on the pavement on one side of the driveway. Abandoning the bag the gunmen ambled up the driveway, turned to the glass door entrance vacated by the darban moments ago. After firing at the entrance, they walked through it. The clock at the reception showed the time was 9.51 p.m.

They first took a left, walked down a few paces and upon seeing no one along the gallery they let go a few stray bullets. Turning around, they walked up to the baggage section where the bellboy and one more hotel employee were cowering in fear. Pointing their rifles at them the two gunmen opened fire. The grand lobby of the hotel reverberated with screams and shrieks and the blood from behind the baggage counter gushed out on to the marble floor. The two once again turned their attention and guns on the punctured glass doors, sprayed another round of bullets to sound off a threat to anyone on the outside. The gunmen now walked straight to the reception counter and sent more bullets flying. A computer monitor crashed on the floor. The staff manning the reception had already fled. As they were crossing the main lobby, doors of one of the elevators to the left slid open and four guests, one of them a Japanese, emerged. Seeing the gunmen they ran back but the Japanese was hit by bullets. But he along with the other three managed to get back into the lift and escape. However, the Japanese guest later succumbed to his injuries. Walking past the plush lobby, a sprawling open restaurant called Veranda and a piano to the left, the two walked up to the Opium Den restaurant at one end of the lobby. They entered the restaurant and opened fire. Most of the diners and staff had already escaped into the back office and systems room. One guest was still around and was immediately shot dead. The two gunmen then went inside the systems room and killed four people – three members of the hotel staff and one guest.

Then they came out and walked back towards the Trident lobby. They spent a few moments in front of the elevators and turned around and went up the carpeted stairs, walking along a corridor lined with shops. This route led to the Oberoi hotel, a twenty-one storey building, adjacent to the Trident, part of the same complex. They first came across a garment showroom called Bruni. Though the shop was closed they still sprayed a few bullets on the glass-walled showroom. Suddenly, they turned back and walked down the stairs they had just climbed, and looked around the deserted lobby, ensuring no one was chasing them. The two now again climbed up the stairs and stopped at a jewellery shop called Tijori. A foreign guest who was hiding there was gunned down. Then the two walked towards the Tiffin restaurant. Before they entered Tiffin, they sprayed bullets on the glass walls and doors of two shops that sold watches, leather accessories and clothes. The time was 9.57 p.m. Upon entering Tiffin, a multi-cuisine restaurant, they fired several rounds, giving the victims no chance to escape. Most of the diners present at the time had perhaps mistaken the sound of gunshots to be that of firecrackers and had stayed put. While some diners were fortunate not to be hit, twelve bodies were recovered from Tiffin later, some bending over their tables, some sprawled on couches, some lying under the tables and others spread on the floor.

Coming out of Tiffin, the duo planted a bomb in the lounge area of the upper lobby of the Oberoi, behind a magnificent grand piano that overlooks a garden and beyond it the sea. Having planted the second bomb, the two headed to a spa and gunned down two women employees working there. Then they went towards Kandahar restaurant that was on the pool level. There were over fifty diners present in the restaurant at the time. The waiters at the Kandahar had by now evacuated most of the diners who had gone down through the service staircase. But many others, despite repeated requests from the stewards, opted to go upstairs using the service staircase. After walking into the Kandahar, the gunmen first threw grenades and then opened fire. There were only two stewards present in the restaurant. The other staff members and guests had already escaped. The terrorists caught hold of the stewards and told them to set the restaurant on fire. They obeyed and started setting the furniture and table cloths on fire. One steward's hand got singed and he hesitated a bit. The terrorists shot him dead instantly. They took the other steward, Pradeep, as a hostage and at gunpoint told him to lead them to the upper floors. The gunmen and Pradeep walked up to the elevators. There are two sets of elevators on the pool level. The central shuttle elevator is from the lower lobby level to the pool level. The other set of elevators are the guest elevators that start from the upper lobby level (on which Tiffin restaurant was situated) and go up to the twenty-first floor. Pradeep pressed the button of the central shuttle elevator. But there was only one button for this elevator with the arrow pointing down. The terrorists figured that this elevator would only go down. They told Pradeep to not act smart as they had told him they wanted to go upstairs. Seeing his bluff being called Pradeep then hurriedly pressed the button of the guest elevator.

Outside the hotel, in the meantime, a police mobile van had pulled in under the porch. Two more police vehicles – white SUVs with yellow and red stripes and a Mumbai police emblem on either side – came and stopped at the foot of the driveway. The time was 10.05 p.m. Getting off one vehicle, API Kishor Shinde spotted the white bag left behind by the terrorists. On lifting the bag Shinde immediately knew it had a bomb. He placed it in a corner at the end of the driveway and sent an SOS to the bomb disposal squad. Sub-Inspector Bhagwat Bhansude and Constable Marne came out from another vehicle and ran into the hotel through the main entrance of Trident. Bhansude and Marne ran up the stairs and as they reached the upper lobby of the Oberoi, Bhansude spotted the two terrorists standing near the elevators and fired one round from his service revolver. The gunmen were taken by surprise. Ducking for cover, the two hurled a grenade towards the policemen. Taking cover, Bhansude fired one more round. The terrorists threw one more grenade. In the meantime, the doors of the shuttle elevator slid open and Pradeep jumped into it and went down.

Two grenade explosions forced the ill-equipped cops to beat a hasty retreat. The gunmen took the guest elevator and went up to the twelfth floor. As they were walking down the corridor they heard some noise coming from the service staircase at the rear. They went in the direction of the noise and saw fifteen people in the service staircase. These were the guests who had escaped from the Kandahar and had opted to go up. The gunmen spirited these fifteen hostages to the twenty-first floor, which is the last guest floor. Here, they lined up ten hostages facing the wall along a small, narrow staircase that goes towards the covered terrace that houses machine rooms. The hostages were told to raise their hands and place them on the wall. A woman among the hostages asked the gunmen why they were doing this. One gunman replied: Do you remember Godhra? The two then called their superiors on the phone and asked for further instructions. The order was to shoot them all which they duly obeyed. Presuming that all ten were dead they hauled the remaining five down to the nineteenth floor, using a staircase. Here they went into a room and spent a few hours with their hostages, questioning their identities, in between handling calls from the LeT's top brass who were incessantly calling from Pakistan, issuing instructions. Of the five hostages, three were women and one old Turkish couple, who implored their captors to let them go on the grounds that they were Muslims. The timely disclosure saved the couple. After locking them inside room no. 1979, the gunmen killed the three non-Muslim women in the corridor. While locking the Turkish couple, the duo accidentally left a bag in the room. Then they moved down to the eighteenth floor. The time was around 4 a.m.

Scene 2

Additional Commissioner Parambir Singh had hardly walked into his house, a spacious apartment in one of the government-owned residential buildings at Nariman Point, when he got a phone call from K. Venkatesham, additional commissioner South region, who informed him that there were near simultaneous incidents of firing at Leopold Café and the Taj hotel. Singh, in his wiry five-feet-ten frame looked agile and ready for action. Originally from Chandigarh, Singh was posted at the ATS. For the last three months Singh had been working round the clock on a case involving a terror attack in Malegaon. The bomb attack had happened on 29 September, in the holy month of Ramzaan in a crowded marketplace, killing five Muslims, including a young boy. The investigation led to the arrest of eleven Hindu radicals including two retired army personnel and a serving lieutenant colonel. The Malegaon blast triggered by the Hindu extremists was, the ATS claimed, in retaliation to the many bomb blasts perpetrated by the Indian Mujahideen – an amorphous Muslim terrorist group that the Indian police believed was behind more than half a dozen major terrorist strikes in the country over the last three years. The arrests of Hindu radicals by the ATS, however, had led to a smear-campaign launched by a Hindu right-wing party Bharatiya Janata Party and its many affiliate organizations. The entire ATS and its chief Hemant Karkare had been under intense media scrutiny.

Reaching out for his Glock pistol and thirty rounds of fire, Singh summoned his bodyguard and rushed for his car. Singh would have hardly gotten into the car when Venkatesham again called to update him that a few gunmen had opened indiscriminate fire outside the Trident and Oberoi hotels as well. Singh told his driver to head for the Oberoi hotel, which was barely 500 metres from his home. Driving past the Vidhan Bhavan and other commercial towers Singh found the streets nearly deserted. As his car hit the lane that led to the Oberoi hotel Singh heard faint sounds of gunshots that seemed to come from the direction he was headed in. The gunshots grew louder as the car inched closer to the main entrance of the hotel. Parking his car a few metres ahead of the iron gate that opened to the driveway of the hotel, Singh got out and walked. There was a lull in the hotel as the firing had stopped. Singh saw some policemen standing outside, numb and in shock. Only one of the policemen was carrying a pistol, while the others were lathi-wielding constables. Across the lane where Singh was standing, on Marine Drive, the main road along the seashore, API Shinde and Bhansude were waiting for additional forces and the bomb disposal squad to arrive. The timer attached to the bomb inside the bag – that Shinde had lifted and placed at the foot of the driveway – was ticking.

The irrepressible Queen's necklace, facing the vast expanse of the Arabian Sea, was glittering with sepia coloured street lights. The sea was quiet. On any ordinary evening, the promenade's concrete stretch would be thick with walkers, camera-wielding tourists, and hawkers. But now the place was unrecognizable. After the initial wave of gunshots an eerie silence had befallen the place. Soon, Venkatesham also pulled up on Marine Drive, parking his vehicle before the two SUVs of the nearby police station. He then crossed the median that divides Marine Drive and stood on the promenade looking up at the hotel. A few moments later a fusillade of gunshots ripped the lull. Only to be followed by a deafening silence. Again, a few minutes later three loud explosions, one after another, sent shards of glass flying all over the place. From years of training in anti-terror operations, Singh could tell these were grenade explosions. He then decided to enter the ground floor lobby of the Oberoi hotel.

The scene was like a well-constructed movie set: furniture had been toppled over, the floor was littered with broken glass, the most populated parts of the hotel – the reception counter and its adjoining seating area – were now deserted. After pacing the lobby for a few minutes Singh came out and saw the chief security officer of the hotel, Sushil Nagmote. With the help of the maps he was carrying, Nagmote explained to Singh the layout of the hotel complex – the twenty-one storey Oberoi and the Trident hotels – and the various entry and exit points. The conversation between Nagmote and Singh was interrupted by more ear-splitting grenade explosions, followed by a rapid succession of gunshots. More than twenty minutes had passed since Singh had arrived at the scene but there was still no sign of additional forces. Shaking off this overpowering despair of just watching the carnage unfold, Venkatesham called Singh outside to show him that two platoons of the SRPF had arrived at the hotel and a bomb disposal squad had also reached the spot. The squad first placed a blast containment ring around the swollen bag stuffed with over 5 kg of RDX and then covered it with a bomb suppression blanket – an armour to minimize damage to life and property from an explosion.

With the newly arrived manpower, the first thing Venkatesham did was to thwart any possible attempt by the terrorists to escape. He issued orders to cover several exit points of the hotel with members from one battalion of the SRPF. Singh began positioning two SRPF personnel each at over half a dozen exit points marked by the hotel security staff. Suddenly, there was a huge explosion that stopped everyone dead in their tracks, the bomb in the bag outside had finally exploded. The impact was massive; the blanket soared and landed in the sea, a flight of fifty metres from the spot where the explosion had taken place. A few minutes after the explosion, which had left all the glass windows on the ground floor of the Trident and Oberoi hotel shattered, ATS chief Hemant Karkare called Singh and asked him if the QRT had reached the spot. On getting a negative reply, Karkare, who at this time was at the CST, assured Singh that the QRT would soon join him. Minutes after the phone call from Karkare, there was another booming explosion that seemed to rattle the very foundations of the building. The bomb inside the hotel lobby had also exploded. Scared SRPF personnel ran from their positions and took shelter near the boundary wall of the NCPA building.

Moments later, hordes of terrified people came pouring out of the Oberoi hotel. Some were dressed in pinstripe suits, some in bathrobes, a few had faces smeared with dust and smoke. Singh tried to stop and engage a few to get some on-site information. But they were too shocked and scared to share any solid information. He then severely reprimanded the SRPF personnel who had run away and told them to take their respective positions. In the meantime, the sounds of grenade blasts and gunshots once again rent the air. An assault van with around six police personnel who were equipped with one AK-47 rifle, one carbine and one SLR, pulled up outside the hotel. Something strange happened at this point. More sounds of gunshots were heard, only this time they emanated not from inside the hotel but from the side of Vidhan Bhavan, 400 metres off to the south of the Oberoi complex. Grabbing an AK-47 from the assault van, Singh along with a couple of policemen jumped into a police SUV and rushed towards the site.

Singh saw a police SUV stranded on the road adjacent to Vidhan Bhavan. On taking a few steps closer to the vehicle and training searchlights on to it, Singh saw that one of the tyres had come off, the right side of the vehicle was riddled with bullet holes, and blood was oozing out of the doors. A moaning voice implored for help from the dark inside of the vehicle. Singh and his men were initially apprehensive, so they asked the man to establish his identity. The voice said it was Arun Jadhav, Inspector Vijay Salaskar's bodyguard. Singh told his men to break the glass of the rear door and pull Jadhav out of the vehicle. Soaked in blood, Jadhav said two terrorists had hijacked the vehicle in which he along with Salaskar, ATS chief Hemant Karkare, Additional Commissioner Ashok Kamte and two constables, were travelling. But where are Karkare and the others, hollered Singh. They were all dead. It could not be true. Only an hour back Singh had spoken to his chief, Karkare. 'Get out of your shock and recollect exactly what had happened,' Singh shook Jadhav holding both his arms. 'Sir, I am telling the truth. They killed Karkare and the others and hauled the bodies of Karkare, Kamte and Salaskar out of the vehicle before hijacking it. I lay buried under the bodies of two constables in the rear, which they did not bother to pull out,' informed Jadhav. It was around 12.40 a.m.

Jadhav was rushed to the hospital. Singh then got a message on the wireless that the two terrorists who had hijacked the police vehicle had been intercepted at Girgaum Chowpatty, 4-5 kilometres north of Vidhan Bhavan. Singh rushed to the spot of the encounter and saw two terrorists being shifted into a police vehicle. A silver Skoda – which the two terrorists had hijacked after abandoning the police SUV near Vidhan Bhavan – was parked against the police barricades with its nose brushing the median dividing the road. Singh went closer and slapped the two terrorists on their faces. One did not respond, the other betrayed signs of life. Singh pinched their noses, one gasped for air. 'This one is still alive. Take him to the hospital,' ordered Singh to the assembled policemen. In the meantime over a dozen officers of the ATS led by DIG Sukhvinder

Singh reached Girgaum Chowpatty. DIG Singh split the team in two. One was sent to JJ Hospital to enquire about Karkare and the others. The other team comprising eight ATS officers accompanied Singh to the Oberoi.

Scene 3

Additional Commissioner Singh and the team of ATS officers drove back to the Oberoi and parked their vehicles on the road between the NCPA and the hotel. He formed two teams, one comprising four ATS officers – Sachin Kadam, Arvind Sawant, Sunil Jadhav and Bala Kadam – and another comprising five QRT commandos – and told them to storm into the Oberoi hotel. Accompanied by the hotel's security chief Nagmote, the ATS team entered the deserted lobby of the Oberoi. They went through the lower lobby and using the fire exit reached the upper lobby where they scanned over a dozen store rooms but did not come across anything suspicious; then they came back to the lower lobby and saw that the two lifts were still in operation. Sachin Kadam instructed the Oberoi security chief to immediately put the lifts out of service. Then Kadam and the others scanned the lower lobby and after some time the team went to the pool level.

The floor was submerged in half a foot of water with an assortment of things floating around: bags, shoes, mobile phones – evidence of the people who had been here just a few hours ago. (A wildfire had enveloped the Kandahar and the tea lounge, where a bomb had exploded, and was threatening to spread to other parts of the hotel. But the fire brigades had reached on time and successfully put out the fire.) The team of cops went into the Tiffin restaurant where a ghastly scene unfolded: blood, blown-out bits of flesh and hair were splattered on the floor and the walls, bullet-ridden bodies were slumped all around. Meanwhile, the team of five QRT commandos, accompanied by the Oberoi assistant chief security officer Rajesh Kadam, went towards the reception where PBAX phones were installed. Rajesh wanted to make calls to the guests holed up in different rooms and give them security advisories. But soon the terrorists started hurling grenades from the top; a few of them landed in the lobby. The trajectory of falling grenades made it clear to the team that the terrorists had taken a strategic position high up in the Oberoi. In the face of intensified grenade attack from the top, both teams decided to retreat.

Outside the hotel, Singh along with two ATS officers went to the top of the Express Towers, a high-rise building a few blocks to the north of the Oberoi. Armed with night-vision goggles and assault rifles, Singh remained positioned there for over half an hour. Another team of two ATS personnel – Vijay Wakudakar and Rahimutullah Sayeed – armed with Kalashnikovs and night-vision goggles took position on the terrace of the NCPA building situated across the road facing the Oberoi. The two teams – one under Singh atop the Express Towers and the other on top of the NCPA building – now started exchanging notes. Singh shared that since Express Towers was at the rear of the Oberoi he was not getting a clear view of the hotel. On the other hand, PSI Sayeed and Wakudakar had an excellent view of the hotel. They saw that the windowpanes of the room in the extreme corner of the eighteenth floor, facing the NCPA building, were broken, from which a gunman was sticking out his rifle, taking aim below, and opening fire. Again, on the extreme corner of the same floor facing the sea, were broken windowpanes indicating another gunman. In each of these rooms the curtains were drawn, and a silhouette of a person would intermittently appear. The rest of the rooms on the same floor had guests holed up inside, waving for help from their window. Singh then decided to abandon his position from the Express Towers, as it was not providing a strategic view of the hotel. As Singh was walking across the road towards the promenade he saw a shadow move on the ledge of a room on the eighteenth floor, apparently trying to cross over to an adjacent room. Though it was dark, Singh believed that the moving silhouette was that of one of the terrorists. Snatching an SLR from a constable standing a few feet away, Singh aimed and opened fire at the silhouette. The bullet missed the target but the moving silhouette jumped back into the room and disappeared.

At around 2 a.m., two columns of the Western Command of the Army and eight Army commandos reached the Oberoi hotel. Lack of coordination among different units within the police, and among the police and other agencies and the armed forces was a continuing problem. The lieutenant colonel who was leading the platoon deployed his men in groups of two along the stone promenade by the seashore. Singh tried to prevail upon the Army head to move the deployment closer to the hotel. Because if the terrorists decided to escape, they could easily vanish into the many back-lanes surrounding the hotel, without giving the Army personnel (who were taking cover behind shrubs and small trees lining the promenade) a chance. The Army did not oblige. At around 3 a.m. two platoons of the RAF (each platoon has thirty armed personnel) reached the hotel. Venkatesham and Singh strategically positioned the RAF on the median dividing the Marine Drive road.

By now about half a dozen relatives and friends of guests locked in different rooms had gathered outside the hotel. Singh took the cellphone numbers of all the trapped guests and distributed the numbers among his officers, assigning them the task of keeping in touch with the guests over the next forty-eight hours, assuring them of safety and advising them about the do's and don'ts. The next reinforcement to arrive was the MARCOS. Venkatesham and Singh briefed the commandos about the possible location of the terrorists. None of the floors of the Oberoi was equipped with CCTV cameras and there was still no clarity on the total number of terrorists inside. The two IEDs left by them – on the driveway and inside the lobby of the Oberoi – had already exploded. But the police feared that more explosives may have been planted inside the hotel. The MARCOS formed two crack teams that included experts of the Explosive Ordinance Demolition and moved inside the hotel.

One team with a dog squad started combing the main lobby of the Trident in search of any planted explosives. The other team started blocking all the entry and exit routes from the hotel complex so that the terrorists could not escape. First the MARCOS blocked the corridor from the main lobby of Trident leading to the Oberoi. There were a few entrance and exit points connecting the pool level of the Oberoi to the Trident. They too were blocked. The main entrance of the Oberoi facing the NCPA building was also being manned. Two commandos went all the way to the twenty-first floor using the service staircase but they did not enter the corridor around the rooms. They saw bodies along the staircase, which they thought wise not to remove, and after some time they returned. The team of MARCOS with the dog squad combed the entire main lobby of the Trident but did not find any hidden explosives. Once this was done, the hotel staff, through the phones installed in the main lobby of the Trident, informed all the guests there to stay put in their respective rooms. But grenades kept landing in the upper lobby of the Oberoi intermittently, preventing the hotel staff from issuing the same advisory to their guests in the Oberoi. The terrorists were possibly hiding in some room and were simply tossing the grenades towards the atrium through the door. Hours went by. The MARCOS and the police just kept vigil around the hotel. Everyone was waiting for the NSG to reach the spot.

Scene 4

At around 9 a.m. the next morning, the Turkish couple who had been hauled up along with thirteen other hostages from the Kandahar restaurant by the terrorists, somehow got in touch with a friend in Mumbai who in turn managed to speak to Singh. The friend put Singh in touch with them; they had been locked by the terrorists in room no. 1979 on the nineteenth floor. In their faltering English, the couple managed to give Singh a first-hand description of the two terrorists. 'One is in blue clothes and the second in black, the one in blue seems more cruel. Each is carrying an assault rifle, maybe also pistols, and a bag full of hand grenades. They are constantly speaking to someone on the phone,' explained the Turkish couple. They also told Singh that the duo had forgotten a bag in the room. Singh asked the couple to open the bag. They found a few grenades and live cartridges inside the bag. Singh assured the couple that security personnel would soon reach them and they would be evacuated.

At around 9.30 a.m., the NSG motorcade roared in on the Marine Drive. Two NSG officers – Colonel B.S. Rathi and Lieutenant Colonel R.K. Sharma – went around the hotel complex a few times, taking a hard look at the neighbouring buildings, the topography, getting a feel of the place. Colonel Rathi was the supervising commander of the soon-to-be started Oberoi operation and Lt Col Sharma was its task force commander, responsible for chalking out the ground strategy and the operational moves. Singh and Venkatesham gave Rathi and Sharma a briefing of the chain of events till then. They also told them that whenever suspicious of any operation inside the hotel, the terrorists would intensify their grenade attack. As per the first-hand account of the Turkish couple there were at least two terrorists, armed with assault rifles and grenades. But the police and hotel staff suspected that more terrorists could be hiding inside the hotel. They told the NSG that the terrorists could also be hiding on the fourth floor of the Oberoi as they had received phone calls of guests and other hotel staff stranded on that floor, who said they had seen some suspicious movements there. Then maps of the hotel were laid out before the NSG team. For over an hour Rathi and Sharma raked their brains, discussing the possible strategies, the approach to be adopted and the route to be followed for entering the hotel. The hotel staff heard the two discussing the option of NSG commandos being dropped from helicopters but Sharma ruled against it as they wanted to catch the terrorists by surprise.

After an hour-long brainstorming session Rathi ordered Lt Col Sharma to storm into the hotel using one of the three interconnecting routes from Trident to Oberoi – through the main lobby of Trident to upper lobby of Oberoi; at the pool level; and through the basement. All night there had hardly been any activity or sound of gunfire emanating from the Trident. The three passages between the two hotel buildings had been secured by the MARCOS earlier. It was safe to assume that there were no terrorists in the Trident. Rathi and Sharma decided to adopt a top-bottom approach combing operation for the Oberoi that would start from the topmost floor, treating every room, every hall, every corridor, every corner in the hotel as a suspected hideout of the terrorists. Every room or enclosed space on each floor was to be scanned and sanitized. On the request of Lt Col Sharma, Additional Commissioner Venkatesham had moved the TV cameras and crew beyond the 1 km periphery of the hotel. (The NSG told Venkatesham they did not want the cameras to capture any close-ups of their operation.) On the instructions of Lt Col Sharma the TV cable of the hotel was also disconnected. Around sixty NSG commandos assigned for the Oberoi operation were waiting at the Maharashtra Secretariat building, about a kilometre from the hotel complex. After Rathi's go-ahead, they were brought to the hotel from a route where there was no media presence.

Half a dozen NSG snipers armed with sniper rifles and carrying secured communication channels were positioned at several vantage points in the adjoining buildings including the NCPA. Finally at around 10.30 a.m., two NSG teams of fifteen to twenty commandos each, one led by Major B. Bharat and another by Captain Yadav, armed with MP-5 submachine guns, Glock pistols and grenades, entered the hotel. The Trident and the Oberoi were interlinked at three different levels. The NSG took one of these routes and headed towards the topmost floor of the Oberoi. Heavily armed NSG took over from the MARCOS who were deployed at all the entry and exit points in a bid to prevent any attempt by the terrorists to escape. Oberoi security personnel Rajesh Kadam, acting as the ground guide, accompanied the NSG teams showing them the way around.

Scene 5

Till 10.30 a.m., police sub-inspectors Rahimutullah Sayeed and Vijay Wakudakar had been perched on the terrace of the NCPA building. Assault rifles leaning against the boundary wall, night-vision goggles glued to their eyes, Sayeed and Wakudakar had been alternating the duty of keeping a watch on the windows of the rooms visible to them. The two ATS officers relayed to Singh on the ground about how guests in several rooms on different floors had drawn their curtains open, and throughout the night had kept waving, trying to attract the attention of the forces on the ground. They also told Singh about how the two rooms on the extreme ends of the eighteenth floor had their curtains drawn shut. Nevertheless, Sayeed and Wakudakar were trying to detect any suspicious movement behind these drawn curtains. Silhouettes appeared fleetingly and vanished but there was nothing more substantial. The nightlong vigil had caused the ATS officers' eyes to burn and fatigue was slowly getting the better of their instincts. At around 11 a.m., the terrorists holed up on the eighteenth floor suddenly opened several rounds of fire at the NCPA terrace that got the ATS personnel diving for cover. The bullets came thick and fast, and punched holes into the concrete wall of the terrace. While the daylight had revealed the cops to the terrorists, the cops too got a brief glimpse of the blue clothing of a terrorist in one of the rooms. The terrorist had compromised by giving away his exact positions: he was in the third room from the side of the lane behind the Oberoi, on the eighteenth floor. The incident of fresh firing by the terrorists was immediately reported to Singh and their position was then communicated to the NSG commandos.

Taking some ATS officers with him, Singh ran towards the NCPA terrace. Since the terrorists now knew that the police were on the terrace, it was dangerous for the security personnel to be positioned there anymore. Singh spoke to DGP A.N. Roy, briefed him about the firing episode and urged him to arrange a few apartments in the NCPA building, ideally between the eleventh and thirteenth floors – that would give the officers a direct view of the eighteenth floor of the Oberoi – where he could position ATS personnel for keeping a watch and also if the opportunity arose take aim at the gunmen. Within five minutes Roy called Singh back telling him that two flats, one on the thirteenth and another on the eleventh floor, had been arranged and Singh with his men could move in right away. Two teams of ATS personnel were stationed on the two floors. Soon two teams of NSG snipers joined the ATS staff.

Scene 6

The two NSG teams under Lt Col Sharma's leadership went to the twenty-first floor. On reaching there the commandos sighted around half a dozen dead bodies lying along a narrow staircase. There was no electricity and the place was reeking with the stink of the fast decomposing bodies. Sharma decided against moving the bodies as they might have been booby-trapped – explosives placed under the bodies could have exploded the moment they were moved. The NSG commandos passed by the bodies and went up to the terrace floor. They combed the entire floor but did not find anybody. Nor did they find any explosives or ammunition. Around this time Lt Col Sharma was informed that the terrorists had opened fire in the direction of the NCPA building. He was told that it seemed that the fire was opened from a room on the eighteenth floor of the Oberoi. The location of the room as spotted by the ATS personnel from the NCPA rooftop was also communicated but it was difficult to figure out the exact room number from their description. Also, it was not clear if there was one or more than one terrorist on that floor. What if the other terrorist was hiding on some other floor? Or if the terrorists were opening fire from the eighteenth floor and then taking refuge somewhere else?

It was possible that the terrorists were trying to trap the commandos by making them believe that they were in a particular room on that floor. There was every possibility that if the NSG had gone straight to the eighteenth floor room they would have been ambushed. It was dangerous for the commandos to go to the eighteenth floor directly because in a gun-battle if a terrorist sneaked out from a particular floor and took position on an unsecured higher level he would create havoc. Moreover, there were guests who needed to be evacuated from the twenty-first, twentieth and the nineteenth floors. The NSG was also receiving conflicting inputs about the possibility of terrorists being holed up in the lower floors. Some of the hotel staff had told the NSG about the disappearance of some of their employees in the lower levels of the hotel building (a few waiters and room attendants had gone to some rooms on third and fourth floor but had not returned or established any contact). Lt Col Sharma finally decided that he would first secure the top floors before moving to the eighteenth floor.

The NSG commandos then began their operation on the twenty-first floor. There were thirty rooms on each guest floor – from the twenty-first to the tenth floor. (Both the Trident and the Oberoi have guest rooms only from the tenth floor upwards. Moreover, there is no thirteenth floor in the hotel industry.) Stealthily the commandos moved from one room to another, announcing themselves as 'Police' to the occupants of the room, requesting them to open the door. While many guests responded, an equal number refused to let the NSG in despite their best efforts. At the threshold of every such room they placed light explosives and the door was exploded to make a forced entry. Once inside the room the NSG frisked the occupants, scanned their belongings and only after their identity was established were they moved out of the hotel accompanied by a few NSG commandos and hotel staff.

Additional Commissioner Venkatesham had established a command centre at the adjoining Air India building which acted as the information centre for friends of guests stranded in the hotel and later on the place where all documentary formalities like *panchanamas* were conducted. Evacuated guests were taken to this command centre where a police team did further verification, cross-checking their identities with the details mentioned in the hotel guest list. It took the NSG several hours to sanitize each floor. Though the NSG had adopted a top to bottom approach, a few distress calls from some guests holed up in lower levels of the hotel who needed immediate medical aid (people with high blood pressure, diabetes or other ailments got in touch with their relatives who in turn requested the security personnel) forced the NSG to divert some of their commandos to other floors to evacuate such guests. The NSG commandos were taking details like name, identity, physical characteristics and the room number of such guests from their relatives and once they were outside their rooms, they would call them by their name thus assuring them that they were commandos and not terrorists. By the time the twenty-first and twentieth floors were cleared and declared sanitized it was around 3.30 p.m.

The NSG now moved to the nineteenth floor where they came

upon semi-decomposed bodies of three women. The NSG had already been informed about the Turkish couple who were locked up in room no. 1979. There was a high probability that the terrorists were present on this floor. Sequentially, all the rooms were opened and all guests including the Turkish couple were evacuated but there was no sign of the terrorists. The NSG commandos now moved to the eighteenth floor where they had been told the terrorists were holed up. Besides, as a result of over eighteen hours of incessant gunfire and explosions, the lights in some parts of the hotel had gone off. By the time the NSG commandos trooped in on the eighteenth floor, it was around 4.30 p.m. and the daylight – which was filtering through the fibre rooftop – had started fading. On reaching that floor, the NSG found that some patches along the corridor were dimly lit while one side of the corridor was completely dark. They began scanning the rooms starting from the right side, which was lit.

Suddenly, Lt Col Sharma received a wireless communication from the snipers positioned in the NCPA building that they could see four suspicious persons on the rooftop of the Oberoi hotel. The snipers asked if they should open fire but Sharma told them to just keep a close eye on the four and give him a minute-by-minute update on their movements. A few minutes elapsed before the NSG snipers called again saying that the four persons were waving out a white cloth. One NSG team was immediately dispatched to the rooftop and found the four in a dishevelled state with their clothes soaked in blood. After thorough frisking and questioning, the four were escorted out of the hotel. Interrogation by the ATS revealed that they were among the fifteen diners who had been taken hostage by the terrorists the night before. Their names were: Amardeep Sethi, Ketan Desai, Siddharth Tyagi and Apoorva Parikh. As the terrorists shot at the ten hostages lined on the service staircase leading to the terrace, they all fell over each other; these four were luckily not hit by the bullets and got buried under the collapsing bodies. For the following eighteen hours they hid themselves in a cooling system on the rooftop, and finally came out at around 4 p.m. when they realized that commando force had come into the building.

On the eighteenth floor, in the meantime, more rooms were cleared. It had been more than half an hour since the team had started scanning the floor. Like the other floors, a few rooms – whose occupants did not respond and who had put a double lock from inside – were forcibly entered into by the NSG commandos after blasting open the doors. Until now, since the beginning of the operation, around 110 rooms had been cleared. As over two dozen commandos were tiptoeing around the eighteenth floor, a volley of bullets zipped across the corridor followed by a few grenades. The bullets were fired from one of the rooms situated on the side which was not illuminated. Kadam, the hotel security staff, who accompanied the NSG team, told Sharma that the room from which the fire had come was in all probability room no. 1856. After more than six hours of a painstaking combing operation the location of at least one of the terrorists was finally known.

The NSG commandos took positions at three different corners of the floor and started shelling the room. But the terrorists, undeterred by the heavy retaliatory fire, kept firing back. One bullet hit Major Saurabh on his thigh and he had to be quickly taken for medical aid. The NSG snipers positioned in the NCPA building were immediately provided the location of the room where terrorists were holed up and ordered to fire at the windows of the room. But the terrorists had drawn the double-layered curtains making it impossible for the snipers positioned dozens of feet away to take a clean shot. Still, the snipers opened several rounds of fire aimed towards the windows; the terrorists, one of them was probably hiding underneath the window, fired back in the direction of the NCPA. Bullets pierced through the windows of the kitchen and bedroom of the eleventh floor NCPA apartment. Inside the hotel too, heavy firing continued from both sides. The NSG commandos positioned on the nineteenth floor also opened fire from the railings. Both the terrorists and the commandos kept hurling grenades at each other. Captain A.K. Singh's eye was damaged by a splinter from one of the blasts. But Singh kept firing till he fell unconscious and was later carried down through the service staircase. Major Bharat, positioned on the nineteenth floor, also got hit by the splinters and had to be sent down for medical aid. Despite three commandos getting injured the NSG team kept firing incessantly in the direction of room no. 1856, in a bid to keep the terrorists pinned down in the room.

Scene 7

Like other floors of the hotel, on the eighteenth floor too there are rooms on all the four sides of the quadrangle shaped corridor running around the central atrium – standing in the corridor of any floor one can see the floors above till the covered roof and all the floors down below to the level of the central lobby. The balustrade along the corridor is made partly of glass and partly of concrete – the central portion of all the four sides of the balustrade is a three feet high concrete railing flanked by glass on both ends. In one corner of the floor are the elevators. NSG commandos kept firing from three different directions towards room no. 1856, giving the terrorists no chance to escape. But relentless firing and grenade explosions by the terrorists made it equally impossible for the commandos to storm the room. The stalemate continued for some time. Then the hand grenades being thrown by the NSG started a fire inside the room and soon it was up in flames. But the automatic fire system came on and water flowed out of the sprinklers in the room. To fight the ravaging fire the terrorists also opened all the taps and showers inside the room, sending waves of water gushing along the corridor. The entire floor was soon under four inches of water. The inundated floor worked in favour of the terrorists as it neutralized all incendiary tactics being adopted by the NSG. The rush of water soon doused the fire inside the room.

At around 12.30 a.m., the NSG saw a shadow shuffling along the dark patch of the corridor. After a few feet the shadow opened fire. Since all the NSG commandos had taken positions behind walls and pillars no one was injured. One NSG commando who was positioned towards the left side of room no. 1856 shouted at the shadow, 'Kya pagal ho gaya hai? Kyun fire kar raha hai? (Have you gone mad? Why are you firing?)' In response the shadow opened fire again. A bullet brushed past Commando Manish's right temple. By this time the shadow became brighter as he came under a dim light near the exit door. Sharma, who was positioned on the extreme end across room no. 1856, took an aim and pressed the trigger. The bullets met the target. The terrorist got hit on his legs and limped back and hid near the lift behind the concrete banister which gave him cover. In a bid to provoke the NSG personnel, the terrorist shouted, 'Chhup ke kya lad raha hai, dum hai to saamne aa ke maar. (Why are you fighting under cover, if you have the guts, come out and fire.)' Sharma retorted, 'Tere andar zyada dum hai to tu saamne aa. (If you have more courage, then you come out in the open.)' Neither Sharma nor the terrorist took the bait. The NSG threw a few grenades in his direction but the concrete wall kept him protected. In retaliation the terrorist also kept throwing grenades in the direction of the NSG personnel.

After the terrorist's exit from room no. 1856, gunfire from inside the room had stopped. Had the second terrorist also escaped and hidden inside one of the rooms along the dark patch or was he still inside the same room, injured, lying low or dead? Nothing was clear. Throughout the night the terrorist and the NSG kept exchanging fire. However, relentless firing by the NSG kept the terrorist who had sneaked out of the room pinned down in the corner near the lift. But the darkness that enveloped the area prevented the NSG from taking a clean shot. While the eighteenth floor kept blazing with cross-gunfire, over two dozen NSG personnel continued combing the other floors below the eighteenth, sanitizing one room after another, evacuating guests locked inside, and escorting them out of the hotel. All the exit doors from the eighteenth floor were also locked and manned from outside. With the approaching sunrise the place started getting bright. At the break of dawn, at first light as the NSG calls it, the NSG commandos got a clear view of the terrorist and fired several rounds. A few bullets hit him on his torso while one bullet pierced through one of his eyes. When the NSG went close to him they saw he was dressed in tight dark green outfit, the ring and middle fingers of his left hand were missing (a birth defect or lost during terror training), his AK-47 rifle was placed across his stomach and a pistol was lying next to him. A cellphone was peeking out of the left pocket of his cargos. Two magazines of AK-47 and a fake student identity card were also found.

Having secured his body the NSG now moved inside room no. 1856. The room was dark and wire ducts were hanging loose. Next to the door was the bathroom. On entering the bathroom the NSG commandos saw the second terrorist lying in a corner. They fired a few shots at him. He did not retaliate. It seemed the terrorist was already dead when the NSG went into the room. The body was secured and was sent down on a stretcher. Meanwhile, the combing on other floors continued and guests from the Trident too began to be evacuated. The operation was finally over in the evening when both the hotels were declared clean and handed over to the police. Ajmal Amir Kasab identified the two terrorists from their fake ID-card pictures shown to him as Fahadullah alias Abu Fahad (who was killed near the lift) and Abu Rehman Chhota.

'I went up assuming that my husband would follow me but he didn't make it out of the door.'

Eyewitness Accounts from CST, Leopold Café, Taj and Oberoi

Harsh Joshi

At 9.45 p.m., the local train from Thane crawled into the Chhatrapati Shivaji Terminus (CST), better known by its former name, Victoria Terminus (VT). Assistant Sub-Inspector Sudam A. Pandharkar of the railway police alighted from the women's compartment and walked towards the station office to report. He hadn't yet crossed the platform when he heard some loud bangs and saw a sudden commotion building up.

'I was confused. I could make out a bomb had detonated. People were running madly in no particular direction. I knew someone was firing but couldn't see the source,' Pandharkar says.

He was then summoned to the end of platform no. 6 by his superior, Inspector Shashank Shinde, also of the railway police. He shouldered his .303 rifle and ran.

'There were just three of us – a police personnel in plain clothes, Shinde and I. We took position in a corner near the end of platform 6.'

For fifty-seven-year-old Pandharkar, it was a situation he had never encountered in his three decades of police service.

'Shinde had a service revolver. Between the three of us, we just had one rifle – mine – and five bullets. We took turns firing from the rifle. But most of the time, we were just waiting in confusion.'

The bolt-action Lee-Enfield .303 caliber rifle, a World War I era weapon and a legacy of the British Raj, carried by the Indian police force, has a five-round magazine. But Pandharkar, caught in an emergency, realized his magazine wasn't loaded.

'I had to load the bullets one by one. Shinde had summoned all the men armed with rifles to the end where we were positioned, but apparently no one else was prepared.'

By this time, the platforms were nearly empty. The three cops then moved toward platform no. 7. Pandharkar recalls seeing the two gunmen firing indiscriminately, only stopping to reload.

'I fired a shot and then dodged. We were short of ammunition.'

After over fifteen minutes of shuffling, Pandharkar caught a bullet on his right side – the shot passing through his ribcage.

'I fell on the ground, feeling faint. I was bleeding a lot.'

There was no one around to carry him to safety. After a few minutes, he summoned the strength to get on his knees and then with the help of a pillar, he got to his feet. 'I walked to the police control room in the station and then fell down again. Someone later took me to St George's Hospital.'

Pandharkar's son, a constable in the crime branch of Mumbai police, came to visit him in the early hours of the morning and shifted him to another hospital where he spent the next twelve days recovering.

'Later, the reinforcements must have arrived. I don't know much about that. But during the first thirty minutes, there were not more than five cops in the area,' Pandharkar recalls, his bullet wound now almost healed. The other two cops, who made feeble attempts to counter semi-automatic weapons with vintage rifles, did not survive.

The two men came in a black and yellow taxi, one of the thousands that trawl the Colaba market daily, ferrying shoppers, tourists and office-goers, on one of the liveliest stretches of Mumbai. It was 9.40 p.m. and Leopold Café in Colaba was packed, buzzing with cheerful conversation, music and the clinking of beer mugs.

'The two guys got off in front of the entrance,' says Eric Anthony, manager of the popular hangout. 'They hugged each other and then lobbed a grenade into the restaurant.' The blast was severe as it hit the front of the ground floor. Almost every glass window and some tables were blown to pieces. Eric, who was standing at the smaller entrance, saw the men calmly walk into the restaurant through the haze and pull out their guns. 'They fired randomly, without aiming at anyone. They sprayed the entire ground floor,' he recalls.

Thirty-three-year-old Eric ran to take shelter in the adjacent Vrindavan Bar. There was a minute's silence and Eric, for that minute, believed it was over. However, the gunfire resumed; he hid in the patio and saw the unbelievable horror unfold.

'They had only stopped to reload. One of the waiters got shot in the arm; he ran toward where I was standing and collapsed right in front of me.' Eric tried to revive him and then asked him about others. 'He told me another waiter had been shot and was unable to get up. But there was little I could do to help.'

Summoning all the courage he could find, Eric stepped out from the shadows of the building. The next moment, he heard a fresh round of gunshots. These were aimed at him. 'I felt bullets just brush past me. One grazed my ear ... I could feel my blood dripping down.'

Eric hid there for the next fifteen minutes as the terrorists continued to empty their weapons into everybody they saw before them. The two men then walked away (as Eric later found out, they were headed to the Taj hotel) while Eric went to the hospital. He wasn't around when the watchman entered the café and saw the devastation – ten dead bodies, smoke, glass, wood and the stench of blood.

K.R. Ramamoorthy, a sixty-nine-year-old veteran banker, after impatiently waiting for room service to bring him drinking water, decided to walk down to the business centre and pick up a bottle himself. That's when he got the first indication that this evening, at his preferred Taj hotel, was spinning out of control.

'I saw four policemen in their khaki uniform, accompanied by a man in a mufti suit. He could have been a hotel employee. They told me to get back into my room. Their hushed tones and the urgency puzzled me. I thought some thieves had gotten inside the hotel,' Ramamoorthy says.

It was around 10 p.m. that Ramamoorthy turned on the television in his hotel room to find chaotic news flashes about 'gunshots' at the Taj and the Oberoi hotels. He called home to tell his wife and children that he was safe.

Responding to the call of duty: Firefighters rescue guests from the burning Taj hotel on
Thursday, 27 November 2008. At least 173 people (civilians and security personnel) were killed
in the attacks. Among the dead were 30 foreign nationals from 10 countries. *(AP Photo)*

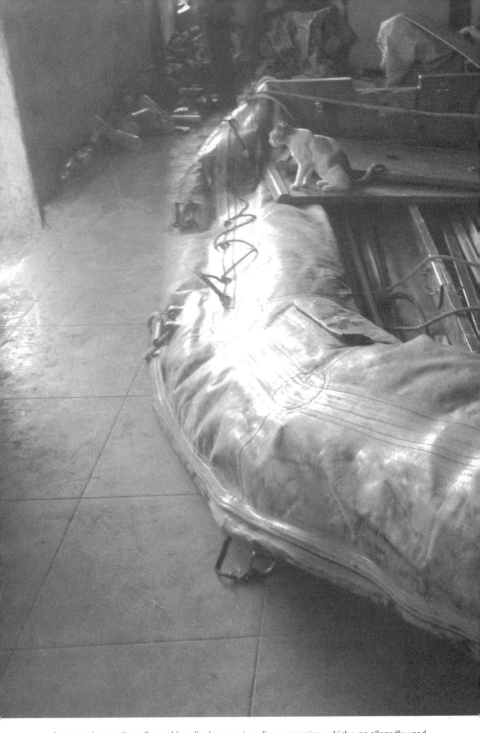

A cat perches on the yellow rubber dinghy, now in police possession, which was allegedly used by the ten terrorists to reach Badhwar Park in Mumbai, after abandoning the Indian trawler MV-Kuber, 4 nautical miles off Mumbai coast. *(AP Photo)*

A creaking shell: The inside of Nariman House after a three-day standoff between the NSG commandos and two of the terrorists that left six hostages dead. Hitherto unknown, the Mumbai centre of the ultra-orthodox Jewish Chabad-Lubavitch movement, was targeted for

the community's rigid stance in the Arab-Israeli conflict. This attack exposed the vulnerability of Jews in India, who had never faced anti-semitism till now. *(AP Photo)*

In the line of fire: An Indian soldier prepares as the Taj hotel burns during the gun-battle with the terrorists. Inside, the hotel staff showed immense courage and valour while guiding people to safety at great personal risk. The siege at the Taj hotel came to an end after 60 hours of rescue

operations by the Mumbai police, RAF, SRPF, the marine commandos, and the NSG. *(AP Photo/David Guttenfelder/FILE)*

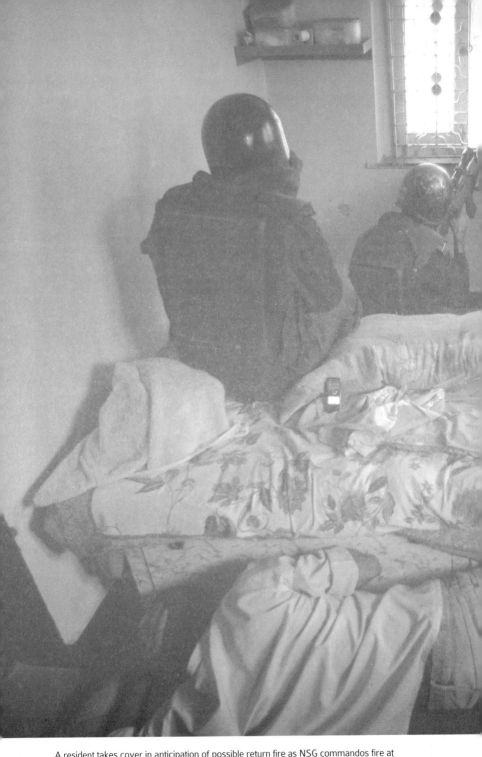

A resident takes cover in anticipation of possible return fire as NSG commandos fire at suspected militants holed up at Nariman House. *(AP Photo/Saurabh Das)*

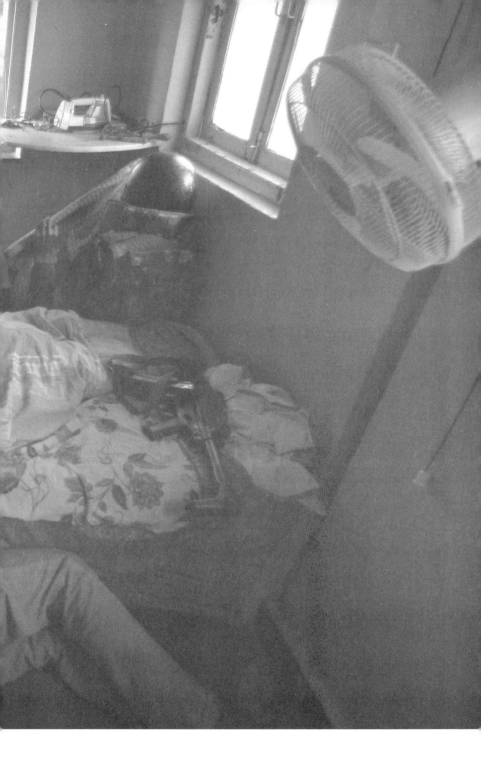

Caught in a crossfire with the terrorists, Major Sandeep Unnikrishnan of the NSG told an injured colleague, 'Don't come behind me,' and ventured alone into the Palm Lounge at the Taj hotel. Giving cover to two commandos, Major Unnikrishnan fearlessly surged ahead to face the

terrorists. The bereaved mother of Major Sandeep Unnikrishnan, touches her heroic son's forehead at his funeral. For his exceptional bravery, he was posthumously awarded India's highest peacetime gallantry award, the Ashok Chakra. *(AP Photo/Aijaz Rahi)*

Some of the items recovered from MV-Kuber, the Indian fishing vessel hijacked by the terrorists near Porbandar.

Tissue paper made in Pakistan.

A Pakistani made diesel container.

PAK detergent powder, made in Pakistan.

Milk powder packets, made in Pakistan.

A sack of wheat flour, made in Pakistan.

A namaz scarf.

Courtesy: Crime Branch, Mumbai Police

INTERCEPTED CONVERSATIONS:

28 November 2008, 7.23 a.m., Nariman House

HANDLER: *Kya haal chaal hai pasha?* (How are you doing pasha [a term of endearment]?)
TERRORIST: *Mere khayal se team utaar di gayi hai.* (I think the team has got off.)

HANDLER: *Aapke chhat par pandrah bande abhi utre hain helicopter se.* (Fifteen men have climbed down on your roof right now.)
TERRORIST: *Khidkiyon ke saamne bhi kuchh khade hain.* (They are standing in front of the windows as well.)

HANDLER: *Kya keh rahe hain? Aapko nazar aa raha hai kuchh udhar?* (What are you saying? Can you see anything there?)
TERRORIST: *Saamne kuchh firing ho rahi hai.* (They are firing in the front.)

GPS (Global Positioning System) recovered from the Nariman House.

27 November 2008, 1.15 a.m., Taj Hotel

HANDLER: *Aag lagi ki nahi lagi?* (Has the fire started or not?)

TERRORIST: *Nahi aag nahi lagi.* (No the fire has not started.)
Woh gadde-shadde . . . parde-warde . . . ikatthe kar raha hun aag lagane waaste. (I am collecting mattresses and curtains for the fire.)

GPS recovered from the Taj hotel.

The 9mm pistol recovered from the terrorists.

Detail of the pistol which bears the trademark of 'Diamond Nedi Frontier Arms Company, Peshawar'.

One of the unexploded hand grenades recovered by the Mumbai police. It was found to be manufactured by an Austrian company named Arges which had given a franchisee to a Pakistani ordinance factory near Rawalpindi.

The Thuraya phone that the terrorists used to communicate with their handlers in Pakistan.

GPS recovered from Kuber.

INTERCEPTED CONVERSATION:

27 November 2008, 1.15 a.m., Taj hotel

HANDLER: *Aur launch ka kya kiya tha?* (And what did you do with the launch?)

TERRORIST: *Bas aise hi chhod di thi.* (We had just left it like that.)

HANDLER: *Kyun? Woh valve nahi kholi thi pani bharne waaste?* (Why? Did you not open that valve to let the water in?)

TERRORIST: *Nahi woh kholi nahi jaldi jaldi mein ... kaam kharab ho gaya tha.* (No, we couldn't do it in a hurry ... some things went wrong.)

HANDLER: *Kya kaam kharab ho gaya tha?* (What had gone wrong?)

TERRORIST: *Woh jis jagah utarna tha na wahan mauje bahut zabardast lag rahi thi aur udhar ek kashti bhi aa gayi thi. Saare bole navy hai, navy hai, to jaldi jaldi doosri boat mein utre; samaan utara. Ismail bhai ka satel-lite bhi wahin rah gaya.* (A powerful tide had risen where we were to get off and another boat had also come there. Everyone said, it's the Indian Navy, so we quickly got onto an-other boat with the baggage. Brother Ismail's satellite phone also got left there.)

Front and back of the SIM card that was found in the phone used by the terrorists.

An Indian soldier takes cover during gun-battle with the terrorists in an apartment adjacent to Nariman House. (*Michael Rubenstein*)

NSG sniper commandos wait on the roof of a building across the street from Nariman House.
(Michael Rubenstein)

The NSG takes control at Nariman House for the final assault resulting in a pitched battle for 46 hours. *(Michael Rubenstein)*

Abu Fahad alias Fahadullah, the terrorist killed near the lift on the eighteenth floor of the Oberoi hotel. *(Courtesy: Crime Branch, Mumbai Police)*

BREAKING NEWS
NAVY CHIEF HINTS AT PAK NAVY LINK TO 26/11

Picture of the only terrorist to be captured alive, Mohammad Ajmal Amir Kasab, who is now in police custody. *(Courtesy: Times Now)*

Sometime afterwards, the channels went off air. The telephone lines died. Ramamoorthy counted minutes as he lay restless on his bed in room no. 632.

'It's so testing seeing incomplete pictures on the television but not knowing what's really going on around you; totally cut off,' he says. 'I must have waited close to an hour with anxiety growing every minute.'

Around what he guesses to be 11 p.m., he heard knocks on his door and the words 'room service'. He felt a quick surge of relief thinking that everything was, perhaps, back in control.

'But I didn't have the courage to open the door. I didn't respond. After a few minutes of silence, the caller again said "shoe polish", "shoe polish". I responded immediately saying "*nahi chahiye*", and held my breath, waiting. Within a few minutes, I heard a gunshot at the entrance of my door.'

Ramamoorthy rushed into the washroom to hide but everything was so sudden that he didn't have time to lock the door. Two men had stormed into the washroom, held a gun to his temple and ordered him to kneel down.

Ramamoorthy describes the next few minutes the scariest moments of his ordeal. In a matter of minutes, the horror unfolding on TV had become his personal nightmare.

'They looked in the age group of twenty-one to twenty-five. They were armed with assault rifles and one of them carried a large rucksack. I pleaded for mercy but they roughly silenced me. I was ordered to undress. They tied my hands and legs with my kurta-pyjama and shoved me back into the room. One guy gave me a couple of heavy blows on my neck and the other one stomped on my back twice with his heavy boots.'

The terrorists then set up his room as some sort of 'temporary control room', making phone calls and organizing themselves.

'The language was unfamiliar but from their tone, I sensed that they were updating someone superior about their movements so far and receiving instructions. I heard the word "grenade" being repeated often.' Lying on the floor, Ramamoorthy was gripped with a sudden raw terror as he thought that he was going to be the first target of these men.

Another half an hour passed before he heard voices in the corridor. A young man in the hotel uniform was forced into the room. Another hostage, Ramamoorthy realized. Over the next thirty minutes, three more hostages – all of them hotel staff – were brought in. A third militant came in sometime during this point and the interrogation began.

'The terrorists asked us our names, occupation, residence and phone numbers. I gave them the details but I was hesitant to reveal my profession, so I told them I was a teacher. One of them retorted, "How can a teacher afford to stay in the Taj?" and then slashed me hard, thrice on my back with a rope.' In pain, Ramamoorthy gave them the truth – that he is the chairman of the board of a private bank and the director in a few companies.

The terrorists immediately conveyed this information by telephone to others. The men stayed in Ramamoorthy's sixth-floor room, for over three hours; made themselves comfortable on the bed and used the phone to make intermittent calls. 'They appeared cool, relaxed and very confident. There was no stress in their gestures or tones,' Ramamoorthy recalls.

After nearly three hours (Ramamoorthy was later told they were holed up in room 632 from some time after 11 p.m. up to around 2 a.m.), the terrorists ordered the captives to move downstairs. 'They marched us down to the fifth floor, using us as a human shield. I was nearly naked. When I tried to walk a bit faster, I was hit again on my back.'

On the fifth floor, the hostages were taken into another vacant room. Fearing a spray of bullets any minute, Ramamoorthy obeyed the orders given to him, lying down once again on the floor.

'I heard them talk for some time in low tones. I was not even sure if all the terrorists who were in my room had come here or some had dispersed to other areas.'

Then silence descended on the room, only to be shattered sometime later by a deafening explosion. Ramamoorthy, badly shaken, could see the room fill up rapidly with smoke. The terrorists were nowhere to be seen.

'It was getting difficult to breathe or even see clearly. I was nearly choking. Since my hands and legs were tied, I couldn't pick myself up from the floor. The hotel employees managed to get up with great difficulty but they were coughing and suffocating too.'

In retrospect, Ramamoorthy says that it is when survival instinct kicks in that man finds incredible strength in himself. No wonder he managed to crawl to the edge of the bed; he leaned on it and tugged to free his hands.

'With great difficulty, I managed to free my right hand from the knot. Quickly, I loosened the knots on my legs and rushed to the business kit, usually kept in hotel rooms, to look for a pair of scissors.'

Using a pair of scissors he freed himself and then the other hostages. Together they managed to force open the windows.

'The room was facing the pool. Two of the hotel staff immediately jumped out of the windows, sat on the angular roof and asked the others to help them to remove the cloth behind the window curtains. They tied all the cloth, even the linen on the bed, to the spire above. With this, they all safely landed on the concrete floor overlooking the pool.'

But Ramamoorthy, unable to descend by himself, waited at the window alone. 'I could hear gunshots intermittently. After about an hour of waiting, I started shouting for help. There was an inaudible response from the other wing of the hotel but no help came.'

Even as he thought out his options, another shock was in store for him. Flames started bellowing out from the sixth floor, right above him.

'In a matter of minutes, the fire grew enormously and charred remnants – metal and wood – were falling down. I could now feel the searing heat.'

He contemplated jumping down the domed roof from the fifth floor, but then backed out. He could also not stay where he was, with the fire spreading every minute. With great effort, he climbed back into the room, covered himself in whatever clothes he could find – a pyjama and a T-shirt, probably left behind by the occupant.

'I stumbled to the door and ran out of the room. The entire fifth floor was filled with smoke. I realized it would be hard to navigate through the long corridors and take the stairs down. It was also possible that the fire had spread to the steps. Yet, I took courage and ran through the corridors, pausing to breathe fresh air at some corners.'

Ramamoorthy ran down two flights of steps through the dense smoke, all the while fearing he'd be shot any moment.

'Then I saw the door of a room which was open, and saw the street through the window. I rushed into the room and ventured to the window. Seeing a fire engine outside, I started waving my hands and fortunately the fire fighters spotted me. They helped me get onto the railings of the ladder and rescued me.'

At about the same time when Ramamoorthy was waiting for room service to bring him water, thirty-odd senior executives of Hindustan Unilever Ltd were sitting down for dinner in the Gateway Room of the old Taj. The occasion was a farewell for the outgoing CEO of Unilever Ltd Patrick Cescau, and his wife, and a welcome to his successor, Paul Polman.

'We had finished the soups and just started the first course when we heard a series of bangs, like firecrackers, outside,' recalls M.K. Sharma, retired vice-chairman of Hindustan Unilever. But it soon became clear that the sporadic bursts were not part of any innocuous celebration that Mumbai witnesses almost every evening. 'The staff realized this as well. They started locking all the entrances to the room. This was difficult, as many of those large, ornate doors don't have a latch, just big, brass handles.'

Sharma says the hotel staff promptly used anything they could to block and barricade the doors, including tablecloths and napkins to tie around the handles.

'The employees were precise in their directions and very prompt. They asked us to lie down on the carpet and not to sit under the beams.'

As the gunshots continued to ring outside, punctuated by grenade blasts, the people trapped inside used their phones to communicate with the outside world.

'We kept thinking it was a severe gang war but there was no panic amongst us. By then the media had started covering the incident and even though there was chaos, there was some comfort in being able to communicate and not be cut off.'

Close to midnight, there was a tremendous blast. 'It was the worst during all the time we were inside,' Sharma recalls. 'It shook the entire building.'

Hours passed and the group inside – known faces of India's business community and some investment bankers who had escaped from their rooms to join them – sat huddled on the plush carpeted floor.

'The hotel employees were marvellous. They continued to serve us water, even wine. They erected makeshift toilets in the corner using table cloths and empty water bottles,' Sharma adds.

Then, around 2.30 a.m., smoke started seeping into the room.

'It was coming in thick and fast. We were in danger of suffocating.'

Paul took the lead and suggested that the group shatter the windows using the furniture.

'It wasn't easy. Those thick windows facing the seaside are designed to withstand storm-gales. Paul hurt his forehead from the back of a chair when it bounced back from the glass.' However, the group did manage to break the windows on the back side of the hotel, facing Colaba streets.

'Within five minutes of this, the fire brigade also arrived. Firemen entered the room and gave us instructions for escaping.'

The group exited, with the ladies leaving first, using ladders. They were among the first to be rescued, just six hours after the carnage began.

At the Oberoi hotel, Ashok Kapur and his wife Madhu were hosting a dinner for their friends from Singapore, at the famous Kandahar restaurant. They had just finished eating when the ordeal began. 'Gunfire erupted suddenly. We shrugged it off, not realizing what it was, but soon the restaurant staff asked us to leave through the fire exit,' Madhu Kapur recalls. As the restaurant manager opened the fire exit door through the kitchen, the couple called their daughter to let her know they were safe. From the time of the call, she remembers that it was 10.06 p.m.

Reaching the fire exit, some people went up while some went down the narrow steps.

'I went up, assuming that my husband would follow me but he didn't make it out of the door,' she says.

The stairs took her and a Spanish couple up to the fourteenth floor, where the door opened into the atrium. They looked down and could see that the lobby was on fire. 'We looked back and saw that the door through which we had come was now closed.'

The group, frantically searching for an exit, saw another fire escape opposite to the one they had emerged from. This one took them down to the swimming pool. They rushed out and hid themselves in the bushes on the periphery of the pool.

'I was trying Ashok's number. It kept ringing but no one picked up.'

After some time, they noticed a service entrance near the pool area.

'We met some more people hiding in there, including some

hotel staff. They took us to the security guards' office. From there, we were led to the Regal Room.'

The Regal Room had become the central refuge for hostages in the Oberoi. Nearly 200 guests and employees were huddled in the cavernous chamber and tried to discern explosions, gunshots and the rage of fire down below.

'The lights and the air-conditioning were switched off. We were asked to keep our voices low.' As the hours passed, Ashok's phone stopped ringing and a mechanical voice told Madhu that it was 'unreachable'.

The group waited for about fifteen minutes before rescue operations materialized. They were asked to take the service stairs, which led to the road outside facing the Inox multiplex. Here, they waited for their cars to take them away from the nightmare.

Madhu kept trying her husband's phone for the next two days, long after it began blurting the mechanical 'switched off' message.

His body was discovered on Friday evening; over forty-eight hours after the couple last saw each other.

Life Beyond the Pain

A month later, the rush on the platforms of Victoria Terminus makes it hard to believe that many people lost their lives here on the night of 26 November 2008. There are no hesitant glances, no pauses at the plastic barriers as an unbroken stream of people flow past the doors towards their respective purposes. Security is minimal, hardly any different from what it has always been. At the makeshift desk and chairs that serve as their base, a couple of commandos have joined the usual group of cops. They occasionally glance at the crowd passing through the scanners, which beep every now and then. Here, life has shrugged off fear; it has been forced to overpower the terror within and move on because of the very little value it has left, after getting battered in jammed trains, bus queues, broken pavements and getting churned endlessly around the pole of survival.

The Leopold Café is bustling again; employees squeezing past chairs and tables to serve the two floors of the restaurant, jam-packed with customers. They hardly have time to stop and chat. Inside the café and on the crowded pavement outside, amid shops selling bluetooths and *bindis*, life is getting back to normal. The only reminder of the nightmare that claimed ten lives here a month ago is, perhaps, the candle burning in a vase outside the doors of the café. I am sitting on the same corner seat I was perched on the weekend before the attacks. Nothing has changed, I muse, not even their music CD. The Eagles end their rendition, *'You can check out any time you like, but you can never leave.'*

The Taj has reopened its doors partially to its guests. People are thronging to it again, as much out of curiosity as loyalty to their favourite hotel. There is a hefty X-ray baggage scanner at the entrance where a month ago, there would be a lone turbaned guard with a smile on his face. The foyer is swarming with a small army of security staff. The smiles are in place but the screening takes nearly fifteen minutes. 'Welcome to the Taj, sir,' the valet says, after finding only pens, pencils and a tape recorder in my bag.

The alley behind the hotel is chock-full of cars and pedestrians. Eyes turn again and again in the direction of pointed fingers, to the façade of solid stone where one can barely discern any marks of the sixty-hour long battle. The windows are pitch-dark and below there are piles of charred and twisted metal.

At the junction near one of the many police blockades, some teenagers are lighting candles under a tree. Cameras try to capture the vague movements of construction workers behind the enclosure that says, 'We are working to restore the symbol of Mumbai's enduring spirit and dignity.'

I notice a balding man trying to film the activity; capturing the cops, the scanners, their weapons and the crowd bustling on the fringes of the still secured site, while talking to a woman, probably his wife. When I ask him if there are personal memories he's trying to revive, he shakes his head.

'I have to return to the US next week. People there know I was in India when it happened. They'll want to see something.'

'But this ... everything looks normal now,' I begin to protest, pointing at the sea of faces flowing past, each in their own stride, with only occasional glances at the building that's supposedly their 'icon'.

'For Mumbai, maybe, nothing. For the world, it is still chaos,' he replies.

'Inflict maximum damage and don't be taken alive.'

Karachi to Mumbai: Terror, Step by Step

ASHISH KHETAN

The First Interrogation

Additional Commissioner Tanaji Ghadge is fifty-one and more than half his age has gone into policing. A smile always lingers on his cherubic face but tonight it is sombre, almost mournful. Dyed black hair parted neatly down the side and hands held across the chest, he is staring into the camera, waiting for the cue. Above his right shoulder, the word 'Police' is painted on the wall in Marathi, in bold black letters. He is seated at a police desk outside the emergency ward of the Nair Hospital, a corner assigned to the police for fulfilling legal formalities and paperwork for cases involving accidents, shootout injuries, anything that falls under medico-legal cases. The time is 1 a.m., the date 27 November 2008.

On cue, Ghadge begins: 'I am the additional commissioner of Girgaum division. There were incidents of indiscriminate firing at the Taj Mahal hotel, the Oberoi hotel and the VT station last night which appear to be a well-coordinated terror attack. In an encounter with the police at Girgaum Chowpatty one terrorist has been killed while another has suffered injuries and has been brought to the hospital. It is important to interrogate him and therefore I am proceeding to question him.'

Next frame. A youth, seemingly in his early twenties, lies prone on a green plastic, the sheet being a protection from bloodstains for the white sheet that covers a mattress. A fine brown blanket has been pulled close to the chest of the young man who lies naked underneath. His thick mop of hair, greasy and dishevelled, is pressed against the bed's headrest. Wheatish in complexion, the youth is well built – round arms, pumped-up biceps, and thick neck. His clean-shaven oval face bears a high forehead. There is a fresh injury on the chin smeared with an ointment, and a sledge-shaped bandage covers the right side of his neck. Apart from both the arms, which are bandaged from wrist to biceps, the torso bears no injury. He shows no signs of physical pain, only his forehead is creased and eyes are tightly shut, the stiffness of his face making clear that he is not asleep.

'*Maine bahut galat kiya* (I have committed a big mistake),' move the parched lips, catching a glimpse of the policeman walking into the room before shutting his eyes again. No question was posed, but Ghadge's walking in inspired the unsolicited admission.

'On whose instance?'

'Chacha *ke kehne pe.* (At the behest of Uncle.)' Eyes still closed; the voice betraying an effort to exhibit pain and earn empathy, more beseeching than replying.

'Who is this uncle?' Ghadge is staring down with bewilderment, still standing by the right side of the bed, near the young man's shoulder.

'The one from Lashkar.'

'Lashkar what? Which village he is from?'

'I don't know about his village. But he has an office … he keeps visiting the office,' the voice relaxes for a second.

'Who sent you here?'

'My father said we were very poor … our condition would improve … we will have food to eat … clothes to wear,' an emotional explanation, an excuse embedded in the reply.

'Was he your real father?' an incredulous Ghadge enquires.

'Real father … real father,' the man seemed determined to condemn his father.

'What's your name?' asked Ghadge, a fountain pen ready to scribble on a writing pad.

'Ajmal.'

'What's your age?'

'Twenty-one.'

'Where is your *gaon* (village)?'

'Faridkot in *tehsil* Depalpur (administrative division), district Okara.'

'Who all are there in your family?'

'Mother … sisters.'

'Mother's name,' asks Ghadge, hardly looking at him, concentrating hard on the writing pad.

'Noor Illahi.'

'Her age?'

'*Wahi koi chaalis ke aas paas.* (Must be around forty years.)'

'What's your father's name?' Ghadge continues.

'Amir,' eyes still closed, head at ninety degrees to the pillow, body, hands and legs stiff like dead.

'What's his father's name?'

'Shahban.' His eyelids open for a split of a second before closing again.

'What's the surname?'

'*Kya?* (What?)'

'What's the surname? *Khandaan ka naam kya hai?*' Ghadge makes his question simpler.

'Kasab.'

'Are you a butcher?'

'No. We are not in this business … just the name has stuck.'

'So, Amir Shahban Kasab, that's your father's name.'

'Yes.'

'What's his age?'

'Somewhere around forty-five years,' head jerks a trifle, before stiffening again.

'What does your father do?'

'He sells *dahi-wade*. Sometimes in the village … sometimes he goes to Lahore city … It's difficult to run the family,' Kasab now opens his eyelids, catching a glimpse of his interrogator from the corner of his eyes.

'How many brothers are you?' Ghadge determined to know every bit about his family.

'*Hum teen bhai hai.* (We are three brothers.)'

'What are the names of your brothers?'

'Afzal and Munir.'

Questions and answers continue like this in one-liners.

'What are their ages?'

'Afzal is around four years elder to me. Munir is around four years younger to me.' The recording and remembrance of age he seems to do only in relative terms.

'Which means Afzal is twenty-five and Munir is eighteen?' Ghadge gets his math wrong with the younger brother's age.

'*Haan* sahab. (Yes, sir.) You can deduce that,' Kasab not the least interested to correct him.

'What do your brothers do?'

'Afzal works as a farm labourer in the village itself,' Kasab replies with a groan, remembering he is injured and in pain.

'Is Afzal married?'

'Yes. He is married to Safia. He has two children: one son and one daughter. Son's name is Ali. He must be around seven to eight years. Daughter's name I don't know. She is just one-year-old. She was born when I was away from home for training. I don't know what they have named her,' Kasab, for the first time makes a departure from one-line replies.

'Where is Safia's paternal home?'

'She is my maternal uncle's daughter. They are from Lahore.'

'What's the name of the village?'

'There is no village. They stay in Lahore city. At Safawala Chowk, near Nizam Adda in Lahore. Her father's name is Manzoor. She now stays with her parents. They had a fight, my brother and his wife. After that she stays with her parents,' Kasab, on his own, provides the unsolicited information about the break-up between his brother and his wife.

'Why was there a fight?' Ghadge asks, showing interest.

'Don't know exactly. *Paise ke kharche ko lekar jhagda hua hoga.* (Must have been over how money was being spent.)' Kasab puts it down to the money, or the lack of it.

'Where did you say her father's home is?'

'At Safawala Chowk, near Nizam Adda in Lahore. I have been there many times. After getting off at Nizam Adda it's quite close by. It's near a bank.'

'What's the name of the bank?'

'Don't know; it is a big bank. Anybody will tell you.'

'What does Munir, your second brother, do?'

'*Woh sakool-wakool jata hai.* (He goes to some school.)' Kasab doesn't attach much importance to his younger brother's occupation.

'*Sakool* means?' Ghadge fails to get Kasab's pronunciation.

'*Sakool ... sakool,*' Kasab tries his best, surprised the cop is not getting it.

119

'*Sakool* ... school, you mean?'

'Yes.'

'What about your sisters?'

'I have two sisters – Rukaiya and Suraiya.'

'Where are they?'

'Rukaiya is married. She is around one and a half years elder to me. She lives with her husband in Pathankot.'

'Where in Pathankot?'

'It's a small village, adjacent to Havelilakha. You ask anybody about my *taye* (elder uncle). His name is Nisaq. Anybody will tell you. It's a small place.'

'You said she is married?'

'She is married to my *taye's* son. Her husband's name is Hussain.'

Ghadge, as if he has had enough of his family, skips enquiries about Kasab's younger sister Suraiya and switches back to Kasab's own life, at the time the centre of Ghadge's curiosity and in days to come of an entire nation.

'How much have you studied?'

'Till fourth standard. In 2000 I quit *sakool.*'

'Which school was it?'

'A primary village *sakool.* In my village.'

'And after that?'

'I first worked as a labourer in my village. After some time I moved to Lahore and started working there.'

'What labour job?'

'*Mazdoori.* Cement, etc. Bricks, etc. Working with a *mistri.* Construction work. For five years I stayed in a *mohalla* called Tohidabad, *gali* number *chauranja, makaan* number *baraah.*'

'*Chauranja?* One and four?' Ghadge fails to get Kasab's alien dialect.

'No, *chauranja*: five and four,' says Kasab correcting Ghadge, seeing that his wretched past is recorded correctly. 'There was a *subzi mandi* close to that house. I stayed there till 2005, along with other labourers. We stayed there on rent. Now I have heard they have razed the quarters and constructed a building in its place.'

'You came back to your village in 2005, after five years?'

'In between also I made a few trips. But in 2005 I returned to my village.'

'Then?'

'Sometime in 2007 my father took me to Zaki chacha and asked me to work with him.' Kasab, cutting straight to 2007 from 2005, skipped details of the two years in between.

'Who is Zaki chacha?'

'He is the big man of Lashkar.'

'Where was his office?'

'In my village. In Depalpur.'

Then Kasab, in an accusatory tone, added, 'Zaki chacha would say: Work with me. You will bring a good name to your family. You will get money. It is Allah's work.' Kasab implies he never believed in what Zaki told him – either an honest admission or a clever ploy to blame it on Zaki, having been misled by him. 'My father said: You will live the way they live. You will eat well. Clothe well. Live a life of comfort. Your brothers and sister will get married,' says Kasab, implicating his father too.

'You went along with Zaki.'

'No, I worked at Lashkar's office in the village ... '

'Was your father from Lashkar?'

'No. No. He just introduced me to those people. I told you they have an office in my village. Many people used to visit the office.'

'What would Zaki say?'

'*Fala fala ho jaayega. Fala fala ho jayega.* (This will happen, that will happen.) After waging jehad we will earn a lot of respect, lot of money. ... *Yeh sabaab ka kaam hai.* (This is a virtuous task.)"

'What else he would say?'

'*Ajar milega.* (You will be rewarded.) *Izzat milega.* (And respect.) You have to wage jehad.'

'What will you get after waging jehad?'

'*Paisa, izzat.*(Money, respect.)'

'What else did Zaki say?'

'He told my father to leave me in the office. From then on I was in Allah's custody.'

'When did you join this?'

'I don't remember ... possibly a year and a half back.'

'And when did you receive training?'

'It was snowing.'

'So it was around January or December?'

Sabaab means 'virtuous deed which results in Allah's reward'.

'Possibly ... (pause). When Benazir Bhutto was killed. Then we were receiving the training.'

'Were these people involved in killing Benazir?'

'I don't know. They do many things. In Afghanistan ... I don't know.'

'How many people were there in training?'

'Twenty-four to twenty-five people were there.'

'Where was this training organized?'

'In Mansera. In the hills. Near a village called Battan. They trained us in pistols, *kalashan*, magazines that are attached with it, in grenades.' Kasab calls Kalashnikovs '*kalashan*'.

'Do you know the names of others who were with you at the training?'

'No, I know just one boy. He was also from Lahore. We became friends. We were not allowed to know about each other. They were very strict.'

'Did Zaki come to train you?'

'No, he would come only occasionally ... You see, he is a very busy man. He would say we will go to heaven. I said, *bhago yaar, main yeh nahi kar sakta*. (Let's run ... I can't do this).'

'Where were you all supposed to go after today's incident?'

'Nowhere. We were meant to die.'

'How many people did you kill at the CST station?'

'Don't know. I finished two-and-a-half magazines. Don't know how many I killed. Just kept firing. Zaki had told us to keep killing till we were alive.'

'For how long were you supposed to carry this out?'

'As long as we could. Until we died.'

'How many of you have come to Mumbai?'

'We were blindfolded. We came in a ship. And then we got into a launch. You know where the launch from India and Pakistan meet, there we got into an Indian launch,' Kasab tries to evade the question on the total number of his accomplices.

'Who provided you support here in Mumbai?'

'I don't know. There are some *mujahids* who come to India and settle down. We don't know about them. We were sent to die.'

'You have come to wage jehad in India?'

'What jehad saab?' Kasab breaks down. No tears. Just the face contorts as a rhythmic, nasal sound of crying comes out.

'There is no point in crying now,' Ghadge sounds a little

sympathetic. 'Ordinary people, just like you, have been killed ... Why didn't you think earlier? Where else have you waged jehad before coming here?'

'Nowhere. Nowhere,' Kasab interrupts his crying.

'What were you told?'

'Just keep shooting, keep shooting till you die,' he now stops crying.

'What were you supposed to get in return?'

'Money. Zaki chacha was supposed to give money to my family.'

'How much money have you got for this?'

'He would give money to my family. He had promised to give a big amount to my family for this.'

'How does Zaki look?'

'He has a black beard with strands of white. His age would be forty to forty-five years. He went to Afghanistan and finished *Roos* (Russia),' Kasab reiterating the legend of Zaki he must have heard a thousand times.

'What lecture he used to give?'

'He would give lectures only once in a while. *Bada masroof rahta tha.* (He would keep very busy.) "You are Muslims. You have to get rid of poverty. Look at India. They have raced ahead of us. They kill your people. You have to wage jehad against India."'

'What is the meaning of a jehadi?'

'I don't know.'

'Just try explaining it to me?' Ghadge insists.

Kasab keeps mum.

'If you don't know then why have you come here?'

'Because he used to give me money ... Otherwise you tell me, *khate-peete ghar ka bhala koi jaayega?* (Will a well-to-do person go for such work?)' Kasab blames his poverty again.

'What has Zaki chacha got in return?

'He is a jehadi ... he does this for jehad.'

'What is the meaning of jehad?' Ghadge returns to his original question.

'To try to do something for the Muslim religion,' Kasab tries explaining seeing that the policeman won't relent.

'What do you understand from jehad?'

'Don't know ... we just got money. You don't have clothes to wear ... don't have food to eat ... and Zaki chacha would throw *davats* (feasts) ... for the first few months we just ate ... poor boys

… not-so-poor boys … we all just ate and had fun … and then he picked a selected few and sent us for the training … but all who came were poor,' Kasab returns to his favourite topic, his poverty, having failed to elucidate the theological cum religious subject of jehad.

'Where were you before you came to India?'

'We stayed in a lodge in Karachi. We would go fishing and have fun. I thought I would continue to work as a security guard there. Family back home was also getting some money. Suddenly one day he summoned all of us and said that the time had come to do big deeds, to become big. We would get money. We would get *sabaab*.'

'You got *shabaab*?'

'*Dekho babu. Agar masrufiyat na ho, ghar me khane ko na ho to kya karoge?* (See, if you are not busy with work, there is not enough to eat, what will you do?)'

'So did you get *shabaab* in Pakistan?' asked Ghadge, confusing *sabaab* with *shabaab*, the former implying reward, the latter women, finally unable to resist the question on account of the repeated mention of the word.

'What *sabaab*? What to say saab?' Kasab fails to comprehend the query.

'No. But did you get *shabaab*? *Majaa kiya?* (Did you enjoy?)' Ghadge puts it across explicitly. (Later, he told this journalist he wanted to know if the terrorists had also been lured with women.)

'*Chee, chee. Gande kaam main nahi karta.* (I don't do dirty things.) *Sabaab maane ajar.* (*Sabaab* means virtuous deeds.)'

'What kinds of weapons were you trained in?'

'*Peeca-meeca*, grenade, pistol, *kalashan* and the equipment that fits in *kalashan*.'

'*Peeca-meeca*?'

'*Peeca … peeca.*'

'After training were you allowed to take the weapons with you?'

'No.'

'Were Pakistan army personnel used to train you?'

'I don't know. The organization is being run for a very long time. They said the work first started from Afghanistan.'

'Did you ever ask Zaki if he ever had done jehad himself?'

'Yes. He said he had done it … in Afghanistan.'

'Didn't you feel for the innocent people you fired at?'

'To become a big man you have to do such things.'

'How did you reach Mumbai?'

'In a launch. In an Indian launch. There were four-five fishermen in the launch. We abducted them near the border of Indian and Pakistani waters. After that when we were just some miles off from the Mumbai coast we got into a speedboat and sailed towards Mumbai and got off near a fishermen colony.'

'From where did you start in Pakistan?'

'In Azizabad. There is a place called Kasmabaad. It's close to the sea. Kasmabaad is a big place. It's a jungle. Well, not exactly a jungle, since there are shanties and shacks and villagers. What's that place called? Yes, Buharo. There's a place called Buharo. It's a jungle. A road goes to that place. We all sat in a jeep with black, tinted glasses and went to the sea.'

'When was it decided to attack Mumbai?'

'A month back. Ismail and I were called. … We were shown the target. A video CD was shown to us. We were shown the VT station … And the road that goes towards the station, from the side of Azaad Maidan. We were supposed to go on that road to Taj Mahal hotel. We were told Azaad Maidan would come. We were told about the work we had to do.'

'What work?'

'Of VTS,' said Kasab. (VTS implying VT station.)

'VTS or ATS?' Ghadge wanted to know if the terrorists had a specific plan to target the ATS office or its officers.

'The place where there is a station,' explains Kasab.

'What kind of office was there in the CD?' Ghadge probing further into the possibility of ATS office being one of the targets.

'There was no office. There was a man. You can't see his face. He was walking around the station and a voice in the background was narrating, explaining the layout of the station.'

'Who were you supposed to kill?'

'Ordinary people. We were meant to kill anyone who would come in sight. Ismail and I had the same target.'

'How did you get hold of the police vehicle?'

'We wanted to escape. We came down from the terrace of the hospital. We were shuffling along, hiding along the way. We would walk some distance, again hide, like that. Then this police vehicle came. They fired at us. I fell down, I suffered bullet injuries on both my hands. Ismail did his job. He fired at the policemen in the vehicle. Then he hauled me up into the vehicle and he drove.'

'How did you get the Skoda car?'

'We took it from there, don't know the name of the place. Our vehicle got punctured. Then we saw this Skoda car. We took the vehicle at gunpoint.'

'Did Zaki chacha come with you on the ship?'

'Chacha came only up to Karachi.'

'What's the name of your *sangathan* (group or organization)?'

'What?' Kasab doesn't understand the Hindi word.

'What's the name of your *sangathan*? Gang?'

'Lashkar-e-Toiba,' murmurs Kasab, the word 'gang' striking home the question.

'And what is Deccan Mujahideen?'

'I don't know.'

'How many weapons did you have?'

'We had one AK-47, one pistol, eight hand grenades and six magazines.'

'What was your plan?'

'To kill people. And then take a stronghold. Take people hostage. And then make demands.' The use of the word, stronghold, takes Ghadge by surprise.

'Make demands to whom?'

'To the government.'

'What demands?'

'*Woh peeche se batane waale the.* (They were supposed to inform us later on.)'

'How would they have informed you?'

'On the phone.'

'How much money did you give the cabbie who drove you to the VT station?'

'100 or 1,000. Don't remember,' says Kasab.

'How much money in all did you have?'

'5,400 rupees each we had on us.'

At this point of time it was also important for the Mumbai police to question Kasab about the other terrorists who were part of one of the most daring terror attacks on Mumbai. Kasab finally surrendered to the persistent questioning about the other eight terrorists and blurted out the details about them. The police already had details of Ismail Khan, who was with Kasab and was shot dead in the encounter.

'One is Abu Rehman. He is around twenty-five years. His eyes are brown. I think he is wearing a red shirt. Also "Yeshu" is written on his cap.'

'Yeshu?'

'Yeshu ... yeshu ...'

'You mean Christ?'

'Yes.'

'But you are all Muslims?'

'Yes. But you see, you have to look like them, to look like them he was wearing the cap.'

'Okay. Continue.'

'Abu Rehman is from Multan city. He had more *kalashan* magazines on him than any of us. The second man is Abu Fahad. He must be around twenty-eight years. He is slightly taller than me. He is from district Okara.'

'Tell me about the others.'

'Then there is Abu Rehman Bada (elder). He is also from Multan. Then Abu Ali from Okara district. Then Abu Soheb from Sialkot. And Abu Umer from Faisalabad.'

'What about the remaining two?'

'The other two are Abu Umar from Faisalabad and Abu Aakasha who is from Multan.'

'Where is your bag that you brought with you?'

'My bag is lying on the terrace of the Cama Hospital. I left it there.'

'What was there in your bag?'

'*Kalashan.*'

'AK-47?'

'Yes. One pistol. Two magazines for the pistol. Three double magazines of AK-47. Each magazine carries thirty bullets. So, in all 180 AK-47 bullets. The pistol magazine had seven bullets each. Eight hand grenades. Two hand grenades were of plastic cover. Three were big, of Arges make. *Badaam ... kishmish* (almonds, raisins). Mineral water.'

'*Badaam, kishmish, pista?*'

'No, only *badaam* and *kishmish*, together weighing not more than half a kilogram.'

'How many hand grenades did you use?'

'Just two. The others fell out of my bag. Ismail must have used more grenades. He was leading. I was giving him cover. Ismail was in

127

charge of this operation. He was the senior-most. *Woh hamse pehle se jamaat me hai.* (He was in the association before all of us.)'

'Where did you assemble the Kalashnikov?'

'No, it was already assembled. I just took it out of the bag and removed the safety pin.'

'Around what time did you reach Mumbai?'

'At around 8.15 p.m. we got off the dinghy and landed near a fishermen colony. We were told to launch the attack between seven and eleven in the evening. Zaki chacha had told us that if we somehow land in Mumbai late in the night, then to postpone it to the next day. And if we had landed early morning, then to start it by 11 a.m.'

'Where would you all have met after the operation?'

'*Milne wale nahi they. Marne wale they.* (We were not going to meet anywhere. We were supposed to die.)'

'Tell me about the ship you sailed in from Pakistan.'

'Arms and ammunition were already stored on the ship. We just boarded it on 22 November and after a few hours of sailing we got into the Indian launch.'

'Who owned the Pakistani ship?'

'Zaki chacha.'

'What was written on the ship?'

'*Husseini … Al-Husseini.* Then we got into an Indian launch. When we were only some distance off the Mumbai coast, at around 7 p.m., we downed a speedboat, an inflatable one, and got into it and landed in Mumbai.'

'Who was driving the speedboat?'

'Ismail. You see, *woh hamara amir tha.* (He was our leader.) We first got off and hailed a taxi and came to CST. The others must have gotten off after us.'

'Where is the CD of the footage of the CST station?'

'It's in Lakhvi chacha's laptop. *Agar koi banda ho na jo unki field me ghus jaye to bahut maloomaat ikhatha kar sakta hai.* (If some guy infiltrates their group he can get a lot of information.)'

'Can you take us there?'

'Yes, I can take you there, provided you give me enough security cover. Zaki can be beaten in his game by his own men.'

'Are you also linked up with Jaish-e-Mohammed?'

'No. Jaish-e-Mohammed *doosri tanzeem hai* (is another movement). We are Ahle-Hadis. *Aur woh sala Deobandi hai.* (And those rascals are Deobandis.)'

'What date was fixed for this attack?'

'Earlier we were told in Pakistan that we would do this during Ramzan. Then I don't know what happened. It was put off. We were not told the reasons. Then as I said we sailed out on 22 November. But no date was fixed. We did not know how many days, four, five or seven, it would take in the waters before landing in Mumbai. But we were told to take care of the timing before we began the attack. If we had landed early morning then we were supposed to start the attack by eleven in the morning and if we arrived in the afternoon, or say evening, then between 7 and 11 p.m.'

It is almost four in the morning. Ghadge has had enough of Kasab. He gestures towards the cameraman. The camera stops rolling. Kasab takes a deep breath and closes his eyes.

At the ATS Office

Vijay Singh (name changed due to security reasons), thirty-eight, standing just under five-feet-eight with dense black hair, well-oiled and slicked to the side much like a schoolboy. Despite having a thick moustache, it is the youthfulness of his eyes that dominate his face. He could be mistaken for a professional in the corporate world, a young IT professional perhaps – which is in fact what he intended before he became an inspector with the Maharashtra police. The last few years of his posting with the Mumbai ATS, though, had hardly given him an occasion to wear his khaki threads – as a key member of the technical section of the ATS. Although he did not have a degree in computer technology, with his technical bent of mind and aided by the formal training provided by the ATS, Singh had become an expert in cyber and electronic intelligence gathering. Singh loved his job: intercepting phone calls, hacking into email addresses or social networking profiles of computer-savvy terrorists, collecting cyber intelligence on terror modules.

However, lately things had been tough for him and for that matter all of ATS, particularly its chief Hemant Karkare. But this evening, the evening of 26 November, was different. After a long gloomy period, the smile had returned on Singh's face. Tonight he wanted to celebrate, in his own inimitable style, by feasting on *pav bhaji* and milkshake at one of his favourite food joints behind the Byculla railway station. He had just ordered one more *masala pav* and some *faluda* when his boss, Hemant Karkare called on his cellphone (Karkare spoke directly to all inspectors, assistant inspectors and sub-inspectors posted at the ATS). 'You call eating *pav bhaji* and *faluda* partying? Keep Friday evening free and I will show you what a real party is,' said Karkare bursting into laughter. It had been a while since Singh had heard his chief this relaxed and cheerful. Singh was delighted that he had done his bit in bringing the smile back on Karkare's face.

The same afternoon a Mumbai court had granted the ATS three more days of police custody for Dayanand Pandey, prime accused in the Malegaon terror attack, the case that had led to the arrest of almost a dozen Hindu radicals accused of carrying out a bomb blast in Malegaon in rural Maharashtra. The evidence produced by the ATS left the court with little choice than to extend Pandey's police custody. The ATS had shown the judge a video clip wherein Pandey and his accomplices could be seen plotting the terror attack. The video clip was shot by Pandey using the webcam of his laptop (Pandey had this queer habit of recording meetings and telephonic conversations held with co-conspirators and storing them on his laptop). It was Singh and his colleagues in the technical section who, after two weeks of rummaging through the data on Pandey's laptop, had retrieved the video clip. The audio and video evidence was now expected to demolish the disparaging campaign kick-started by the Hindu right-wing parties, accusing the Mumbai ATS of being anti-Hindu and victimizing saffron activists without any evidence. The discovery of the video had changed everything: incontrovertible and clinching, it was going to steal the thunder of its detractors.

A few minutes after Singh spoke to Karkare he got a phone call from his friend informing him about the firing at the Oberoi hotel. His *vada pav* half-eaten, Singh rushed towards the Oberoi. As he parked his car on the road opposite the hotel he saw smoke billowing out of the upper lobby of the Oberoi; then a few foreigners, screaming and pleading for help, came running out of the hotel. A few minutes later there was an ear-splitting explosion. Another blast followed – lesser in decibel volume – perhaps that of a grenade, but loud enough to send people scurrying for cover. Singh decided to call up Karkare but the latter disconnected the call. A few minutes later Addl CP Parambir Singh of the ATS called Singh and asked him to rush to the ATS office and get cracking with other staff members at the technical room. The time was 10.50 p.m.

In less than fifteen minutes Singh walked into the technical room of the ATS, equipped with modern gadgets, high-end computers and advanced technology for intercepting phone calls and electronic communication. Assisted by three more inspectors and half-a-dozen police constables, all technically trained, Singh started coordinating with different cellphone service providers, scanning their international gateways for any suspicious calls, concentrating on the calls originating or ending in the localities surrounding the Taj hotel, the Oberoi hotel and Colaba. But there were thousands and thousands of telephone calls passing through the international gateway and also the cellphone towers in the area around Colaba and Nariman Point. The ATS staff sucked out a few conversations from the air – whispery voices speaking Arabic or some other Middle Eastern language – but soon they were found to be of tourists or businessmen, all above suspicion. More calls were taken on 'listening' but they too turned out to be clean. Soon doubts started creeping into Singh's mind. Maybe the terrorists were not using telephones. Maybe they were not communicating at all. But the technical staff of the ATS had to stay on the job. ATS chief Hemant Karkare and the second-most senior officer, Parambir Singh, were both out in the field, in the middle of operations. A small TV set kept in a corner was telecasting the unfolding carnage live. Pictures of blood, bodies, burning hotel rooms, fire, smoke, injured people were being aired in rapid succession.

At around 12 a.m. the news flashed that Hemant Karkare along with a few other senior police officials had been seriously injured in an exchange of fire with the terrorists near Cama Hospital. A few seconds later the news flashed that Karkare had been shifted to JJ Hospital and his condition was critical. Singh felt his blood freezing. For Singh and the other inspectors Karkare was more than just a boss; he was their mentor, a father figure, the patriarch of the ATS family. An eye on the breaking news section of the TV screen, Singh and his colleagues kept toiling for the next one hour, without much luck. Dozens of calls were put under observation but none had anything suspicious.

Then at about 1 a.m. the ATS received a phone call from the IB. The IB had managed to find three cellphone numbers that were being used by the terrorists at the time. The agency passed on these numbers to the ATS which in turn immediately put them under observation. After the first breakthrough there was no looking back for the ATS technical staff. They found out that these three numbers were receiving phone calls from the number 00-120-1253-1824 which turned out to be a virtual number allotted by an international VoIP provider, in short, known as net telephony. Thereafter, all the calls made by this number to India or received from India were put on interception. Soon the virtual number flashed on the screen of Singh's computer. It was making a call on an Indian cell number whose then current location was the Taj hotel. The time was 1.05 a.m.

Terrorist: Hello.

Handler: *Salaam ailekum.*

Terrorist: *Wailekum as-salaam.*

Handler: *Yaar, tumhara kamra 360 ya 361 number jo hai woh pata lag gaya in logon ko … Kya* camera *laga hai?* … (Your room, 360 or 361, they have come to know about it. Is there a camera?)

[The conversation continues as recorded in the Taj Operation section (see page 69), till the handler asks them to put the bed-sheets, etc., on fire.]

Terrorist: *Lekin baaki kamre na band hain; hamare paas ek hi kamra hai. Agar idhar aag laga di to kidhar jaayenge?* (But the other rooms are closed; we have only one room. If we set this on fire, where will we go?)

Handler: *Achha aur kamre nahi khul rahe hain.* (Oh, so the other rooms are not opening.)

Terrorist: *Na ji.* (No sir.)

Handler: *To na gali mein ja ke kaalin mein aag laga do. Aag lagane ke kaam mein der nahi karni hai.* (Then go and put the carpets in the corridor on fire. We cannot delay setting the place on fire.)

Terrorist: *Inshallah.* (Allah willing.)

Handler: *Aur jab mein* phone *karoon to* attend *karna.* (And attend the phone when I call.)

[The call disconnects.]

It was the first call between the terrorists and their managers that the technical staff had intercepted. The handler was keen to be in control of the situation. It was now clear to Singh that though the carnage, the mayhem was being carried out in Mumbai, the director, the puppeteer, the invisible hand was in some safe haven, monitoring the TV, and planning the next move, like a football coach or an army general. The conspiracy had been orchestrated to the last detail. The

Indian intelligence and investigative agencies had their own version of 9/11 to contend with.

The terrorists holed up in the Taj, the Oberoi and the Chabad House soon stopped using their own phones (the Indian SIM cards which they had brought with them) and started using the cellphones of their hostages. But as they kept switching over to different cell numbers, the ATS too kept trailing these calls, putting the new numbers under surveillance.

Time: 1.15 a.m., Taj Hotel

[The phone number 00-120-1253-1824 again flashes on Singh's computer screen. A cellphone in the Taj hotel rings.]

Terrorist: *Salaam ailekum.*

Handler: *Wailekum as-salaam. Aag lag rahi hai ki nahi?* (Is the fire on yet?)

Terrorist: *Bas kapde ikatthe kar rahe hain.* (We are just collecting the cloth.)

Handler: *Jaldi laga do. Aur* launch *ka kya kiya tha?* (Light it quickly. And what did you do with the launch?)

Terrorist: *Bas aise hi chhod di thi.* (We had just left it like that.)

Handler: *Kyun? Woh* valve *nahi kholi thi pani bharne waaste?* (Why? Did you not open that valve to let the water in?)

Terrorist: *Nahi woh kholi nahi jaldi jaldi mein ... kaam kharab ho gaya tha.* (No, we couldn't do it in a hurry ... some things went wrong.)

Handler: *Kya kaam kharab ho gaya tha?* (What had gone wrong?)

Terrorist: *Woh jis jagah utarna tha na wahan mauje bahut zabardast lag rahi thi aur udhar ek kashti bhi aa gayi thi. Saare bole* navy *hai,* navy *hai, to jaldi jaldi doosri* boat *mein utre; samaan utara.* Ismail *bhai ka satellite bhi wahin rah gaya.* (A powerful tide had risen where we were to get off and another boat had also come there. Everyone said, it's the Indian Navy, so we quickly got onto another boat with the baggage. Brother Ismail's satellite phone also got left there.)

[The call ends.]

The Cuffe Parade police station had taken a speedboat into possession that was found drifting near the fishermen colony at

Badhwar Park a little earlier that night. It was not the large motorboat the terrorists were referring to. Singh immediately passed on this piece of information – the fact that the terrorists had come by sea and had abandoned a launch on the high sea, though on the phone the Taj terrorist did not mention where they had abandoned it nor did he specify what kind of a launch it was – to senior officers. Singh and his colleagues tried to intercept as many calls made by terrorists as they could, recording all the conversations as they would soon form critical evidence.

At around 1.20 a.m. the news broke on TV: 'ATS chief Hemant Karkare *shaheed*.' For a few moments it seemed time had stopped. A stunned silence enveloped the room. Frozen to their seats, they all kept staring at the TV. Singh in a late reaction picked up the phone and called up Karkare's driver. '*Saab khatam ho gaya hai*,' said the driver, confirming the news. A glacial rush flowed through his veins. He was hoping Karkare's injuries were not serious. Hoping he would survive. But no. It was over. Tears started rolling down his eyes. For Singh and his colleagues in the ATS, the death of Karkare signalled the end of an era. Karkare, who was being maligned by Hindu radical organizations, and accused of appeasing Indian Muslims, was killed by a bunch of Islamist terrorists sent allegedly from across the border. When alive, Karkare had often said that terror had no religion. His death exemplified his credo.

Seconds after Singh had put the phone down, the number 00-120-1253-1824 again blipped on his computer screen. Singh picked up the headphones, though his mind was numb, his eyes bleary, his senses stunned; despair and defeat writ large on his face. The time was 1.25 a.m.

After exchanging some details about starting the fire in the hotel with bed-sheets and mattresses, the handler informed the terrorists about the scenario in Mumbai.

Handler: *Mahaul bahut achha bana hai. Poore shahar mein tabahi machi hai. Dhai sau se zyada log zakhmi hue hain. Terah-chaudhah jagah firing ho rahi hai, to pareshan mat hona ...* Allah *aapke saath hai. Achha ek* commissioner *bhi maara gaya* hai ... media *kah rahi hai. Achha sun*, ATS *ka* chief *bhi maara gaya hai.* (A conducive environment has been created. The whole city is under destruction. More than 250 people have been injured. There is firing in thirteen-fourteen places, so don't worry. Allah is with you. One commissioner has been killed, the media is reporting. And listen, the ATS chief has also been killed.)

Terrorist: *Achha. Lo,* Umer *aur* Ali *aa gaye hain.* (Ok, Umer and Ali have returned.)

[Another handler comes on the line and inside the Taj hotel the terrorist called Umer takes over the phone.]

Handler 2: Umer, *salaam ailekum.*

Umer: *Wailekum as-salaam.*

Handler 2: *Achha ghabrane wali koi baat nahi hai.* Allah *ke fazal se jo* Bombay *mein* operation *karne wala* chief *hai na, woh mara gaya hai; abhi thodi der pehle.* (Ok, there is no need to panic. By Allah's grace, the chief who ran operations in Bombay has been killed, just a little while back.)

Umer: *Kaun maara gaya hai?* (Who has been killed?)

Handler 2: Chief *maara gaya hai* Bombay *ka;* commissioner *mara gaya* Bombay *ka. Bahut saare log zakhmi hain ... mar rahe hai. Poore shahar mein* firing *ho rahi hai ... aag lagi hui hai ...* Allah *ne aapse bahut achha kaam liya hai.* (The chief of Bombay and a commissioner have been killed. Many people are injured, many are dying. Firing is on throughout the city; there is fire at many places. Allah has extracted very good work from you.)

The call ended at 1.47 a.m. As Singh listened to the call, the terrorists shared the news of Hemant Karkare's death. For them, the death of the ATS chief, who they knew as someone who ran operations against terrorists, was a big victory.

At around 2 a.m. a deputy director of the RAW, Subodh Jaiswal joined the ATS technical staff. Together, they put to use all their technical know-how to intercept the communication between the terrorists. The terrorists were speaking in Punjabi Urdu. The Mumbai ATS only had one officer, Parambir Singh, who knew the language well. But he was camping at the Oberoi, coordinating the police action there. Jaiswal's arrival at the ATS office gave the technical staff the much-needed moral boost. Until a few months back Jaiswal was serving as an additional commissioner in the Mumbai ATS and knew all of them well. Being from Punjab, Jaiswal was also well versed with the language and was able to catch the idiom the terrorists were using. For the next two days, along with the ATS staff, Jaiswal intercepted and recorded over six-and-a-half hours of telephonic conversation between the terrorists and their handlers.

Hundreds of miles away from the Byculla based headquarters of the Mumbai ATS, the operations room of the IB situated in a sprawling complex at Sardar Patel Marg in Delhi was buzzing with activity. Parallel to the interceptions being made by the Mumbai ATS, the IB was doing its own interceptions. The three Indian cell numbers which the terrorists had first used after landing in Mumbai were already under the IB's watch. Ironically, these numbers had been provided to the LeT activists by undercover security personnel who had managed to infiltrate the ranks of the LeT in India. The LeT operatives in India had sent these numbers to their masters in Pakistan. The Indian intelligence agencies believed that since these numbers were under observation they would know in advance what the terrorists were up to. But the ten terrorists switched on these numbers only after landing at Badhwar Park a little after 8.15 p.m. By then it was too late.

Time: 2.48 a.m., Taj Hotel

Terrorist: *Salaam ailekum.*

Handler: *Wailekum as-salaam. Achha tumhare* hotel *mein wazir hai teen – kisi kamre mein teen wazir hain aur ek* cabinet secretary *hai … Jo saari* cabinet *ka* secretary *nahi hota, woh bhi hain tumhare* hotel *mein.* (Listen, there are three ministers in your hotel – in some room – and one cabinet secretary.)

Terrorist: *Oye, oye, oye! Badi khush-khabri sunai hai.* (Oh, that's great news!)

Handler: *Yeh teen-chaar bande dhoond lo, fir jo marzi manwa lo* India *se.* (Find out these three-four men, then you can make India agree to anything.)

Terrorist: *Inshallah … bas dua karo* Allah *se.* (Allah willing … just pray to Allah.)

Handler: *Aur* grenade *feko … Bahar shayad* navy *aa gayi hai. Khidki se* fire *karo aur* grenade *feko.* (Throw grenades. Probably there is Indian Navy outside. Fire and throw grenades from the window.)

[The phone call ends.]

Time: 3.53 a.m., Oberoi Hotel

Handler 1: Brother Abdul. The media is comparing your action to 9/11. One senior police officer has been killed.

Terrorist 1: We are on the eighteenth or nineteenth floor. We have five hostages.

Handler 2: Everything is being recorded by the media. Inflict maximum damage. Keep fighting and don't be taken alive.

Handler 1: Kill all hostages except the two Muslims. Keep your phone switched on so that we can hear the gunfire.

Terrorist 2: We have three foreigners including women from Singapore and China.

Handler 1: Kill them.

27 November afternoon, Chabad House

Handler: *Baat karao.* [The handler in Pakistan instructs the Chabad House terrorist to put the hostage on line.]

Terrorist: *Haan, bolein.* (Here, speak.)

A woman hostage: Hello ... Who is that?

Handler: Did you spoke ... Did you speak to the consulate?

Hostage: I am talking to the consulate ... they are doing ... they are making phone calls ... just now ...

Handler: Already made it or you are going to make it?

Hostage: Yeah ... [She starts sobbing and then recovers to talk.] I've already talked to them ... I was talking to the consulate just a few seconds back and they are making their phone calls. They have said to leave the line free so that they can get in touch with you anytime and tell you that we are pleased with you [again starts crying] ... You understand?

Handler: Come again ... come again. No I don't understand.

Hostage: They will get in touch with you anytime.

Handler: Don't worry ... just sit back and relax and wait for them to make contact ... Okay?

Hostage: [Cries]

Handler: Save your energy for good days ... Maybe if they can contact right now ... maybe you will celebrate Shabbath with your family.

Hostage: [Cries again]

Handler: Give the phone back to the guy.

[The terrorist takes the phone back from the hostage.]

Handler: *Iski baat hui hai ... Abhi kissi bhi waqt* phone *aayega un logo ka.* (She has talked to them ... Anytime now their phone call will come.)

Terrorist: *Mere* number *par*? (On my number?)

Handler: *Haan, aapke* number *par* ... authorities phone *karenge. Poochhenge, "Kya chahte ho aap log?" To aapne sabse pehle yeh kehna hai ki yeh jo aasu gas ki shelling ho rahi hai ... firing ho rahi hai, yeh silsila band ho. Matlab paanch minute ke andar Army ilaka khali kar de. Matlab yeh silsila agar chalta raha to hum log sabr, intezar nahi karenge ... Aap likho in cheezo ko. Achha, jo* operation *ho raha hai,* Taj Mahal *mein,* Oberoi *mein aur aapke oopar – teen jagah – in teeno jagah par* operation *fauran roka jaaye ... Achha, doosra, inhone kaha hai hamara ek banda giraftaar kiya hai kal; unse yeh kehna hai ki banda fauran yahaan aapke paas lekar aayein. Aur khana-wana khaya?* (Yes, on your number the authorities will call. They will ask, "What do you people want?" So, first you ask them to stop shelling tear gas and firing. That is, within five minutes the Army should leave. If this goes on, we will not be patient, we will not wait ... You write these things down. And the operations they are carrying out in the Taj Mahal and the Oberoi and above you – at three places – should be stopped with immediate effect. And, another thing, they are saying they arrested one of our guys yesterday; tell them to hand him over immediately to you, here. And food – did you have your meal?)

Terrorist: *Thoda bahut.* (Little bit.)

Handler: *Thoda bahut? Yeh log to badi* party-*sharty karte hain ... khana to hona chahiye. Achha yeh log halal hi khate hai, haraam nahi khate yeh log, to woh koi masla nahi hai ...* (Little bit? These people hold lot of parties, there should be food around. These people eat *halal* meat, not *haram* [forbidden], so that is not an issue ...)

27 November, 2.33 p.m., Chabad House

Handler: *Salaam ailekum?*

Terrorist: *Wailekum as-salaam.*

Handler: *Kya haal chaal hai?* (How is it going?)

Terrorist: Allah *ka shukar hai.* (Things are fine by Allah's grace.)

Handler: *Koi* phone *aaya?* (Has any phone call come?)

Terrorist: *Koi* Inspector Patil *tha* Mumbai police *ka; uska* phone *aaya. Maine kaha* inspector *winspector kya hota hai – koi* higher authorities *se baat karao.* (It was some Inspector Patil from Mumbai police. I said I will not talk to some ordinary inspector – get the higher authorities to talk.)

Handler: *Kaho* area *khali karao. Aur* grenades *feke bahar aapne?* (Tell them to clear the area. And did you throw grenades?)

Terrorist: *Haan ji feke.* (Yes, we did.)

Handler: *Kab feke?* (When did you throw them?)

Terrorist: *Abhi koi ek-do* minute *hua hoga.* (Just a minute or two back.)

Handler: *Koi halchal huyi?* (Did anything stir up?)

Terrorist: Grenade *fekne ke baad koi jawabi* firing *nahi huyi hai.* (There was no firing in response.)

Handler: *Kis taraf* grenade *feka hai?* (In what direction did you throw them?)

Terrorist: *Woh ...* Merchant House *ki taraf.* (Towards Merchant House.)

Handler: *Achha ab aap* gun *ki* barrel *bahar nikaal ke gali mein* fire *karein ek-do. Sirf* barrel *nikaalni hai, apna jism saamne nahi karna hai; neeche gali hai na* open fire *karein.* (Now you push out the gun barrel and fire once or twice in the lane outside. Don't expose your body, only the barrel; there is an open lane below – fire there.)

Terrorist: *Haan* open *hai. Lekin hum daaye, baaye aur* back *mein* fire *kar sakte hain,* front *nazar nahi aa raha hai.* (Yes, it is open. We can fire in the left, right, and back, but we cannot see anything in the front lane.)

Handler: *Achha, to darwaza khula nahi abhi tak aapka?* (Ok, so you have still not opened your door?)

Terrorist: *Nahi abhi tak nahi khula.* (No, not yet.)

Handler: *Achha jo bhi bahar harkat karta hua banda nazar aaye na usko* fire *maaro. Apne aapko bachana hai; ek banda oopar chhat pe rakho, aur koi bhi* movement *nazar aaye to* fire *karo.* (The moment you see someone doing something outside, open fire. And, you have to protect yourself; put a man on the rooftop, and the instant you see any movement, open fire.)

Terrorist: *Achha yeh jo aurat hai agar iski hum khud* media *mein baat karaaye? Yeh khud* media *ko bataaye ki hamare saath yeh ho raha hai aur hamein bachaya jaye.* (Ok, what if we get this woman to talk to the media herself? She will tell the media what is happening with her and that she needs to be saved.)

[The instructor in Pakistan stops to watch TV for a while.]

Handler: *Abhi aapne jo* grenade *feke hain usse* media *mein shor mach gaya hai.* (The grenade you just threw has created a commotion in the media.)

[A third person now takes the phone.]

Handler: *Salaam ailekum.*

Terrorist: *Wailekum as-salaam.*

Handler: *Kaise ho bhaiya?* (How are you brother?)

Terrorist: Allah *ka shukar hai.* (Things are fine by the grace of Allah.)

Handler: *Jo baatein maine aapko batayi thi yaad hai na? Agar* media *waale poochhe kahan ke ho to kehna* Hyderabad Deccan *ka hoon;* Hyderabad city *ka hoon.* (You remember all that I had told you? If the media asks where you are from, tell them you are from Hyderabad in the Deccan; that you are from the city of Hyderabad.)

Terrorist: Hyderabad.

Handler: *Haan. Aur kehna* Toli Chauki area *ka hoon; aur kehna* Mujahideen Deccan *se mera talluk hai. Kis tanzeem se?* Mujahideen Hyderabad Deccan. *Aur woh pooche yeh sab kisliye kiya … aap likh rahe hain na?* (Yes. And say you are from the Toli Chauki area; say you are associated with the Deccan Mujahideen. And if they ask why you did all this … are you writing all this down?)

Terrorist: *Haan ji.* (Yes.)

Handler: *Kehna hukumat ki dohri* policy *… hukumat to peeth thapthapati hai aur prashasan to sar par tole marti hai … iski taza misaal* Sachar Committee *ki sifarshat hai … hukumat kuchh aur ailan karti hai aur prashasan uska amal* Muslim *naujawano ko pakad-pakad kar karti hai.* (Say it is the duplicitous policy of the government – on one hand they pat our backs, on the other they beat our heads with hammers. The latest example of this is the Sachar Committee Report. The government declares one thing but the administration executes its reverse by wrongly arresting Muslim youth.)

Terrorist: Muslim …

Handler: *Yuvko ko …* (Youth)

Terrorist: *Yuv …*

Handler: Muslim *naujawano ko … giraftar karta hai … unka jo* future *barbaad karta hai. Aur unko* ultimatum *de de ki yeh abhi hamara* trailer *hai, asal* film *to abhi baaki hai. Aur sun itminaan ke saath baat karna … khali apni baat karni hai; unko sawaal karne ka mauka kam dena hai.* (Muslim youth … are arrested … their future is ruined. And give them the ultimatum that this is only a trailer, the full film is yet to be shown. And listen, talk confidently, and only allow yourself to talk; don't let them ask too many questions.)

Terrorist: *Theek hai. Inshallah.* (All right.)

Handler: *Ek* (one) minute.

[The voice goes into consultation with other voices in the room. Some other voice now takes over the phone.]

Handler: *Woh poochhenge aapki* demand *kya hai.* (They will ask what is your demand.)

Terrorist: *Ji.* (Yes.)

Handler: *Aap kehna, jitney bhi* Musalmaan *jailon mein band hai aap unko riha karo,* number *ek;* number *do,* Muslim state Musalmaano *ke hawale kar diya jaaye.* Number *teen* ... Kashmir *se fauj bulayi jaaye aur* Kashmiriyon *ko unka haque diya jaaye* ... Babri Masjid *par fauri taur par* masjid *ka kaam shuru kiya jaaye* ... *uss jagah ko* Musalmaano *ke hawale kiya jaaye.* Israel *ke saath gathbandhan na kiya jaaye.* (You say, first, release all the Muslims in the jails; second, hand over the Muslim state to Muslims. Third, call back the Army from Kashmir and give Kashmiris their rightful due. Begin the construction of Babri Masjid immediately. The land of the masjid should be handed over to Muslims right away. Do not maintain ties with Israel.)

Terrorist: Israel *ke saath* ... ? (With Israel ... ?)

Handler: Israel *ke saath gathjod na kiya jaaye; aur* Israel *hukumat ko yeh* ultimatum *diya jaaye ki* Musalmaano *ke oopar zyadti band karein.* (Break off ties with Israel; and give the ultimatum to the Israeli government that it should stop the injustice on Muslims.)

Terrorist: *Musalmaano ke khoon se khelna band kiya jaaye.* (Stop playing with Muslim blood.)

[The terrorist gives his own poetic touch to the last bit while jotting down the notes.]

Handler: *Aur* Israel *agar yeh nahi karega* ... *Bas, bas, yahi baatein theek hain, theek hai?* (And if Israel doesn't agree ... No, no, this much is enough, okay?)

Terrorist: *Theek hai.* (Okay.)

[Another voice takes over the phone.]

Handler: *Jo aapki jagah hai na, kehna* Nariman House *se baat kar raha hoon.* Media *kah rahi hai ki* Nariman House *mein aatankwadi hai.* (And the place you are at, say you are calling from Nariman House. The media is saying there are terrorists in Nariman House.)

[The terrorists and the planners knew the place as Chabad House, which is the commonly known name of Nariman House.]

Terrorist: Nariman House.

Handler: Nariman, Nariman. *Aur saath saath khayal rakhna bahar ka bhi.* (And also keep track of what is happening outside.)

Terrorist: *Inshallah. Aur jo baate likahyi hain sirf utni hi karni hai?* (And, what you have instructed, we have to say only that much?)

Handler: *Utni hi; ek* minute hold *karein,* number *likhein. Yeh* Zee TV office *ka* number *hai* – 0120-2511064. *Aur aapka* number *jisse aap* call *karenge bataoon aapko?* (Yes, only that much; hold on one minute, write this number down. This is the Zee TV office number … And should I tell you the number from which you will call them, because they will ask you?)

Terrorist: *Haan ji, bataien.* (Yes, tell me.)

Handler: *Aapka* number *hai* (Your number is) 9819464530.

Terrorist: 9819464530. *Maine usko bolna hai mein bol raha hoon* Nariman House *se aur mujhe iss* number *par* phone *kare.* (I have to tell him I am calling from Nariman House and he should call me on this number.)

Handler: *Haan aap kahein aapke paas* hostage *hai, aur aap iss* number *par fauran* call *karein.* (Yes, you say you have a hostage, so call me on this number right now.)

[The phone call ends.]

Later in the evening, the terrorist, Babar Imran (Abu Aakasha) finally managed to get through a telephone number of India TV which was provided to him by his handlers. In a fake Kashmiri accent, he first spoke to the receptionist and thinking he was on live television, he rattled off all the lines he had memorized. The receptionist was flabbergasted. She asked Imran to be on the line as she transferred the call to the newsroom. The moment a male news producer said 'Hello', Imran again rattled off all the demands he had been told by his handlers to speak on TV. The news producer told Imran that the conversation was not being broadcast live and asked him to pause so that they could talk normally. After consultation with others present in the newsroom, the producer finally put Imran through to a female anchor. Imran announced his demands to the world over the live telecast. Throughout his conversation Imran maintained the fake Kashmiri accent he had assumed for the interview. Soon after he ended his telephonic interview, the handlers in Pakistan called to congratulate him for the job well done.

28 November, 7.23 a.m., Chabad House

Handler: *Salaam ailekum.*

Terrorist: *Wailekum as-salaam.*

Handler: *Kya haal chaal hai* pasha? (How are you doing pasha – [a term of endearment]?)

Terrorist: *Mere khayal se team utaar di gayi hai.* (I think the team has got off.)

Handler: *Aapke chhat par pandrah bande abhi utre hain* helicopter *se.* (Fifteen men have climbed down on your rooftop right now.)

Terrorist: *Khidkiyon ke saamne bhi kuchh khade hain.* (They are standing in front of the windows as well.)

Handler: *Kya keh rahe hain? Aapko nazar aa raha hai kuch udhar?* (What are you saying? Can you see anything there?)

Terrorist: *Saamne kuchh firing ho rahi hai.* (They are firing in the front.)

Handler: *Aapke oopar se unhe neeche aana hai. Aapne seedhiyon par aisi* position *banani hai ki aate hi aap unhe gher lein: unhe seedhiyon se utarna hai neeche. Lekin aisi* position *banaye ki unke oopar aane se pehle aap* grenade *feke. Aap aisi* position *banaye ... ki matlab kamre mein rahein lekin jo seedhi hai na ... Achha, aapko daaye baaye koi fauji nazar aa raha hai?* (They have to climb down to reach you. Take such positions on the staircase so you can corner them as soon as they come: they will have to get down from the stairs. But you throw grenades before they come. You take such a position ... you stay in the room but the stairs ... Listen, can you see any Army personnel to your right and left?)

Terrorist: *Hamare saamne saaf nazar aa rahe, ... khidkiyon mein baithe hain.* (We can see them clearly in the front, sitting in the windows.)

Handler: *Maaro,* fire *karo,* burst *maaro. Achha, baat suno, aap abhi kamre mein ho na, aap* fire *karo. Ek banda bahar darwaje ke paas* position *leke rakhe, ek andar se* fire *kare.* (Hit them, fire, open burst fire. Ok, listen, just fire from the room. Let one person take position by the door and you fire from inside.)

Terrorist: *Lekin hamara aage ka kamra* damage *ho gaya hai.*

Hamare paas position *nahi baachti hai.* (But the room in front of us is damaged. We don't have a position left.)

Handler: *Lekin aapko woh nazar aa rahe hain. Kyunki jaise hi unhone aapko dekh liya unhone aap par* fire *shuru kar dena hai.* (But you can see them. Because if they see you, they too will start firing immediately.)

Terrorist: *To issi liye keh raha hun ki oopar chhat par jayein aur wahan ladayi kare.* (That's why I'm saying, we should go to the roof and fight there.)

Handler: *Aapne oopar nahi chadna hai. Do baatein yaad rakhni hain:* number *ek, jo* sniper *baithe huye hai na khidkiyon mein, jahan se mauka mil gaya wahan se inhe* fire *karna hai; doosra, jo log upar utre hai, pandrah log* helicopter *se, woh aapki taraf aa rahe hain. Unpar* grenade *feke.* (No, you do not have to climb up. Remember two things: one, as soon as you get the chance, fire at the snipers in the window; two, the fifteen people who have got off the helicopter are coming towards you. You have to throw grenades at them.)

Terrorist: *Hamare paas* grenade *sirf chaar bache hain.* (We have only four grenades left.)

Handler: *Achha, aap log apni* positioning *bana lein aur shuru ho jayein.* (Ok, you take your positions and begin.)

Terrorist: Positioning *mujhe samajh nahi aa rahi ki kaise banani hai.* (I cannot understand which positions to take.)

Handler: *Seedhiyan* corner *mein hai na* pasha? (The stairs are in the corner, aren't they?)

Terrorist: *Haan ji, ek* side *mein hain.* (Yes, they are on one side.)

Handler: *To ek banda seedhiyon ko* cover *kare aur doosra* cross *baithe; jaise maine shaam ko samjhaya tha. Jaise koi agar neeche aata hai to dono taraf se ghir jaaye.* (So one of you has to cover the steps and the other has to sit across; the way I had explained it in the evening. So that if someone comes down, he is surrounded on both sides.)

Terrorist: *Lekin woh agar* grenade *fekte hain to hamare paas* grenade *se bachne ke liye aad nahi hai.* (But if he throws a grenade, we do not have any cover to protect ourselves.)

Handler: *Meri baat suno* pasha. *Agar aap deewar se chipak kar khade ho jaate ho, aur agar* grenade *fekte to kya aap tak aa sakega?* (Listen to me, pasha. If you stick to the wall, can the grenade reach you?)

Terrorist: *Deewar maine bataya na ...* (I told you about the wall.)

Handler: *Achha aapke paas aur kya hai – koi* sofa, furniture *ya* foam *ka gadda*? (Ok, what else do you have – any sofa, furniture, or foam mattress?)

Terrorist: *Haan,* foam *ka gadda hai, ek* minute. (Yes, there is a foam mattress, one minute.)

[Another man comes on the phone.]

Handler: *Aap ek kaam karein. Aap* grenade *fekte huye neeche utarna shuru karein.* (You do this. While throwing grenades, you start climbing down.)

Terrorist: *Hamare paas* grenade *nahi hai.* (We don't have grenades.)

Handler: *Do to bache hai na? Woh istemal karein aur neeche wali manzil mein chale jaayein.* (You have at least two left, don't you? Use those and go to the floor below.)

Terrorist: *Hum darwaze ke peechhe chhup jaayein aur jaise hi woh andar aaye to hum* firing *karein?* (Should we hide behind the door, and the moment they come, should we fire?)

Handler: *Aap alag alag chhup sakte hain?* (Can you hide at different places?)

[Another man takes the phone.]

Handler: *Aap ek kaam karein. Aap chhat ki taraf chalein;* grenade *feke aur unki taraf* fire *karein. Woh aap par* fire *kare isse pehle aap unpar fire kaare. Aap Bismillah karein.* (You do this. Go towards the roof, throw the grenade at them; and fire at them before they can fire at you. Do this now, in the name of Allah.)

Terrorist: *Theek hai ja rahe hain* Allah *ka naam leke.* (Okay, we will go, remembering the name of Allah.)

Handler: *Bismillah-e-Rehman-e-rahim.* (In the name of Allah, most Gracious, most Compassionate.)'

28 November, 08.47 a.m.

Terrorist: *Salaam ailekum.*

Handler: *Wailekum as-salaam.*

Terrorist: *Mujhe aag lag gayi hai.* (I have got burnt.)

Handler: *Kahaan lagi hai?* (Where?)

Terrorist: *Baju mein aur pair mein.* (On the arms and on the legs.)

Handler: Allah-*talla aapki hifazat kare*. (May Allah protect you.)

Terrorist: *Unke log bhi zakhmi ho rahe honge*. (Their people also must be getting hurt.)

[A loud gunshot rings in the background.]

Handler: Allah *hafiz*. (Allah protect you.)

[The phone disconnects.]

The RAW later identified five Pakistani handlers who were giving instructions on the phone: Wassi, Zarrar, Jundal, Buzurg and Kahfa. Besides these five there was one more handler who was being called Major General by the terrorists. Though the Indian investigative agencies know that Zaki-ur-Rehman Lakhvi, Muzammil, Abu-al-Qama and Abu Kahfa were some of the conspirators of the Mumbai terror attack, they don't know much about most of the other handlers – the demonic voices who directed the bloody mayhem – and of their positions in the LeT and their background.

The Indian government has handed over parts of the intercepted conversations between the terrorists to the Pakistani government. After much procrastination and many wishy-washy statements, the Pakistani government, on 15 January 2009, finally announced the formation of a special team to investigate the Mumbai terror attack. Foreign office spokesman, Mohammed Sadiq said that Pakistan has formed an enquiry team led by the Federal Investigation Agency that will conduct the probe into the matter.

Terror's Trail

It was around 10.30 p.m. when the inspector general of Indian Coast Guard, Western region, Rajendra Singh – in charge of the coastal security of 3,473 km of coastal belt along the western coast of India: a total area of 9,73,000 sq. km of Arabian Sea extending from Koteshwar in Gujarat to Mattam Point in Kerala up to the International Maritime Boundary Line (IMBL, an imaginary boundary separating Indian waters from Pakistani waters) – received a phone call from the Operations Room Centre of the Coast Guard in Mumbai. 'Sir, there appears to be a coordinated terror attack in Mumbai; the Taj hotel, the Oberoi hotel, the CST station and a place called Chabad House in Colaba have been attacked by armed terrorists.' Singh, who had just come back to his small room in

Mayur Vihar, Delhi, from a routine departmental meeting at the Coast Guard Headquarters in the capital, was packing his bags to fly back the next morning to Mumbai – the official base of the Western region.

Singh immediately turned on the television set. Hysterical anchors and reporters across different channels were giving sketchy, varying facts of the unfolding terror attack. 'More than twenty terrorists have stormed the city.' 'The Taj, the Oberoi and the CST have been attacked.' 'Few bomb explosions have occurred across Mumbai.' 'The terrorists are setting the Taj on fire.' 'Nine terrorists have been reportedly arrested by the police.' 'Terrorists had checked into the Taj and the Oberoi days in advance and had stored explosives in hotel rooms for the impending terror attack.' Singh, bewildered and shocked, remained glued to the TV as horrifying, fleeting images of burning hotel rooms and sounds of grenade explosions kept beaming on news channels.

Hundreds of miles away from the Mayur Vihar apartment in Delhi where Singh was staring at the TV, Bharat Dattatraya Tamore, fifty-eight, was sitting at a small, rickety desk in a badly lit, grimy police station at Cuffe Parade in Mumbai. Tamore had been staying at a fishermen colony – a cluster of flat-roofed, matchbox styled houses in the squalor of an urban slum along the seashore – at Cuffe Parade in South Mumbai since his birth. It was something that Tamore had seen that very evening at around 8.20 p.m. that necessitated his presence at the police station. Not far from the Taj President – another five-star property of the Taj Group in Mumbai – he had seen eight, maybe ten (it was dark and the occasion did not present a chance for a head count), strongly built, smartly dressed youth emerge out of the dark sea at the fishermen colony. The scene was odd enough for Tamore to register it; faces grimy and hair sticky from days without a bath, the youth made their way hurriedly with bulky rucksacks on their backs and additional bags in their hands.

'What else did you see?' asked Assistant Police Inspector Vilas Bhole, taking down notes on a white sheet of paper. 'They came in an inflated speedboat. Came right up to the shore, by the rocks and then got off the boat and walked towards the main road. They split up in groups of twos, each group went away separately, in different directions,' replied Tamore. Ironically, the men Tamore had seen were headed to wreak carnage at the Taj hotel, Tamore's workplace for the last thirty years, where he was employed as a steward. As

Tamore sat narrating his eyewitness account to API Bhole, a few feet from him, his neighbour Bharat Kashinath Tandel, fifty-two, resident of *kholi* number 18 in the fishermen colony, was sitting across Sub-Inspector Anil Kamble.

Tandel had his own story to tell which was similar to Tamore's except for one additional, important detail. Tandel had sensed that they were not from Mumbai, their rubber speedboat was not like those used by the fishermen in the area, the anxiety on their faces making them all the more suspect. A curious and suspicious Tandel asked the men who they were and where they were headed. To this, one of them replied: '*Hum pehle se hi tang hain. Hume pareshaan mat karo.* (We are already quite stressed. Don't pester us.)' Tandel and Tamore were alone at the time these men came to the shore. 'Normally, at that time of the evening, the place is buzzing with people. But this evening because of the day-night cricket match between India and England most of the men were inside their houses, watching the match on TV. If there were more people around we would definitely have had an altercation with them,' said Tandel.

Not just the cricket match, it seemed that everything went the way of those ten men who came in the speedboat. That evening because of the high tide, seawater had come right up to the rocks, just 60-70 metres off the main road. Had it been a low tide the water would have ended 150 to 200 metres away from the rocks, leaving in between a thick and slippery muddy stretch, one foot deep and difficult to manoeuvre. But the elements made everything a breeze and the strangers hauled their heavy bags off the boat and approached the road unhindered – luck was on their side. Tandel observed, 'The way they anchored their boat, the loop of the rope was different from the one tied by us fishermen.' Unfortunately, despite the peculiarities Tandel and Tamore had spotted, they did not inform the police. Both went back to their houses and like the others sat down to enjoy the cricket match. Only after news of the terrorist attack broke out on TV, did Tandel inform a police van patrolling the area. Police Inspector P.N. Jagtap, Sub-Inspector Anil Kamble and Sub-Inspector Rajendra Kamble, all attached to the Cuffe Parade police station, reached the spot.

With the help of the fishermen the cops retrieved the speedboat from the water, which had got unhinged and was drifting more than 200 feet away from the shore, and a bomb disposal squad soon arrived and rummaged the boat in search of explosives. Though no explosives or arms or ammunition were recovered from the boat, an assortment of seemingly harmless articles, which would soon form crucial material evidence, was recovered from the boat: eight yellow life jackets manufactured in China, an off-white drum of twenty-five litres capacity containing approximately twelve litres of diesel, some tools in a polythene bag, a yellow coloured tube of adhesive manufactured in Pakistan for fixing punctures, two eight-foot-long rowing sticks with a one-and-a-half-foot-wide *patta*. The boat had a Yamaha engine, and had been painted yellow, the colour recently applied – as investigation would later reveal – to make the boat look old. There were three valves on either side of the boat which the cops unscrewed to deflate it and then hauled it to the Cuffe Parade police station on a handcart.

The news of the recovery of an abandoned speedboat soon spread like fire. 'The terrorists had come by sea. An abandoned speedboat has been found drifting in the waters near Badhwar Park at Cuffe Parade': the bold words flitted across TV screens. In a flash, Singh's – still glued to the TV – status changed: from a horrified, concerned spectator he became a central character in the bloody terror attack. Exactly six days ago, on 20 November, at around 4 p.m., Singh's office, situated in a three-storey complex at Worli sea face in Mumbai, had received a fax: 'Intelligence indicates suspected LeT vessel sighted in position 24 DEG 16 MIN North and 67 DEG 2 MIN East attempting to infiltrate through sea route. Request: 1) Direct ship in area to exchange surveillance. Launch Dorniers at first light for sea-air coordinated search; 2) Deploy ACV IB to patrol off-creek area.' The fax was sent by principal director (operations), Coast Guard Headquarters, Delhi, who in turn had received this particular intelligence from the IB.

Singh had immediately called up Deputy Inspector General T.K.S. Chandra, the commander of Coast Guard District Headquarters of Gujarat, whose office is at Porbandar, and instructed him to launch a hunt for a suspicious Pakistani vessel which could make a bid to enter the Indian waters. DIG Chandra in turn alerted the three Coast Guard substations under his jurisdiction – Jakhau, Vadinar and Okha, all in Gujarat – and told them to launch their vessels into the waters along the IMBL and search for the suspected 'LeT vessel'. One interceptor boat each from Jakhau and Vadinar, two hovercrafts and one fast patrol vessel from Okha immediately sailed towards the

IMBL. At the time, two joint military exercises – Defence of Gujarat (DGX 8) and Tatraksha XXIV being carried out by the Indian Navy, Coast Guard, Border Security Force (BSF), the Indian Army and the respective ports between 18 and 22 November – were underway in which a total of six vessels of the Coast Guard were participating. After receiving the IB input Singh pulled out all the six vessels that were intended for the military exercise and moved them towards the IMBL. All in all, one offshore patrol vessel with an integrated helicopter (a vessel with a sustenance of twelve to fourteen days in the outer sea without any external help), one inshore patrol craft (sustenance of four to five days), two fast patrol crafts, one air cushion vehicle (hovercraft), two interceptor boats and two Dorniers were asked to patrol the Indian waters from Diu and head to Porbandar to Okha to Kandla to Jakhau across the IMBL. (The Western region of the Indian Coast Guard has a total of fourteen ships, eight Dornier aircrafts, six helicopters, two advance light helicopters, ten interceptor boats and two hovercrafts to patrol the 9,73,000 sq. km of Indian waters across the states of Gujarat, Maharashtra, Goa, Karnataka, Kerala and the union territories of Daman and Diu and Lakshwadeep.)

But after two days of intense patrolling the Coast Guard failed to find any suspicious vessel, leave alone a Pakistani ship. On 22 November, Singh wrote back to its Delhi-based headquarters asking the principal director (operations) for a more specific, actionable intelligence like the colour or size of the vessel, the name or the kind of vessel, and if possible, some coordinates. The Coast Guard headquarters in turn wrote to the IB asking for specifics on the vessel. But the IB had nothing more to add to its first communiqué. On 23 November, the Coast Guard again wrote to the IB asking for 'specific, actionable intelligence', and the latter communicated back saying that if there was any more intelligence on the matter, the same would be conveyed to them.

The first, and in this matter also the last, location of the suspected LeT vessel – as tracked and reported by the IB – was 22 nautical miles (50 km) outside Karachi in the outer anchorage area which was way inside the Pakistani waters. The Indian Coast Guard can only intercept or board a vessel once it crosses the IMBL. However, from 21 to 26 November, boarding parties of *Meera Behn* (fast patrol vessel), *Amrit Kaur* (fast patrol vessel), *Vijaya* (offshore patrol vessel), and one inshore patrol craft boarded and inspected 276 Indian fishing vessels plying in the Indian waters. But all the 276 fishing boats which were boarded and checked by Coast Guard patrolling parties were clean; the sailors on board were bona fide Indian fishermen. At any given time there are 60,000 registered Indian fishing boats in the Arabian Sea, of which roughly 10,000 fishing boats are in the waters around the IMBL. The 276 Indian fishing boats searched between 21 and 26 November were all sailing close to the IMBL. On the night of 26 November, when the terrorists finally disembarked off a speedboat at Cuffe Parade in Mumbai, six Coast Guard vessels and two Dorniers were patrolling the Indian waters along the IMBL.

Through the night Singh made several calls to his commanding officers wanting to know how the terrorists had sneaked in by the sea (by now it was quite clear that the speedboat recovered from the fishermen colony belonged to the terrorists) and managed to give the Coast Guard patrolling vessels the slip. The terrorists could not have travelled by the speedboat in the high seas and must have definitely been dropped a few miles off the Mumbai coast by some bigger vessel. So, did the suspected LeT vessel the IB had first tipped them about sailed all the way to Mumbai and then lowered the terrorists in a small speedboat? Or did the terrorists sail to Mumbai in some merchant vessel and then got on to the dinghy? The Indian intelligence and investigating agencies were groping in the dark, looking for answers. And these baffling questions kept haunting Singh through the night. DG Coast Guard, Delhi, wanted to know if it was possible for any Pakistani vessel to enter the Indian waters despite the high alert. Singh on his part was assured that he and his team had not left any stone unturned since the IB alert, and for any Pakistani vessel to enter the Indian waters was simply not possible.

The next morning he took an Indian Airlines flight and landed in Mumbai at 9.45 a.m. Singh drove straight to his Worli office; the roads were deserted and an otherwise one-and-a-half-hour journey from Santacruz airport to Worli was completed in twenty minutes. At around 12.30 p.m. the commanding station officer (operations) of Coast Guard at Worli received a call from the Western Command of the Navy asking him to intercept a merchant vessel called MV-Alpha which was headed towards Gujarat. The Indian Navy suspected that the terrorists had used this vessel to cross into Indian waters. Singh immediately alerted one of its vessels called *Samar*, which after three hours of hot pursuit intercepted the said merchant ship that had twelve Ukrainian crew members on board. After eight hours of rummaging, the Coast Guard cleared the ship of suspicion – it was headed to Alang port for shipwrecking.

Then at around 2.10 p.m., Singh received a phone call from the office of joint commissioner (crime) of Mumbai police, Rakesh Maria. Singh was informed that Kasab's – the lone terrorist who was captured alive – police interrogation had revealed that the terrorists had sailed to Mumbai in a brown-coloured Indian fishing boat with a wooden finish and it was abandoned 4-5 nautical miles off the Mumbai coast after which the terrorists got into a speedboat. Maria who was still in the middle of interrogating Kasab told Singh that the terrorist had confessed of having killed the sailor on board and his body was lying in the engine room. Maria asked for the Coast Guard's help in tracking down the vessel. Singh called up the commanding officer of Coast Guard Air Squadron 842 at the Navy base Kunjali at Colaba and told him to immediately fly two helicopters over the coast of Mumbai and see if there was any suspicious Indian fishing boat drifting in the waters. Simultaneously, a Dornier which was doing a sortie close by was also told to look for this suspicious Indian fishing trawler going up north. Within twenty minutes Singh was informed by his officers aboard the two helicopters that they could see an Indian fishing trawler drifting 5 nautical miles south off Prongs Lighthouse, in the outer anchorage of Mumbai harbour. From the helicopter, no one was visible on the boat.

At 2.40 p.m. Singh called up Maria's office and told him about the discovery of a suspicious boat. Maria now asked Singh to ask his men to board the boat and see if there was a satellite phone and a GPS also lying in the boat. Two Coast Guard personnel were dropped from the helicopter on to the boat who on entering the engine room found a semi-decomposed body with hands tied at the back and throat slit from ear to ear. They also saw a dark black Thuraya satellite phone and a GPS with 'Garmin' and 'GPS 12 MAP' written on either side of the screen. At this time a Coast Guard ship called *Sankalp*, an advanced offshore vessel, was entering the Mumbai harbour after three days of sailing. Singh told *Sankalp*, with eighty-five Coast Guard personnel on board, to sail towards the abandoned boat. In the meantime, the two Coast Guard helicopters kept hovering over the boat, ensuring it did not drift out of their sight. By 6 p.m. a team of six sailors, headed by Deputy Commandant Vijay, boarded the boat and recovered a satellite phone and a GPS that were left behind by the terrorists. The deputy commandant retrieved four wave points that indicated the sea route taken by the vessel. The first wave point was 32 nautical miles into Pakistani waters from the IMBL, the second wave point was west of Porbandar, the third wave point was south-west of Diu and the fourth wave point was 10 miles west of Bombay harbour – the point where the terrorists had abandoned the boat and lowered their speedboat.

The Coast Guard now had before them the exact route the terrorists had taken to sail to Mumbai. And it showed that they had got into the Indian fishing boat 32 nautical miles into Pakistani waters from IMBL. That is, the mother vessel carrying the terrorists never entered the Indian waters, giving the Coast Guard no chance to intercept them. Instead, the Indian fishing boat went deep inside Pakistani waters and was probably hijacked there. The Coast Guard found an assortment of items on the vessel: fifteen blankets; the same number of winter jackets and toothbrushes; two engine covers; a raft case on the trawler; a 'Sogo' spray paint; a few empty packets of fifty rounds of bullets for .34 bore gun with a 'Made in China' label; a nylon rope; an empty diesel plastic can of a petrol filling station with a head office address of HO No. 8, Industrial Area, Karachi; a white coloured packet of tissue papers branded 'Tissue The Senses' produced by Zik Brothers, Karachi; a 10 kg packet of wheat flour from a Karachi shop called Qamar Food Products, Plot No 3/3, Raita Plot, Shah Faisal Town; a packet of Pakistan-made pickle; a matchbox made in Pakistan; a floor cleaning brush; a two-litre Mountain Dew bottle; two detergent boxes branded PAK – All Purpose Detergent, manufactured in Pakistan; a white 50 kg gunny bag with 'Pakistan White Refined Sugar, Crop Year: 2007-2008, Expiry Date: December 2009, Net Weight 50.00 KG' embossed on it; a tube of 'Touch Me' shaving cream manufactured in Pakistan; 'Medicam' dental gel made in Pakistan; eight razors of Gillette brand; eight pencil cell batteries of Duracell; black quarter pants labelled South-O-Pole, Made in Pakistan; two packets of Nestlé milk with marking of Nestlé Pakistan Limited; a few black and white *namaz* scarves with the label 'Cashmilan Best Qlty, Phone 0614516729'; a few packets of fairness cream; three handcuffs with steel chains and a metal plate with picture of a gun with instructions in Urdu.

These items, which would become a crucial part of the material evidence of Pakistan's involvement in the carnage, made it clear that all the ten terrorists had sailed from Pakistan with supplies of

Pakistani origin. The papers onboard the boat showed that it was registered in the name of Kuber with the Gujarat fisheries department with the registration number PBR 2342. The maximum speed of Kuber, which had just one engine, was 8 nautical miles per hour. It requires special skills to ride a fishing trawler and with much difficulty the Coast Guard sailors, who are trained in driving hi-tech marine vessels, drove Kuber to Sassoon docks at Colaba – it took them three hours to cover a distance of 5 nautical miles. At 9.30 p.m. on 27 November, the Indian Coast Guard handed over Kuber to the Mumbai police.

The Confession

The crime branch of the Mumbai police – a specialized department in neutralizing and investigating organized crime as well as intricate cases that are beyond the competence of local police stations – have a staff of 150 experienced detectives. The entire bureau is headed by a joint commissioner of police. Since June 2007 the joint commissioner of the crime branch was Rakesh Maria. A tall and broad-shouldered man, every strand of greying hair in place, Maria was known to be a workaholic. But on 26 November he left for the day at 8.50 p.m., two hours before his usual time. Maria wanted to spend some time with his twenty-one-year-old son who was leaving that night for Ahmednagar to participate in an inter-university championship. At 9.40 p.m. Maria's son left home. Ten minutes later, as he was getting ready to retire to bed, he received a call from the police control room: armed gunmen had opened indiscriminate fire at the CST station killing dozens of commuters. By the time he got into his car, reports of firing at Leopold Café, at the Taj Mahal hotel and at the Trident-Oberoi hotels had also poured in. As he asked his driver to head towards Mumbai police headquarters, the commissioner of police, Hasan Gafoor called and instructed Maria to take charge of the police control room. At 10.22 p.m. Maria reached the control room. By the time he walked in there, the command centre of Mumbai police had turned into a war zone.

Dozens of telephone lines and wireless communication channels were buzzing like bees. Beads of sweat were falling off the foreheads of police personnel fielding calls from the public, coordinating among the 45,000 city police personnel and communicating with eighty-six police stations and senior officers spread across Mumbai. A few gunmen had simultaneously attacked different sites throughout the city. Dozens had already died while hundreds of injured needed immediate medical aid. It seemed the city was at war. A giant screen was showing the important city landmarks and locations of over 3,000 police vans patrolling in different areas. Maria started mobilizing the police personnel dispatching police vans to the troubled spots. Around 10.35 p.m., report came that a bomb had gone off in a speeding taxi on the Western Express Highway, close to the Santacruz airport. So powerful was the explosion that the head of the taxi driver got severed from the torso and after shooting thirty feet up in the air, got stuck in the branches of a tree. Five minutes later at 10.40 p.m. another call came that a second bomb had exploded, again in a taxi, this time in Wadi Bunder, approximately 25 km from the location of the first blast. Memories of the 1993 serial blasts were refreshed in Maria's mind. How many more bombs were waiting to go off? Two suspicious looking bags outside the Taj and one bag outside the Trident hotel had already been sighted.

Maria instructed all police stations to comb their areas. Bomb disposal squads were dispatched to different sites. Then reports of police casualties started trickling in. At around 11.25 p.m. Maria got the call that Additional Commissioner Sadanand Date, who had followed the terrorists into Cama Hospital, was injured, while a constable accompanying him had been killed. Between 10.29 p.m. and 12.11 a.m. Maria diverted over 200 police personnel towards Cama Hospital. During that time Karkare, Kamte, Salaskar and others had headed towards the hospital. Not far from there, at the CST station, were three SRPF striking forces, one RCP (Riot Control Police) striking force of around twenty personnel, eight mobile vans, one QRT and one SOS team. In addition, four DCPs and four senior police inspectors were also in the area. But unfortunately, the reinforcements never moved inside the lane where Karkare and the others were waiting.

At 12.25 a.m., Maria received a wireless message from Arun Jadhav, Salaskar's bodyguard. He said terrorists had hijacked the police vehicle in which he and Karkare and the others were travelling, that they had 'injured' everybody and finally abandoned the vehicle outside Vidhan Bhavan with him inside it. Jadhav told Maria that the terrorists had then hijacked a black Honda City. Yet somehow, in that three-minute communication, Jadhav stricken with panic failed to tell Maria that the terrorists had killed Karkare and the others. It was only after Additional Commissioner Parambir Singh reached Vidhan Bhavan that Maria was informed about the outcome of the episode. A little later a senior police inspector of DB Marg police station informed the control room that they had killed one and caught another terrorist alive.

Throughout the night Maria coordinated with the MARCOS, then the NSG, placing dozens of calls to the Maharashtra chief secretary, the Western Navy Command, the Union home ministry, and the Army headquarters in Delhi, besides numerous other offices and bureaucrats.'At around 1.30 a.m. Maria was told to interrogate Ajmal Kasab who was at the Nair Hospital. After Ghadge's interrogation was over, Maria had already been updated by the D.B. Marg police about the revelations made by Kasab. Maria sent one of his trusted detection officers Prashant Marde to Nair Hospital with the brief to just clarify four points: 1) How had they come; 2) How many of them had entered the city; 3) What weapons did they have with them; and 4) What task had each terrorist been assigned?

At around 4.30 a.m., as Maria was busy arranging transport to pick up the NSG commandos from the airport, Marde called and briefed him on the four crucial points. Based on the details provided by D.B. Marg police and Marde, Maria briefed the NSG in his office at around 5.30-6 a.m.

At around 9.30 a.m. a police motorcade carrying Kasab turned into the police headquarters. A posse of two dozen policemen armed with assault rifles escorted Kasab into the crime branch interrogation room. Maria was waiting for him. Though he had been told Kasab was not more than twenty-one years old, he expected a tougher guy, at least in looks. Maria had imagined a withered and rugged appearance. Not a baby-faced, smooth-skinned, blushing jehadi. Kasab, the *fidayeen*, looked like a kid. With the beck of his finger Maria signalled Kasab to sit on the ground. Leaning forward, his six-feet-one-inch frame towering over Kasab, Maria said, 'There is no point in hiding things. We know how to wrench the truth out of you. And you don't think I or anybody here gives a damn about your injuries. So you better start singing now.'

'Sahab, I have already told you that I am a Pakistani and I joined the LeT one and a half years back. As far as other things are concerned I have explained everything to your guys,' said Kasab, sighing and groaning, exhibiting fatigue and pain.

'I don't care for your pain. You look in my eyes and tell me how many of you have landed in Mumbai,' growled Maria.

'We were just ten of us. We came by sea and then split into five teams. Ismail and I were part of one team. The other four teams went to the Taj, the Oberoi and the Chabad House. Abu Rehman Bada, Abu Ali, Abu Soheb and Abu Umer had been assigned the job of the Taj. Abu Rehman Chhota and Abu Fahad were given the task of storming the Oberoi. And Abu Aakasha and Abu Umar had gone to the Chabad House,' Kasab confirmed. He also gave the physical characteristics of each terrorist and a description of their clothes.

'Where are your local logistics providers? Did you get in touch with anyone after reaching Mumbai?' Maria just could not believe that the ten had pulled off an attack of this magnitude without local support.

'No. We did not know anyone in Mumbai. We had no names or numbers. We were just told about our targets. Once we landed, we took taxis and went straight to our targets.'

'What time did you land?'

'Can't tell exactly. But it was somewhere around 8.15-8.30 p.m.'

'Then why did the attack at the CST begin at 9.40 p.m., an hour after you landed?'

'After landing we had a chat among ourselves. We decided that since we all had to reach different locations and we might get traffic on our way, we would begin the attack only after 9.40 p.m. We were sure that all of us would reach our respective targets within an hour and so that was the time decided to begin the attack. Ismail and I had to wait for ten to fifteen minutes before we got a taxi. Ismail and I were the first ones to catch ones, the others were still waiting for the cabs when we left. We got off at the station after which I went to a toilet there while Ismail waited outside. I wanted to pee real bad. Then I came out and waited another few minutes. After my watch showed 9.40 p.m. we removed our guns from the bags and opened fire.'

'What were the arms and ammunition you all were carrying?'

'We had one AK-47, one pistol, two magazines for the pistol, six to eight magazines of AK-47 and ten to twelve hand grenades on each of us. Besides, we had a lot of loose cartridges of AK which we did not count,' said Kasab. He had earlier told Ghadge that each had eight hand grenades and had made no mention of the loose cartridges. To Maria, however, he gave a higher figure for the ammunition.

Twice Maria posed the question differently but Kasab gave the same figure: one AK-47, one pistol, ten to twelve hand grenades, and six to eight magazines.

'Don't you think you are forgetting something here?' Maria narrowed his eyes, moving his face closer to Kasab's.

For a few moments Kasab just stared listlessly into Maria's eyes, his face so close to Maria's that he could not look elsewhere. And then he said, 'Sorry I forgot to mention it. We brought bombs as well. Each of us had one bomb, which we carried in a separate bag. We wanted to plant these bombs on the periphery of our targets so that when the police arrive they would get killed by the explosion.'

Maria finally had a figure on the total number of bombs that had entered the city the previous night. His mind started calculating. Seven bombs had already exploded – one each in two taxis, one on the sixth floor at the Taj, one outside the Trident hotel, one inside the Oberoi, one at a petrol pump near Chabad House and one on the staircase of Chabad House. Two had been defused – one on the promenade facing the Gateway and one in a bylane on the back side of the Taj. But there was still one bomb left. Where was the tenth bomb? Maria's head started reeling.

'Where is the bomb that you were carrying?'

'I had put it in the cab we took for VT station, under the seat of the driver. Ismail sat next to the driver while I sat at the back. On our way I connected the wires, set the timer and pushed it under the seat.'

The riddle of two bomb explosions – one at Vile Parle and the other at Wadi Bunder – on 26 November was slowly unravelling. Laxminarayan Goyal from Hyderabad who had come to Mumbai on business took the same taxi from CST. At around 10.35 p.m., when his taxi reached Vile Parle, the bomb placed by Kasab went off, killing both Goyal and the taxi driver. When the police reached the spot they found just a few rods of the engine section left of the taxi. The taxi driver had just jumped a traffic signal. Had he, like other vehicles, waited for the signal to turn green, the death toll would have been much higher. Around the same time another bomb placed in another taxi had blasted at Nal Bazar in Wadi Bunder, killing a woman passenger and the taxi driver.

'If you wanted to kill policemen why did you place the bomb in the taxi?'

'We thought that taxis would only move around in South Mumbai and their explosions would kill the approaching policemen.'

'Where did Ismail leave his bomb?' Maria asked, as that was the only one unaccounted for.

'He left it at VT station. I don't know where exactly he left the bag but it was somewhere at the station.'

But the bomb had not exploded. It was finally recovered six days later, on the evening of 3 December, when railway personnel were sorting out the 150 odd bags left behind by the dead, the injured and other passengers who had been caught in Ismail's and Kasab's line of fire. All the bags had been dumped by the railway police in a parcel room on the first floor of the CST. After Kasab's revelation the Mumbai police tried to locate the black and white bag as described by him but they could not find it. Luckily, the timer of the bomb had malfunctioned and it had not caused further damage.

'How did you reach Mumbai? I want to know each and everything that happened on the high seas. Take me through your entire sea journey. Don't cut the long story short.'

'All ten of us had been kept in isolation for the last three months in a LeT safe house in Azizabad, on the outskirts of Karachi. On 22 November, we woke up at the break of the dawn and were taken to a creek area in a jeep with tinted glasses. At around 8 a.m. we all got on to a boat that was waiting for us at the shore. After about forty minutes of sailing we spotted a larger boat called *Al-Husseini* which I was told belonged to Lakhvi chacha. There were seven LeT *mujahids* who were already on board. We were told that the arms and ammunition were already there on *Al-Husseini*. All of us were then escorted into a cabin in the basement where we spent the next thirty hours. We were told to shave and be ready. On the 23rd at around 3 p.m., we felt a thud as if something had come and struck against our boat. An Indian fishing trawler had docked next to our boat. One *mujahid* came running to the basement and told us to hurry up. It was time to leave.

'When we went up we saw four Indian fishermen being hauled from their trawler on to our boat. We hopped on to the Indian trawler. The sailor of the trawler was still on board. Our bags containing arms and ammunition and ration for the journey were also transferred into the Indian boat. A rubber speedboat and a foot pump were also hauled on the Indian boat. We all hugged the *Al-Husseini* crew members and started our journey towards Mumbai. Ismail was our group leader and he assigned us on board duties. Nine of us including Ismail performed watch duties in two-hour shifts. Only Imran Babar was exempted from watch duties as he had to cook. We kept a log book to make entries of our work shifts.

'Finally on 26 November at around 4 p.m. Ismail told us we were now very close to Mumbai. We waited till it turned dark. At around 7 p.m. we inflated the rubber boat with the foot pump and transferred our bags on to the boat. After sailing for over an hour we reached the fishermen colony at Badhwar Park at around 8.15-8.30 p.m.'

'How did the LeT crew members manage to intercept the Indian fishing trawler, Kasab?' Maria probed.

'Sahab, I don't know exactly. But from the snatches of conversation I overheard while crossing over to the Indian boat it appeared that the Al-Husseini crew members waved a broken engine belt towards the Indian boat and asked for help. As the Indian trawler docked next to us, they kidnapped four Indian crew members and transferred them to Al-Husseini.'

'Who sailed the Indian trawler to Mumbai?'

'Amar Sinh Solanki, the Indian sailor, Ismail and Abu Umer. The three of them sailed and navigated the boat to Mumbai.'

'Where is Amar Sinh Solanki?'

'Ismail and Shoaib killed Solanki just before we boarded the rubber boat. Once we spotted Mumbai from the high seas we waited in the waters for some time. As it grew darker Ismail called up somebody higher up in the LeT and told him that we were only 4 nautical miles off from Mumbai. Speaking in coded language Ismail asked what we should do with the Indian sailor. The LeT boss on the other end said, *"Humne to chaar bakre kha liye hain, tum bhi apna bakra kha lo."* It was the coded message to kill the sailor, Amar Sinh Solanki. Ismail and Shoaib killed him by slitting his throat and dumped his body in the engine room.'

Maria immediately relayed the important information to the Indian Coast Guard and requested them to look for the Indian fishing trawler.

'Tell me how Ismail knew he was just 4 nautical miles off Mumbai. What navigation tools was he using?' Maria resumed the interrogation.

'We used a GPS to navigate. We were all trained to operate the GPS. But throughout the journey it was Ismail who operated it and he also spoke to the LeT bosses on his satellite phone.'

'Where are the GPS and the sat phone you used on the seas?' Maria enquired.

'I was the safe keeper of the sat phone and the GPS. But as we were lowering the dinghy into the waters another fishing boat came very close to us. We got scared and thought it might be the Indian Navy. Quickly, we loaded our bags on the boat and set off towards Mumbai. In the hurry I forgot Ismail's sat phone and GPS behind on the Indian trawler. Halfway into the journey Ismail suddenly remembered the sat phone and the GPS. We deliberated if we should go back to fetch it but then decided against it and kept sailing towards Mumbai.'

Halting the interrogation, Maria again left room to update the Coast Guard about the new information.

'Kasab. Tell me everything you know about the LeT,' said Maria on entering the room.

'Sahab, I don't know much. I joined it only a year and a half back. My father pushed me into this.'

'Look Kasab,' Maria interrupted Kasab before he could go into a spell of self-pity. 'We have had enough of your bleeding heart stories. You have been telling my officers that your father pushed you into this. That you were very poor. That you did not have enough to eat. That you did this just for money. You better stop bluffing now. Because we have arrested a few of your colleagues and they have told us everything, about you, the LeT, your training,' said Maria rubbing his forearms and then puffed his chest with a deep breath.

Two of Maria's detection officers pulled up stools lying in a corner and placing them close to Kasab, encircled him.

'I know everything. But I want to hear it from your mouth,' said Maria, his eyes glinting, a know-all smile playing on his lips.

'I don't like lies, Kasab.' Maria's face suddenly stiffened, the smile disappeared, and his broad jaw tightened up.

For a few seconds Kasab kept staring at Maria. Ghadge had never questioned Kasab's tearjerker narrative. But Maria would have none of it. And now he had some of his colleagues in custody too. Who could it be? Kasab wondered.

After a brief silence, Kasab began: 'I studied up to fourth standard and then in the year 2000 I dropped out of school and went to Lahore. I stayed there with my brother Afzal who was staying at House No. 12, Galli No. 54, Mohalla Tohidabad, near Yadgar Minar. I did the job of a construction worker till 2005. In between I visited my village many times. Finally in 2005, I quit my job and went back to my village, thinking I would stay there. But my father scolded me and I left home and went to Ali Hajveri Darbar at Lahore. It was a kind of shelter home for young homeless boys and the management there used to assist us in finding employment. I found employment with a contractor called Shafiq who was in the catering business. For the next two years I worked with him at his shop called "Welcome Tent Service". But the money I earned was never enough. Around this time Shafiq, a friend of mine, and I carried out a few small robberies. We then decided to plan a robbery big enough to fetch us lakhs of rupees in one go,' Kasab revealed.

The transformation in Kasab's persona was radical. A hours back he had portrayed himself as a timid, obedient son waylaid by his greedy, selfish father. Now, with the threat of being exposed by fellow terrorists staring him in the face, Kasab unveiled his true side willingly. Yes. He was a labourer and his father was a poor vendor. But it was he who had taken to crime, prompted by his own needs, initiated into the world of violence not by his father but by a criminal friend. An indifferent father was just a ruse to earn sympathy from the police.

'We wanted to acquire weapons. But it was not easy,' Kasab continued. 'After much deliberation we thought we would join the LeT. We thought we would get both weapons and training to operate them. We filled up a few forms and joined the organization. At Muridke we went through an induction period of twenty-one days. The trainers were very strict and everything from *namaz* to lunch to dinner happened with clockwork precision. But in the first three weeks we were not trained to operate firearms. I was not enjoying it much but Shafiq said that in the next phase we would be imparted the arms training. After the completion of the first phase, we were taken to a small village in Mansera where we were given initial training of handling AKs, Uzi guns and pistols. We were also given lectures on Islam and Hadith. We were told that our religion was in danger and Muslims were being killed everywhere. That was when I decided I would not go back to robbery but would continue with the LeT.

'I went home in between and returned to participate in a training camp at a hilly area called Chelabandi in PoK. Here we were trained to handle explosives, rocket launchers and mortars. At the end of the three months' training period thirty-two of us were selected by

Zaki chacha for waging jehad. Sixteen were sent for some operation, the details of which I don't know. Out of the remaining sixteen, three escaped from the camp. We, the remaining thirteen, were then sent to a training camp at Muridke. Abu Kahfa was our leader. Here we were trained to operate GPS instruments and to navigate boats in the sea. We were conditioned to sail on the high seas for long. We were taught swimming as well. After the training was over I went home to see my mother. After a week I returned to the LeT camp at Muzaffarabad. The thirteen of us were again trained to sail on the seas and navigate boats.

'Zaki chacha then sent six from amongst us for some operation in Kashmir. Three other men then joined us. They had already been *mujahids* for some time and had done operations elsewhere. One among them was Ismail. He was made the leader of our group. In the second week of September we were shifted to a LeT safe house at Azizabad in Karachi. Here we were told to carry out the Mumbai operation. I was only informed about the VT station attack which was entrusted to me. The operation was initially planned for 27 September but then got delayed, the reasons for which I do not know. We then whiled away our time. We were given the best food and the best clothes. Zaki chacha said we could have anything in the world we wanted before setting out for Mumbai. Initially, we knew each other only by our code names. But soon we told each other our real names, though we were not supposed to. But we bonded well and shared many personal details.'

'So tell me all the real names and the addresses of your accomplices?'

'Ismail's full name is Ismail Khan. He is from Dera Ismail Khan in North West Frontier Province. Abu Ali's real name is Javed. He is around twenty-two years old and he and I come from the same district – Okara. Abu Fahad's real name is Fahadullah and he too hails from my district. Abu Aakasha is Babar Imran and he is from Multan. I don't know the name of his village. Abu Soheb is Shoaib and he is the youngest among us. He is from village Shakkargarh Naroval in Sialkot. Abu Umar's true name is Nasir and he comes from Faisalabad. Abu Umer too is from Faisalabad. His real name is Nazeer. He is the oldest among us. Abu Rehman Bada is actually Hafiz Arshad and he is from Multan. Abu Rehman Chhota is also from Multan and his true name is Abdul Rehman.' Kasab finally gave away the real names of his group members.

Later, Maria shared these names with the RAW that, through its undercover agents in Pakistan, collected more information on them.

'Who else besides Zaki has trained you?'

'Abu Hamza, Abu Al Qama, Abu Kahfa and Yousuf alias Muzammil were the other trainers.'

'When you were sailing towards Mumbai who all did you speak to on the sat phone from the deck?'

'Ismail did most of the talking. He was speaking to many in the LeT including Muzammil.'

'Who did he make the last conversation with about the five *bakras*?'

'It was Muzammil.'

'Who provided you the maps of your targets?'

'I don't know. I was just shown a CD of the VT station. I assume others too were shown similar CDs of their respective targets. But we were never told about the LeT operatives active in Mumbai or at other places in India.'

In a few weeks, the crime branch investigation revealed that two LeT terrorists – Faheem Ansari and Mohammad Sabahuddin – who were arrested by the UP police earlier that year, on charges of abetting and aiding in another terror case, had provided the maps and the video footage of the CST, the Oberoi, the Taj and Nariman House to their LeT bosses in Pakistan. They were allegedly involved in the killing of seven paramilitary troops in an audacious attack at a CRPF camp in Rampur on 1 January 2008.

Ansari, originally from Uttar Pradesh but born and brought up in Mumbai, had joined the LeT in 2003 while he was in Dubai. In 2007, he came to Mumbai and stayed there for about three months. Though his parents and brothers were staying in Goregaon he made no contact with them during his entire stay. Ansari later told Maria that he first stayed in a guest house at Grant Road but after a few weeks he had rented a small accommodation. He also told Maria that he wanted to take a place on rent in Colaba but then had to settle at Grant Road as Colaba was very expensive.

Ansari did a reconnaissance of several landmarks in Mumbai including the Bombay Stock Exchange, the Mumbai police headquarters at Crawford Market, the Maharashtra police headquarters in Colaba, the Mahalaxmi temple and the Sidhivinayak temple. He went to the Taj and the Oberoi hotels as a tourist and shot video footage of the interiors. He also captured the CST and the Chabad House on tape. Besides, he hand-drew the maps of all the 26/11 targets. In December 2007, he travelled to Kathmandu, where he met and handed over the material to Bihar-born Sabahuddin. Sabahuddin had also conspired in attacking the Indian Institute of Science in December 2005. Ansari then travelled on a Pakistani passport to Karachi and gave the maps to Muzammil as well. Later, when Ansari and Sabahuddin were arrested by the UP ATS in February 2008, several hand-drawn maps of different roads and buildings and installations in Mumbai were recovered from them. But the video footage and maps of the 26/11 targets had already been handed over to the LeT top brass in Pakistan.

'Did you ever meet Hafiz Sayeed, the chief of LeT?'

'Yes. He came and gave sermons during one of our early training sessions. He told us that Muslims worldwide need to rise in jehad against the infidels.'

'What else did Sayeed say in his sermon?' asked Maria.

'He said that we had to fight the war for Allah. He said if we die waging jehad, our faces would glow like the moon. Our bodies would emanate scent. And we would go to paradise.'

'Did you ever have a one-on-one meeting with Sayeed?'

'No. Never. He was a very big man and I was just one of the recruits.'

Maria, of course, knew by now that Kasab was small fry, just a foot soldier, and this was as far as he could take him in the investigation. As Maria got up to leave the room Kasab said, 'Sahab. Will you tell me who have you arrested besides me?'

'You will come to know,' said Maria and left.

Keeping in mind Rakesh Maria's impeccable record in investigating terror-related cases, the Maharashtra government made him the chief investigator of the 26/11 terror attack on Mumbai. The 1993 serial bomb blasts and the 2003 Gateway of India and Zaveri Bazar blasts were the other terror cases that had been cracked by Maria. Over the next two months, in coordination with the RAW and IB, Maria analyzed the satellite phone, the GPS instruments, the mobile phones, the AK-47 rifles, pistols, hand grenades, and the speedboat, among other things recovered from the scenes of crime.

The speedboat used by the terrorists to cover the last leg of their journey to Mumbai was brand new but was painted yellow to make it look old. The terrorists had also erased the engine number but with the help of forensic experts the police retrieved the original number – 67 CL-1020015 – which was manufactured by Yamaha Motor Corporation, Japan, and imported into Pakistan by a company named Business and Engineering Trends, situated at 24, Habibullah Road, Off Davis Road, Lahore. The 9mm pistols recovered from the terrorists bore the trademark and name of Diamond Nedi Frontier Arms Company, Peshawar. The unexploded hand grenades recovered from different places were found to be manufactured by an Austrian company named Arges which had given a franchisee to a Pakistani ordinance factory near Rawalpindi. Similar hand grenades had been recovered from terrorists involved in the 1993 serial blasts in Mumbai and the attack on Indian Parliament on 13 December 2001.

The email sent to Indian media houses in the name of an organization called Deccan Mujahideen claiming responsibility for the attack was tracked to a proxy server in Russia. Investigation revealed that the account used to send the email belonged to Zarrar Shah, the communications chief of the LeT who was also in touch with the terrorists on the phone while they were holed up in the two hotels and in Chabad House. It was also revealed that Shah had organized a payment of US $ 238.78 to a New Jersey based net telephony company named Callphonex to buy a VoIP connection. While buying the net telephony connection Shah used the fake name 'Kharak Singh' purportedly based in India. But the payment was sent by one Javed Iqbal who had a Pakistani passport numbered KC 092481. The connection thus purchased was used to make dozens of telephone calls to the terrorists while they were shedding innocent blood and unleashing the carnage in Mumbai. The satellite phone used by the terrorists from the high seas was of Thuraya make. It was used to make calls to the LeT higher-ups while the ten terrorists were sailing towards Mumbai.

Over the weeks Maria interrogated Kasab many times. After the first few sessions Maria started speaking to Kasab in Punjabi. (Since Maria's forefathers were from Punjab, he speaks the language very well.) One afternoon, about a month after the incident, Maria summoned Kasab in his office.

'Do you want to meet your other colleagues now?' he asked.

'Yes I would like to see them,' Kasab replied.

Maria called a crime branch officer inside his office and told him, 'Please take him to the place where his others friends have been kept. After their meeting bring him back to my office.'

Kasab was driven in a police vehicle to JJ Hospital. As Kasab entered the building he realized it was a hospital. 'Are they all badly injured?' he asked an accompanying police officer. The officer looked at him and said, 'You can see for yourself.'

Kasab was taken to the mortuary and the bodies of all the nine terrorists were slid out. Bodies of Javed and Shoaib were half charred. Nazeer's body was like a frozen mound of charcoal. Ismail's head had been severely damaged due to his bullet injury. Hafiz Arshad's face was almost completely burnt. Fahadullah had been shot through his eye. Nasir and Babar Imran's bodies were riddled with bullets. The faces of the terrorists were twisted, teeth jutting out, and the skin of the face was deathly pale or scalded and burnt. There was a sickening smell in the room. Kasab could not stay there for long. He told the officers he wanted to leave. He was driven back to Maria's office.

As Kasab entered the room Maria asked him, 'So, did you see the glow on their faces and smell the fragrance of roses emanating from their bodies as Hafiz Sayeed had told you?'

Kasab kept staring at the floor. Tears rolled down his face. Maria told a few constables to escort Kasab back into the crime branch lock-up.

'The Lashkar was obviously not using money to buy flowers for the Indian Army.'

Inside the Headquarters of the Lashkar-e-Toiba

Harinder Baweja

'You are in an educational complex but you are from India, so it will take you time to change your mind,' is what Abdullah Muntazir (my guide and the spokesperson for the foreign media), threw at me within minutes of us reaching Muridke, believed worldwide to be the headquarters of the Lashkar-e-Toiba (LeT). It was perhaps, for the first time, that permission had been granted to any Indian journalist to visit the sprawling campus that lies 40 km out of Lahore. The barricade that leads to the complex is heavily guarded and no one can enter without prior permission.

The guided tour took me through a neatly laid out sixty-bed hospital, schools for boys and girls, a madrasa, a mosque, an exorbitantly large swimming pool and a guest house. Nestled between tall trees and a meshed wire boundary, the 75-acre complex has manicured lawns, turnip farms and a fish-breeding centre. The students who enroll in the school pay a fee while those who study in the madrasa and pass out as masters in Islamic studies can come for free. Learning English and Arabic from class one onwards is compulsory as is a course in computers.

'Welcome to the headquarters of the "Lashkar-e-Toiba". You think a terrorist organization will be based just a few metres away from the main Grand Trunk Road?' is the next loaded statement. The administrators of the complex, drawn from the LeT's political wing,

Jamaat-ud-Dawa, are clearly at pains to disassociate themselves from the group alleged to be behind the terror attack in Mumbai on 26/11. Other foreign journalists were guided through the complex a few days before my visit. During their orchestrated tour, they saw students working in chemistry and physics laboratories, peering into microscopes and connecting electric circuits.

None of us went there thinking we would see firing ranges or target shooting in progress, but the tour itself is surreal, because even as you walk through the neatly trimmed lawns and veer left or right to see the hostel or the mosque or the hospital, the conversation itself is dotted entirely with words like terrorism, Lashkar and in my case, Kashmir. Even though the gates have been opened – after clearance from Pakistan's security agencies (read ISI, the Inter Services Intelligence) – to dispel the impression of Muridke being the training camp that 'India has made it out to be', the conversation is not about the school syllabus but only about how India is an enemy.

A day after I visited Muridke, I met a family whose sister-in-law lives right next to the complex. 'But of course it's a training ground. You can hear slogans for jehad blaring out of loudspeakers in full volume and you can sometimes also hear the sound of gunfire,' members of this family confided. But during the two hours that I spent within the complex, there was enough conversation about jehad even if there were no signs of it being a sanctuary, not just for the Lashkar-e-Toiba, but for Ramzi Yousef, an al-Qaeda operative, and one of the conspirators of the 1993 World Trade Center bombing.

Mohammad Ajmal Kasab, the lone terrorist who was captured alive in Mumbai, is supposed to have studied here according to his interrogators, and it's time to ask some straight questions.

'So did Kasab study here, in Muridke?'

'Even if he did, we are not responsible for what any one of our students does after passing out.'

'Do you support the Lashkar-e-Toiba?'

'We used to.'

'You used to?'

'Yes, we were like-minded but the group was banned after Indian propaganda following the attack on its Parliament, which was done by the Jaish-e-Mohammad and not the Lashkar. We used to provide logistical help to the Lashkar, collect funds for them and look after their publicity.'

'Did you also provide them with arms?'

'They must have bought weapons with the money we gave them. They were obviously not using the money to buy flowers for the Indian Army.'

'The Lashkar has claimed responsibility for the attack on the Red Fort in Delhi and the airport in Srinagar.'

'We do not consider Kashmir to be a part of India. It is a part of Pakistan. Those who attack the security forces are not terrorists, they are freedom fighters.'

'President Musharraf moved away from the position that Kashmir either secede or be given independence. He proposed joint control.'

'Musharraf did not have any legitimacy. He had no business making such proposals.'

'Do you consider India an enemy?'

'Without doubt. India is responsible for the attack on Islamabad's Marriot hotel, for the bomb blasts in Peshawar. Sarabjit Singh has been convicted of being a RAW agent.'

'Your *amir*, Hafiz Sayeed, has given calls for jehad.'

'He supports the freedom movement in Kashmir. We think it is right. It is ridiculous to call him a terrorist. Even when India is pricked by a thorn, the whole world stands up. Why did Condoleeza Rice not put pressure on India for handing over Narendra Modi after the Gujarat carnage?'

'Kashmir is no longer entirely indigenous. Foreign fighters like Maulana Masood Azhar were arrested in Anantnag.'

'He was a journalist and still is an inspirational writer. Anyone from here can go to Kashmir. We don't see it as part of India.'

'Did you sanitize this place before bringing me in?'

'This is an educational complex and the Jamaat-ud-Dawa is a charitable organization. There are very few people here because of the Eid break.'

'Does the ISI support you?'

He just laughs.

Muridke. The infamous address crops up time and again. Several terrorists arrested in Kashmir have testified to having been trained in this 'educational institution'. So has Kasab who has told his interrogators:

There were thirty-two trainees in the camp ... Zaki-ur-Rehman chacha sent the remaining thirteen with a person called Kahfa to the Muridke camp again. At Muridke, we were taught swimming (the same large swimming pool shown to me!) and made familiar with the life of fishermen at sea ... We were shown clippings highlighting atrocities on Muslims in India. I then went to the LeT camp at Muzaffarabad. The thirteen of us were present for training. Then, on Zaki-ur-Rehman's instructions, Kahfa took us to the Muridke camp. The training continued for a month. We were given lectures on India and its security agencies, including RAW. We were also trained to evade security personnel ...

Much as my guide Abdullah Muntazir tried to indoctrinate me into believing that Muridke was only a centre of learning, it is clear from Kasab's interrogation that the worldview of it being the headquarters of the Lashkar-e-Toiba is not misplaced. That the Lashkar has a free run in Pakistan and is closely managed by the ISI too is not a matter of mere speculation. Post 26/11, India has put together enough evidence on the Lashkar hand in Mumbai and the Ministry of External Affairs' dossier has been endorsed by the international community. British Foreign Secretary David Miliband's statement – 'it is clear the responsibility for Mumbai lies with the LeT. Pakistan has to tackle the roots of this organization' – is only the latest testimony of the Lashkar's involvement. So what motivates the Lashkar and what is the agenda of Hafiz Sayeed, its *amir*?

A professor by training, Hafiz Sayeed was hopping from one Pakistani news channel to another, while I was there, till he was finally put under house arrest after international pressure built up. Usually clad in a salwar-kameez, a dress worn by most men in Pakistan, the *amir* of the banned terrorist organization could, at first glance, pass off as an ordinary looking, even humble man. Like so many others, he sports a long beard (only his is coloured with henna), invariably wears a Turkish cap, and actually looks a pious man in his late sixties.

He is pious in more ways than one, for he believes in destroying the forces of evil and is a staunch believer in spreading the message of Islam. Nothing wrong with that, expect for the way in which the professor has interpreted Islam for himself and his many followers.

Till 2002, when the Lashkar was officially banned by America, the website of the parent organization, the Markaz-Dawa-Wal-Irshad (the centre for religious learning and propagation) proudly displayed the cold statistics of death. Then, Hafiz Sayeed would often say, 'Jehad is not about Kashmir only. About fifteen years ago, people might have found it ridiculous if someone told them about the disintegration of the USSR. Today, I announce the break-up of India, *Inshallah*. We will not rest until the whole (of) India is dissolved into Pakistan.' Those were the days the Lashkar also took responsibility for its bloodletting; days it took pride in hitting Indian targets and so proudly claimed the attack on the Red Fort as its own handiwork.

In fact, the attack on the Red Fort in December 2000 was the first indication that the Lashkar's ideology of spreading Islam extended beyond challenging India's sovereignty in Jammu and Kashmir. The group's agenda – outlined in a pamphlet titled 'Why we are waging jehad' – includes the restoration of Islamic rule all over India and of uniting all Muslim majority regions that surround Pakistan. The 'pious' professor of Islamic Studies who taught at a Lahore university considers India, Israel and the US to be his prime enemies and has often given calls for jehad and threatened to launch suicide attacks, just as the Lashkar-e-Toiba, or the 'Army of the Pure', did in Mumbai.

Quite unlike other Kashmiri separatist militant groups operating out of Pakistan, the majority of the members of Lashkar are non-Kashmiris – borne out by the ten who landed in Mumbai. Kasab and his nine accomplices are all from Punjab. Indeed, other Kashmiri outfits distrusted the Lashkar until it raced ahead with the sheer impact of its brutal terror acts by introducing daring suicide attacks on Indian troops. Trained, indoctrinated and armed by serving ISI officers, the infamous outfit was not deterred by the ban of the Lashkar and it soon rechristened itself as the Jamaat-ud-Dawa, which literally means 'a congregation of the calling', and announced it would engage only in nonviolent social and relief work. It was this office of the Jamaat that foreign journalists were invited to tour on 4 December 2008, in yet another alias of the Lashkar that was banned by the United Nations Security Council a week later. Its masters in the Army and the ISI are, however, still in no mood to fall to pressure from India and the international community and the 'Army of the Pure' is said to have re-emerged, yet again, under a different alias:

Tehreek-e-Tahafuz Qibla Awal (Movement for the Safeguarding of the First Centre of Prayer).

Several journalists have commented on the change of names and continued to meet members of the 'Army of the Pure' who also lend a helping hand to the Jamaat-ud-Dawa's extensive charity work. *Washington Post's* former managing editor Steve Coll, a Pulitzer-prize winning journalist who visited Lashkar/Jamaat sites extensively in 2005 and met their operatives again in 2007, says it would be difficult for the US to draw down the group. 'To some extent, Pakistan's policy of banning Lashkar and tolerating Jamaat has helpfully reinforced Lashkar's tendency towards nonviolent social work and proselytizing,' Coll wrote in the *New Yorker* on 1 December 2008. 'In the long run, this work is a threat to the secular character of Pakistan ... ' Coll says he found this year that Lashkar's bank accounts had remained 'unmolested' by Pakistan's government, thus giving the group 'quite a lot of running room'.

Room is what the ISI and the Pakistani Army are giving the Lashkar even after 26/11. Compared to other similar organizations, the Lashkar has proved to be a great success. Since its inception in the '90s, it has managed to attract thousands of young men to its fold. It uses its charity network to create a passion for jehad. The Lashkar, by some accounts has about 1,000 small offices all over Pakistan.

There was one near Kasab's village. When the *Observer* correspondent went to Kasab's village in Faridkot, just off a town called Depalpur close to the border with India, to establish if he indeed was a Pakistani, he was told that 'religious clerics were brainwashing youths in the area and that LeT's founder Hafiz Sayeed had visited nearby Depalpur. There was a LeT office in Depalpur, but that had hurriedly been closed down in the past few days. The LeT paper is distributed in Depalpur and Faridkot'.

The Jamaat-ud-Dawa has a wide base and operates 140 schools and 29 seminaries in different towns and cities of Pakistan. According to the Jamaat's website, 'Islam does not mean following a few rituals like performing prayers, keeping fasts, performing the pilgrimage to the Ka'ba (Hajj), giving alms (Zakat), or donating to charitable works, but in fact, it is a complete "Code of Life". That is why Jamaat-ud-Dawa's struggle is not limited to any particular aspect of life only; rather, Jamaat-ud-Dawa addresses each and every field of life according to the teachings of Islam. It is a movement that aims to ...

establish a pure and peaceful society by building the character of individuals according to those teachings.'

Its appeal extends to urban professionals like doctors who were out in large numbers in Muzaffarabad (the capital of Azad Kashmir or POK, depending on which side of the line of control you are placed) in 2005, after a devastating earthquake. Unlike the Taliban, the Jamaat is modelled after Hamas and is not merely an army with gun-toting members but a complex and intricate organization with a social and political agenda. It has a huge following and reports have often indicated that in its annual congregations, where Hafiz Sayeed gives a call for jehad, as many as 1,00,000 people are present in the sprawling Muridke compound.

Till 9/11, when America turned its attention to Pakistan and Afghanistan and began its war against terror, the annual conference of the Lashkar in Muridke was often attended by the ISI chief. According to Pakistan media reports, the Lt Gen. Mehmood Ahmed, who was removed as the ISI chief in October 2001 by General Musharraf, was seen as a supporter of LeT's jehad. Also considered pro-Taliban, he reportedly attended the yearly conference at Muridke. The conference passed a resolution calling on its cadres in India to emulate the example of Mahmud Ghaznavi, capture Hindu temples, destroy the idols, and hoist the flag of Islam on them.

America turned against the jehadi organizations operating in Pakistan after 9/11 but the Lashkar had reached a level of sophistication because of the covert aid it received from the Central Intelligence Agency (CIA) during the early '90s to fight off Soviet invaders in Afghanistan. The professor has in past interviews admitted on several occasions that he participated in the US-sponsored jehad against Russians in Afghanistan. Perhaps a reason why Abdullah Muntazir is sarcastic in his comment when, at one point, I pressed him on why the professor should not be labelled a terrorist. His cryptic answer, 'America sponsored us with guns during Afghan jehad. If we were not terrorists at that time, then why are we terrorists now?' Muntazir also compared the 'Indian occupation of the disputed territory of Kashmir' to the Soviet occupation of Afghanistan. For him Kashmir is a battlefield for jehad and he makes no bones about hiding that even though he insists Muridke is only a centre for learning.

In fact, the CIA was not in favour of declaring the Lashkar a terrorist organization when the issue first came up in the year 2000.

The US justice department had then determined that the Lashkar was a threat to them too but the CIA opposed it on the grounds that it would threaten its useful links with the ISI. Eventually, after the attack on the Indian Parliament in December 2001, the LeT was finally declared a Foreign Terrorist Organization.

But post 9/11, General Musharraf was pushed into a complete U-turn. The total support he was forced to lend George Bush saw Pakistan take a slow but sure journey that has today placed it on a dangerous crosshair. While Musharraf joined the war against terror – forced to by Bush who had infamously said you are either with us or against us – he got isolated from his own people who took to the streets, openly protesting his support of America that was bombing and strafing civilians, first in Afghanistan and then in Iraq. The last straw on the camel's back – to use a cliché – came when his own Army stormed the Lal Masjid in Islamabad in mid-2007. Reports of machine guns being used against innocents who got trapped in the masjid, converted many within the Army and the ISI and those who had retired from these outfits.

It was a turning point for former ISI chief Lt Gen. Assad Durrani, who explains his changed stance. 'It was the most blatant homage paid to the Americans. The mosque is located under the nose of the ISI headquarter and you can't first allow it to become a fortress and then fire on people who were willing to surrender.'

The storming of the Lal Masjid was a tipping point in more ways than one. If the release of Masood Azhar and the subsequent formation of the Jaish saw the advent of *fidayeen* attacks in Kashmir, the Lal Masjid operation led equally to the birth of intense attacks by suicide bombers. The suicide attacks were not just targeting civilians, they were seeking men in uniform and the figures, in fact, tell the story. The first half of 2007 saw twelve such attacks all over Pakistan between January and 3 July, wherein an estimated seventy-five people were killed. But after the Lal Masjid operation which reduced large parts of it to rubble, forty-four suicide attacks took place between July and December, killing 567 people, mostly the members of the military and para-military forces, the ISI and the police. December also saw the assassination of Benazir Bhutto, a grim reminder of the fact that the militants had declared a war against their ex-masters.

The attack on Islamabad's Marriot hotel, the city's most high-profile landmark, only confirmed the fact that terror can strike at will, any time and anywhere. It also confirmed that terror was not restricted to Pakistan's tribal belt alone. Former President Musharraf himself had, in fact, survived three assassination attempts and now lives under extremely tight security. The terror threat in Pakistan can be gauged from the fact that both President Asif Zardari and the prime minister, Yousaf Raza Gilani, in a complete first, offered Eid prayers at their respective residences on 9 December 2008.

The wave of suicide attacks in Pakistan and neighbouring Afghanistan does not just testify to the revival of al-Qaeda and the Taliban networks but as Ahmed Rashid, strategic writer and author of several books on the jehadi network, says, 'The army is embroiled in fighting these forces in the Frontier and one third of the country is not even in the state's control. This is hardly the time to pick a fight with India.'

The ratcheting up of tension and animosity between India and Pakistan after the Mumbai terror attacks point to another dangerous faultline – while the Pakistani Army joined the global war against terror, it never completely gave up its support to the jehadi network active on its border with India. As Rashid points out, 'Musharraf used to place Hafiz Sayeed and Masood Azhar under house arrest for Western consumption. He may have stopped infiltrating them into Kashmir too under international pressure but there was no attempt to stop their activities in Pakistan after they were banned. They were just allowed to hang loose.' Concurs former interior secretary, Tasneem Noorani, 'There was no effort to mainstream the radicals.'

Kasab's journey from a remote village in Faridkot to Mumbai is a testimony to this. So is his revelation to his interrogators that he was trained by a 'Major'. Zardari may have been right when he attributed the Mumbai attack to 'non-state actors' because the Major does not necessarily have to be a serving officer employed with the ISI. 'Retired ISI officers are helping the Pakistani Taliban and they have become more Lashkar than the Lashkar,' is how Rashid puts it. Any number of strategic and security analysts will testify to this dangerous trend. Admits one such analyst, who prefers not to be named, 'You don't need large training camps. Ex-servicemen are imparting arms training within the compounds of their homes. Different officials are attached with different groups.'

The switch from one alias to another – Lashkar-e-Toiba, Markaz-e-Toiba, Markaz-Dawa-Wal-Irshad, Jamaat-ud-Dawa, to the latest,

Tehreek-e-Tahafuz Qibla Awal – speaks of the Establishment's (as the Army and ISI combine is referred to in Pakistan) more than subtle support of groups that are used against India. The long-standing relationship between the Establishment and the India-bound militants is now under pressure. The overriding message from America after the Mumbai attack is for these groups to be reined in. This is testing not just the Army's carefully crafted support for the militants but has also focused attention on yet another faultline – the equation between the Establishment and the civilian government.

Committed to better relations with India, Pakistan's topmost civilian representatives responded instinctively to the horror in Mumbai, in keeping with what Zardari had told the Hindustan Times Leadership Summit, held a few days before the gun and grenade battle at Nariman House and the Taj and Oberoi hotels. In what took the Indian government by surprise, Zardari committed Pakistan to a no-first-use of nuclear weapons. It was the first major security-related statement to come from Pakistan's government after the 18 February 2008 election and more than just surprise the Indian government, it caused unrest amongst Pakistan's own Establishment. The next statement made by Prime Minister Gilani – confirmed through a press release issued by his office – pertained to the civilian government agreeing to sending its topmost ISI officer, Lt Gen. Ahmed Shuja Pasha to India on Prime Minister Manmohan Singh's request.

The sequence of events following Gilani's offer and Zardari's quick retraction, saying they had agreed to send a director and not Lt Gen. Pasha, speaks of the internal battle of supremacy between the Establishment and the civilian authorities, especially on the crucial issue of national security, which the Army believes to be its exclusive domain. Imtiaz Alam, a peacenick and head of the South Asian Free Media Association, who had dinner with Zardari a day after the Mumbai attack says, 'Zardari is very firm on terrorism. He thinks democracy is a better weapon but the terrorists have succeeded in creating a psychological gulf between India and Pakistan. Instead of Pakistan fighting the jehadis, it has become a fight between India and Pakistan.'

Senior journalists in Pakistan admit that briefings from the ISI changed the post-Mumbai discourse. Reacting perhaps to the loud, jingoistic demands on Indian television channels for action against

Pakistan, the ISI told a select group of journalists that India had in fact 'summoned' their chief. The Jamaat-ud-Dawa *amir*, Hafiz Sayeed – with a clear nod from his handlers – appeared on one news channel after another, making the same points: that the list of twenty most wanted which also includes him, was old hat, that India was playing the blame game without evidence, that India had its own band of 'Hindu terrorists' and India should give freedom to Kashmir and end the matter once and for all. The leak soon after, of the hoax call, purportedly made by the MEA's Pranab Mukherji to President Zardari, sealed the debate – India bashing was back in business. Jingoism overtook the more important debate of the threat Pakistan itself faced from terror networks flourishing on its soil.

Pakistan's news channels went on an overdrive and as some even blared war songs, the question that gained importance through all the din was: Who really runs Pakistan? Who is in control?

The answers to the questions are both easy and complex. Mushahid Hussain, chairman, Foreign Affairs Committee in the Senate, is clearheaded on the answer: 'War on terror, national security and relations with India, Afghanistan and China are the domain of the Army. Thanks to India, the Army has been rehabilitated and the war bugles are all over. No one person, no one institution is running Pakistan. Musharraf ran a one-window operation and the Army and the ISI used to report to him, but now decision making is murky and that is causing confusion. The hoax call and the DG ISI controversy are symptomatic of that.'

There are other examples. Only a few months ago, Zardari quickly retracted on his effort to bring the ISI under the control of the interior ministry. And even as the Pakistan government's response to Indian pressure to rein in the terror networks plays itself out on a day-to-day basis, it is evident that the civilian authorities have had to accept the Establishment's point of view vis-à-vis India. Therefore the talk that India should provide concrete evidence. Therefore Zardari's statement that the guilty – if found guilty – will be tried in Pakistan. That the twenty most wanted will not be handed over. Even on sourced reports put out in the local media that Masood Azhar had been put under house arrest, Prime Minister Gilani went on record to say that no such report had come to him yet.

If India believes that Pakistan's response has been poor – two Lashkar men, Zaki-ur-Rehman Lakhvi and Zarrar Shah have been arrested in Muzaffarbad – it is because the government here is tied down by the Establishment and pressure from its own people. It cannot be seen to be buckling under pressure either from India or the US.

The Pakistani government banned Jamaat-ud-Dawa soon after the UN sanction. But Lashkar was banned in the past, as was the Jaish. Prime Minister Gilani has committed to not allow Pakistani soil to be used for terror attacks, but then Musharraf had made exactly the same promise after the Parliament attack in Delhi.

Former Prime Minister Nawaz Sharif has gone as far as to say that 'Pakistan needs to set its own house in order' but he is in the Opposition and he can afford to make such statements. If Pakistan has begun to resemble a house of terror, it is because the Army and the ISI are yet to change their stance, not just vis-à-vis India but vis-à-vis the terrorists they create and support. Until then, the sprawling compound in Muridke will continue to remain in business. It already is, with the Jamaat-ud-Dawa having got a new alias.

'Like that only and proud, no?'
Mumbai

Bachi Karkaria

'We are having a blast.' In multi-storeyed Mumbai lingo, the statement could come from the penthouse or the basement. Page Three's lofty denizens seem to do nothing other than this, but at more-down-to-earth levels, it could as well have referred to the most recent explosions. This is the usual way of saying things. 'We are having blasts.' Just like 'We are having *batata vadas*'. Mumbai's iconic dome, Mumbai's iconic snack, we say it like this only.

It is not only a matter of syntax or semantics. Mumbai has learnt to live with both kinds of blasts, with both guns and poses. And is none the worse for it. Correction: it is the better for it.

Remember? It was the *Bombay Times* which created the super-deluxe socio-economic section of Page Three People, underdressed and overhyped in direct proportion. With this self-marketing gimmick, the city added not just one more feather, but the whole ostrich to its outrageous hat, making it the ultimate totem of the gilded life. Wannabe cities from New Delhi downwards have tried, even achieved, but they have never caught up with Mumbai's head-start as the uber-cool partying capital of India.

Equally, Mumbai has not just survived the other kind of blast, but extracted its own cachet from it. I am not being flippant, let alone insensitive. We seem to have wrested an RDX one-upmanship too. It wasn't something we sought, but having it thrust upon us, we have distilled a greatness from it. It is called by various names, but the most commonly accepted one is 'spirit'.

Once again we had the first-mover 'disadvantage'. On the surreal afternoon of 12 March 1993, within two hours and three minutes, twelve blasts ripped through the length of the city. They blew up, among other sites, seven of the city's power towers, from the Air India building in Nariman Point's corporate cluster to the Centaur hotel in the sybaritic Western suburb of Juhu, killing 257 and injuring 713. More ominously, this was the very first time that the explosive chemical RDX revealed its mangled face to civilian India; Mumbai had scrawled out the new alphabet of urban terror.

Since then, there has been plenty to test Mumbai's now fabled spirit – and its construction standards – between the deathly dozen of 12 March 1993 and 26 November 2008's six-point terror at CST station, Cama Hospital, Leopold Café, the Taj and Trident hotels and the Chabad-Lubavitch House at Nariman House, which together claimed 174 lives.

Bombs of varying devastation went off near Jama Masjid (28 August 1997), Malad and Virar (24 January and 27 February 1998), and Ghatkopar and Bombay Central station (2 and 6 December 2002). The decadal anniversary, 2003, was marked by five blasts, at Vile Parle (27 January), Mulund station (13 March), Bandra (14 April), in a BEST bus at Ghatkopar (29 July) and at Zaveri Bazar and the Gateway of India (25 August). The combined five-year toll was 78 dead and 349 injured. Then, in just eleven minutes of the evening of 11 July 2006, 181 people died and 890 were injured or disabled for life when seven blasts tore through the suburban commuter network at peak-hour.

Mumbai did not choose to be attacked, but the elected enemy was even more destructive. The cloudburst of 26 July 2005 may have been an act of God, but the resulting deluge could be blamed only on official apathy, ineptitude and corruption. The unrelenting torrent of 944 mm of rain flooded North Mumbai, but still stranded all those trying to make their way home from their offices in the south because no warnings were flashed. Indeed, crisis management looked closer to paralytic seizure.

The water did not flow off because the municipal corporation had neglected the drainage system for decades, and the government had cozied up to builders to turn all natural holding ponds and other open space sponges into non-absorbent concrete. It was the first time that most Mumbaikars got to know of the existence of the Mithi River in their backyard. It had choked to death with filth, and been buried with no rites and several wrongs under, among other violations, an airport runway.

For almost three days, India's most swaggering megalopolis

resembled a marooned village in the Bihari boondocks. It claimed 750 lives, 55 suburban trains, 10,000 commercial vehicles – and Amitabh Bachchan's entire fleet of luxury cars. Transportation, schools, banks and other companies, everything shut down, resulting in losses totalling Rs 5,000 crore, *not* counting man-days. Then, not even a full year after this Biblical-grade flood, it was 'the fire next time', the train blasts of July 2006. And now a new 26th has embedded itself like a bullet in our brain, sharpening memory rather than numbing it into a dubiously welcome oblivion.

Despite this procession of primitive mayhem so incongruous with Mumbai's image of plush sophistication, I can never forget those original balls of RDX, and the way they dramatically altered my perception of this city. I had come to work here from Calcutta, where I was raised on Bengal's intellectual snobbery about all matters materialistic. So, I used to observe Bombay's single-minded philistinism with conditioned disdain. Why, even during its Ganeshotsav, it was business as usual unlike my hometown which shut down completely for the five days of the corresponding mass celebration of Durga Puja. Any fragment of high-thinking which existed here seemed confined to the sterile frames of Bollywood films. It wasn't just me-first, it seemed to be me-only.

Then, on that serrated afternoon, as W.B. Yeats wrote of the Irish Easter Rebellion, 'all changed, changed utterly: a terrible beauty (was) born'. I watched in a disbelief as unwilled as my admiration as ordinary citizens just took over within minutes of the blasts at the Stock Exchange, and everywhere else. They ferried the injured promptly to hospitals, passing cars turned into willing ambulances. Obstructing gawkers were kept at bay. Without being exhorted, they lined up at blood banks, which were filled to the brim by dusk. And, most awesomely of all, the entire city trooped to their workplaces the next day. Even the bombed out offices soon began functioning with a semblance of defiant normalcy. My much-flaunted hometown would have been paralysed in impotent martyrdom or stirred itself only to poetic angst.

Mumbai has had so much practice at being 'bloodied but unbowed' that it has become a tired cliché, and one which itself began detonating in outbursts of rage. Socialite czarinas, without missing a beat of their partying, have denounced this spirit as an impostor. To be fair to them, the real target of their hysteria is official apathy which allows the city to be subjected to serial attacks, and expects ordinary citizens to pick up their own pieces simply because they have shown themselves so ready, willing and able to do so.

Since 1993, bombs have savaged almost every Indian city with varying degrees of viciousness, and its citizens have rallied to pick up the pieces, but it was Bombay which showed the way that very first time. That was the birth of the famous spirit, so widely emulated, but never quite equalled. It has emerged soaked, bedraggled, soot-covered but always shining through in all the serial assaults on our security, our human dignity, our now-most-precious possession, ordinariness. Which is why it pains me so deeply when I hear the angry outbursts which insult this spirit's sanctity, even rubbished its existence.

It is not that other citizens don't dust off the debris, rush to the rescue and rebuild afresh. It's not that the spirit of never say-die lives only in Mumbai. But this sense of get-up-and-go is so uniquely a part of Mumbai's DNA because its DNA is 'like that only'.

Many Mumbaikars struggled for hours to return home through the hell of high water that Terrible Tuesday, and then plunged right back into the filthy swirl to save a schoolchild – several of them contracted leptospirosis for their altruism. On a Wednesday the next July, slum-dwellers gathered up the broken victims in the only sheet they possessed and rushed them to medical assistance when detonations blew up the commuter trains. In every previous conflagration too, ordinary people were the classical fireman, sprinting up the stairs when everyone else was clattering down.

It was again no different during those sixty hours of terror in November 2008. A station constable equipped with only a stave, or a hospital watchman armed only with his presence of mind, saved scores. At the two hotels, chefs, waiters and managers took the terrorists' bullets in their chest to shield their guests and redefine the standards of service. Like the scores of others who had run into the jaws of death to ensure one more survivor in all the previous attacks, they proved, in the words of the chairman of the Taj Group, Ratan Tata, that 'You can knock us down, but you can never knock us out.'

And in his small flat next to the burning Nariman House, Iqbal Singh Jaggi, eighty-three, voiced exactly the same sentiment more earthily when he later told the *Times of India* reporter, 'Two foolish fellows were not going to succeed in driving me out of my house.' Instead, he and his wife Dhanika, seventy-four, busied themselves making tea and snacks for the saviour soldiers.

Terrorism is just an extreme form of the other furnace that daily tempers the Mumbaikar's steel. The quotidian commute in cattle trains, the long hours of struggle in a city that covers the successful in glory and designer labels but gives no quarter to the weak, the sirens' song of promises which drives the citizen to his punishing daily odyssey are all par for the course if you want to be part of the Bombay Dream. And everyone – from pavement to penthouse – wants it, body, mind and Faustian soul, because they have come from the four corners and every cranny of India in search of it.

Yes, Mumbai has been built and shaped by migrants right from the time that Catherine de Braganza's swampy dower was mortgaged by her unimpressed husband, Charles II, to the East India Company. From the hinterland and much further afield, commercial adventurers swarmed in to turn their own fortunes, and a fishing village into a shining city. They have never stopped coming, and, like the quintessential migrant, the city too seized the ambient opportunity to reinvent itself according to the demands of the day – from entrepot and cotton king to financial services, fashion and entertainment hub.

Migrants come for money, and these two drivers of the city found an easy accomplice in what soon became the third deity of the Mumbai Trinity, Bollywood. The commercial Hindi film industry stoked the Bombay dream; indeed, for many on the outside, Mumbai was 'Bollywood only'. When you think about it, it is these three elements which have alchemized to produce that unique 'spirit'.

The migrant will not allow disruptions to come between him and the next rung of ambition's ladder. Money is both a means and an end. So, if you rewind all the way back to not just '93, but to '92, you will see that those communal riots ended for reasons more commercial than secular. Hindus and Muslims were inextricably woven together in the economic fabric, and one couldn't be afflicted without affecting the other's livelihood.

Bollywood, for its part, suffuses every citizen with not just its own glamour, but with its own reel-life certainties. It ordains that everyone can script his or her own destiny. These mantras saw Mumbaikars through all the earlier horrors. And the most recent one, more than any of the past, actually played itself out like a full-length action thriller: heroes and villains *dhishum-dhishuming* their way out of the screens in our drawing room.

This triple-stranded DNA creates a hardy species high

on aspiration, low on surrender. The cardiac surgeon and the construction worker, in the dream are equal made. Like the doughty Mr and Mrs Jaggi they aren't simply going to abandon what they've built with sweat and fantasy just because some dangerous fool takes it into his head to plant a bomb, wave an AK-47 in their face, or make their home go under two metres of water. Ambition and dreams are made of sterner stuff. Yes, the spirit of Mumbai is about survival, but it also elevates that survival to a nobler plane.

Which is why the answer is both Yes and No to the question, *Is this object of media hosannas nothing more than the mundane necessity of making a living?* Yes because no other city is ruled as unbendingly by the bitch goddess, Success, and, No because nowhere else do its subjects pay such willing tribute because that's the promise which brought them here in the first place.

This is why Mumbai is like Bertie Wooster's redoubtable Aunt who 'does not go around wringing her hands and saying, What to do? What to do? She acts.' This is also why Mumbai extracts a positive charge from what would electrocute a lesser city. Dharavi may be Asia's largest slum, but it doesn't fester in deprivation and despair; its inhabitants have turned it into a buzzing hive of entrepreneurship.

Similarly, the punishing daily commute doesn't sap the harried working wife; she converts it into her mobile bazaar, kitchen, social club and psychological safety valve. She buys her vegetables cheap in the station's lane, and has chopped them into pieces by the time she alights. She has also got a new recipe and stressful *saas-bahu* gripes off her chest during the journey.

Each daily two-way trip hammers her into shape to take on anything this city throws at her – and fling it back. 'Move, move, why you are spreading yourself? You're some fancy maharani, or what? Others have to sit, no?' No 'thank you's, please. In a place where push turns to shove as a matter of right, you cannot survive without the gift of the grab.

Yes, the Mum-*bai* embodies and embellishes this envied spirit. You don't mess with her in the fish market or on the 8.17 Fast. This Superwoman has packed her husband's tiffin box and her own, managed to be on time at the station, elbowed herself into the compartment, handed over her toddler to her mother or other babysitter waiting on an en route platform before she is disgorged at CST or Churchgate to join the swell, the jasmine chaplet in her hair bobbing like flotsam on the hungering tide.

She too was back in her usual compartment the day after the terrorists blew up the trains on that insane evening in July 2006. Even if she saw her courage as nothing more than getting her daily *roti*, she too was furthering her dream of prettier *kapda* for the family, perchance some day a 1-BHK *makaan* of their own.

Dismiss not the Bom-babe either who shatters glass ceilings or raises a Daiquiri glass to strawberry lips with *bindaas* aplomb. Page Three butterflies with toned butts are actually made-over worker bees piling up the money, honey. Pretty faces may have pouted vacuously about the loss of Oberoi 'Tiffin' brunches, but these babes are as hard as their abs, cashing in on the ancillary industries which have grown out of that joint venture of glamour and entertainment. Yes, the spirit may manifest itself in widely divergent avatars, but it must always be deified. Defile it at our peril.

Let me conclude with another symbol of regeneration. Jaidev Baghel's 'Tree of Life' sculpture in the Taj lobby survived the grenades and guns. It was fittingly installed as the centrepiece of the hotel's moving memorial to those who fell and those who rose during the November nightmare. This tableau for the latest tragedy was unforgettable, but I would like to turn to a real-life tree from 1993 when Mumbai emerged triumphant from its first encounter with terror.

Worli, the midway point between established South Mumbai and a challenging suburbia, was one of the targets of those twelve fire-balls of RDX. The entire façade of three buildings had been gouged out, and body bits scattered across a cataclysmic radius. Framed by that Armageddon stood a tree, charred and abjectly bowed. Its sudden death, its utter hopelessness was a sight that chilled the blood much more than the wider swathe of destruction behind it. For months, we turned our faces away as we passed, for it was a taunting reminder of our vulnerability; it mocked a city that pretended it had overcome.

Then, suddenly, out of that blackened sepulchre sprang an unbelievable miracle. Overnight, four leaves had sprouted, defiantly green. And, in the next weeks, the foliage had covered the boughs and reclaimed its birthright with manic determination. Our Tree of Death became our Tree of Life. Call it a divine sign, call it a symbol of the Mumbai spirit, or dismiss it as just a natural cycle. Whatever it was, it continues to see us through.

THE TERRORIST AT MY TABLE
Published in 'Erratica' of 30 November 2008,
in the Sunday Times of India

L ast Sunday, I wrote about the two weddings which had just extended our global family. Last Wednesday, global terrorism attacked the remaining of the multiple celebrations. The reception was in the Jeejeebhoy Agiari compound, at the far end of Colaba. The second-last sitting of the traditional dinner was underway, and we were on a high that everything had gone off so perfectly. Then the mobile phones started the end game. It's difficult to distract from *patra* fish and saffron chicken, but the frenzied feeding on rumour began.

Rahul Akerkar got the first message that someone had been shot outside his restaurant, Indigo. Seconds later, someone added 'Leopold', followed by 'Shamiana at the Taj'. 'A lone sniper has gone berserk' escalated to 'It's some gang warfare'. Finally, with calls about 'bombs' at CST station – the possibility of terrorism – blasted our comparative complacency. It helped that my TOI colleagues had arrived by then presuming that they had got the next day's edition under control; fact was easier to distil from wild panic as our news bureau and police sources kept them informed. What didn't help were the intermittent explosions, their chilling sound detonating down the length of Colaba to freeze us in mid-buzz.

We closed the gates, switched off the festive lighting, and, in the flicker of the decorator's *diyas*, remained inside the agiari compound for an hour or so. Then, fearing that the situation might deteriorate, we dispersed in reassuring groups of cars. Now there was no question of the bridal couple spending the night at the Taj as booked. When we got home and turned on the TV, we realized that it had been a very close call for everyone. Everyone except Sabina.

She had come especially for the wedding, like my two other Delhi best friends, Anjali and Pranavi. Fate alone knows what made her leave early, and return to the Taj. Had she stayed on till later, like Suhel and Raian, she would have camped elsewhere, and the rest would not have been history. I called on her cell as soon as I saw the TV images. She answered in a voice I'd never heard from my strapping, no-nonsense friend. She whispered that a lot of firing was going on. No one had yet plumbed the depth, length or the darkness of the nightmare to come.

I never got through again. Instead, it was a continuous, impotent vigil punctuated by unflagging calls and smses from friends and colleagues from all over. The agony of not knowing was excruciating, but nothing compared with the terror in which our dynamic, generous, hospitable, ever-obliging Sabina was trapped.

Then, twenty-four numbing hours later, Jug called with the liberating news that she was safe, and my mobile phone glowed with the relief I relayed. Only to be told soon after that it was premature. I hadn't known till then that she was in the heritage suite which we had seen aflame all day. We pleaded for a miracle, for hope had turned out to be a perfidious ally.

And I prayed. I wished I could turn off my cell, so that I could do so undisturbed, but it was the sole emissary of the news I so desperately wanted – and it was also the link with our common friends and their embrace of dry-lipped concern. They too needed to know. I had brought Sabina to this situation, and I alone was responsible. I owed them the answers, minute by minute.

Now we all know what we did not want to know. And I'll feel responsible for a long, long time.

Bachi Karkaria

'The need is operational independence without political intervention.'
Tackling Terror in Modern Times

Julio Ribeiro

For ages, Mumbai's policemen have referred to the head constable, who prepares duty charts at police stations, as 'Commander'. Around 10 p.m. on 26 November 2008, the 'Commander' at the D.B. Marg police station, was instructed by the senior inspector to muster all available force for a *naka bandi* at Girgaum Chowpatty. The 'Commander' dispatched Assistant Inspector Hemant Bawdhankar, Assistant Sub-Inspector Tukaram Omble and some other constables for this special *naka bandi*. They were told that some terrorists had opened fire at the CST railway station and Cama Hospital and had hijacked a police vehicle which was later abandoned after which the miscreants commandeered a private car.

Literally translated, *naka bandi* means closing a part of the road. The police place removable barriers across part of the road forcing vehicles to slow down and stop. If the people in the vehicle or their movements or appearance arouse any suspicion, they are questioned and sometimes physically checked. *Naka bandis* are conducted quite regularly at random by the city police, to keep policemen and criminals on their toes. However, this particular *naka bandi* was ordered with a purpose and on specific information. Yet, since the magnitude of the task they were to confront had not yet dawned on them, the men deputed for the task were only slightly more alert than when doing routine checks of vehicles crossing the police barriers.

The full purport of the message had not yet seeped into their consciousness when the police party set out to intercept the hijacked vehicle. Terrorists had struck in the city in the past, though not in this brazen manner. Maybe it was the underworld using guns, turning crazy! Mumbai's policemen take these occurrences in their stride. They did not know then, that a *fidayeen* attack had taken place at the Taj and the Oberoi hotels, or the extent of damage done to life and property at the CST railway station or outside Cama Hospital. They were oblivious to the fact that two of their senior officers, Joint Commissioner Hemant Karkare, Additional Commissioner Ashok Kamte and an encounter specialist, Inspector Vijay Salaskar, lay dead somewhere near Cama Hospital.

The stolen car with the terrorists aboard presumably came along at great speed with the obvious intention of ignoring the stop signals of the police party. The police must have reacted quickly in trying to flag down the terrorists, who then emerged from their hijacked vehicle with guns blazing. ASI Tukaram Omble, a fifty-four-year-old veteran and some of the other constables who were armed only with lathis, jumped on the two men. API Bawdhankar, who was armed with his revolver managed to shoot one of them. In the exchange of fire, ASI Omble was shot dead by the second terrorist, before the others finally overpowered him.

It was this capture of Mohammad Ajmal Amir Kasab, which finally succeeded in unravelling the entire conspiracy behind the operation. Indeed, it was the presence of mind and the courage displayed by these ordinary policemen, who probably did not expect the terrorists to attack them, that marked the turning point in the entire tragedy that struck the city of Mumbai on that fateful night. ASI Omble has become a hero in the eyes of the people of Mumbai. There are demands for a junction near his residence to be named after him and it is hoped that he will be given recognition befitting the magnitude of the work he performed.

Mumbai police had been inured to terrorist crime since March 1993, when explosives planted in parked vehicles brought down parts of the Bombay Stock Exchange and Air India buildings, and in eleven other sites, claiming the lives of numerous share brokers, working professionals, customers and bystanders. It was on 12 March 1993 that Mumbai's police force was confronted with the entirely new phenomenon of serial bomb blasts, marking the advent of terror in Mumbai.

After that massive terror attack, Mumbai has witnessed three more attacks at regular intervals – in buses, trains and other public places – with the use of RDX loaded explosives and timers. All along, the culprits did not personally face the law keepers but had to be traced by police investigators; but on 26 November 2008, it was a different story. Men willing to give up their lives mounted an attack that was not only well planned but very meticulously executed. They not only targeted common men, women and children on the roads and in the railway station but also the well-heeled elite dining or partying in five-star hotels. Ten men with AK-47s, grenades and RDX-filled bombs held the city to ransom for three entire days! Mumbai had never witnessed such mayhem or such a bold show of force by fanatical elements.

When the citizenry understood the impotence of the State in the face of such terror, their anger had to be seen to be believed. Television footage showed that the policemen who first arrived at the scene of the attacks at the Taj and CST were clueless, leaderless and hopelessly out-manoeuvered. The cops did not know what they were facing and it dawned on the helpless public that their security was in the hands of an incompetent set of politicians, administering a soft State.

The police in India did not have any experience of terrorism till it surfaced in Punjab in the mid-'80s of the last century. It was a nationalist form of terrorism wherein the community to which the terrorists belonged, harboured some sneaking sympathy for the 'boys' because they felt that these boys were fighting for the community and not for themselves. It is not unnatural or unheard of, for co-religionists or people from the same community as the terrorists, to react in this manner. Very few provide them logistical support like places to hide or to store their arms or food and shelter but the vast majority will not help the authorities to arrest the culprits. Perceived injustice, mostly imaginary but some genuine, was what these 'boys' were fighting against.

In Punjab, terrorists had recruited many criminals in their ranks; they were found to be guilty of numerous human rights violations and atrocities, including the rape of village women. This is when the depredations of the terrorists crossed all limits and militated against the interests of the community in general. When the Sikh Jat peasantry began informing the police about the whereabouts of the culprits, the tide finally turned against the boys, bringing an end to terrorism in Punjab. Hence, the classical response to the nationalist form of terrorism is to win over the hearts and minds of the community while going after the gun-wielding desperados.

What we now call the jehadi form of terrorism is of a slightly different and more complicated form than the nationalist one we encountered in Punjab. The nationalist form was manifested earlier in Ireland, more then two centuries ago and its embers still smoulder. The same form of terrorism was experienced in Palestine, in Spain with the Basques, and in Sri Lanka with the LTTE. Terror was confined to well-defined geographical areas though stray attacks on individuals identified with the State were reported from outside those geographical limits. The difference with jehadi terrorism is that the Umma or Islamic brotherhood is spread across the world and jehadis can be motivated to attack targets in distant places in the US, the UK or India. It is much more difficult to win over communities in this global context. But it can be done if the community in a particular geographical area, such as in India, comes to realize that its interests are not served by the barbarism that defines terrorist acts.

The police in India have got accustomed to terror unleashed by hidden explosives timed to cause maximum damage in crowded localities. They have even experienced a backlash of sorts, mounted by Hindu fundamentalist groups out to counterattack in a similar fashion. However, a *fidayeen* attack – with people willing to die for a politico-religious cause – had been experienced only in the attack on the Parliament in New Delhi, and thereafter in Gandhi Nagar in Gujarat in the attack on Akshardham temple. In both these previous instances the people involved were partly local and the logistical support received by the perpetrators was provided locally. This fact alone dwarfed the complexity of the attacks when compared to the LeT operation of 26 November. No local involvement has yet been proved in the Mumbai attack and the sea route that was adopted for ingress gave the whole episode an air of temerity that was both unexpected and tragically bold.

The Mumbai police and the police in other cities and states of India are not trained or prepared to face a contingency of this magnitude. The criticism that the police was not properly equipped is valid only to the extent that we do not even have men trained to be in the first line of attack or defence, in *fidayeen* situations. A commando force that was trained and set up a few years ago by a previous police commissioner in Mumbai, was disbanded by his successor on unexplained grounds. Since the commando group was not officially sanctioned, the entire exercise was one of futility. If it had official sanction, trained men could have been pressed into action immediately, and even if they had not been properly equipped at least they would have been better trained and more physically fit than their compatriots in the police stations.

In the aftermath of 26 November, there is a crying need to station a platoon or even a company of the NSG in this city and other vulnerable cities of the country, to meet such exigencies. These men should always be under training and readily available at a moment's notice. Attempts to use them for normal law and order duties or for guarding VIPs can be withstood only if the troops are under central command and not answerable to any state government. The states' police, of course, are free to have their own trained men but that will require time, money and an iron will to withstand pressures from the men themselves, who want to be diverted to normal police work where opportunities for earning easy money are available.

The civil police attached to police stations do not have to be armed with AK-47s or even World War II weapons while performing ordinary police duties. A few weapons in the police station armory, available for emergency riot duties, are more than sufficient. The entire question of equipment needs to be re-examined at an expert level to avoid knee-jerk reactions to the public demand of arming the civil police with more sophisticated weapons, bulletproof vests, etc. After all, the great majority of the public is law-abiding whereas terrorists may confront the police only once in a decade or even once in a lifetime. On these occasions specialized forces have to be on hand to take on the attackers.

A lot has been said about the failure of intelligence; an oft-repeated criticism after every terrorist incident. There are central agencies like the IB, RAW, Directorate of Revenue Intelligence and army intelligence with sophisticated eavesdropping and other technological means of gathering timely information. But nothing can substitute human intelligence which is obtained either through informers, men planted in terror cells or from ordinary citizens living in slums and *bastis*, who may have noticed suspicious movements or arrival of suspicious strangers in their localities. Human intelligence, or 'HUMINT' as it is called, is best obtained by beat policemen with good local contacts. If relations between the people and the police are healthy and based on mutual trust and respect, it is possible to get better human intelligence which could obviate a terror attack. For this, a change in the mindset and behaviour of the police is required; rather than feeling superior to the common citizen, they should be on a plane where they are partners with the people.

For improved police-public relations, the imperative need is that of good police leaders at cutting-edge positions. The DG of police and the commissioner of police must be very carefully chosen for their proven integrity and competence. Nobody suspected of corruption or inability to take decisions or inability to communicate should be allowed to go up the ladder and propelled to a position where he is forced to be considered for the top slots. At the age of fifty and then again at fifty-five, the All India Service Rules permit the government to pension-off corrupt or incompetent officers. Unfortunately, this power is rarely used because every officer has a pipeline to some politician or the other, who pleads his case on the grounds of caste, religion or some other consideration.

If good people are appointed at the very top, they should be entrusted with operational freedom to manage their own force and produce the desired results. The National Police Commission in its recommendations submitted in 1981 had stressed the need for operational independence, the freedom to transfer, punish and reward their men without political intervention. This has never truly come about; with the result that today, we have politicized forces in every city and state of the country. Sadly, many police officers and policemen owe their allegiance to different politicians and do their bidding rather than look up to their own superiors for guidance.

Police chiefs who are not sure of getting their orders carried out will not be able to deliver justice according to the law of the land. When we talk of police reforms, it means basically this – no interference of politicians in the transfers and postings of subordinates, and secondly, no interference in the investigation of crime because that may lead to a negation of the rule of law. Unless these two reforms are introduced immediately the system will not work. Strong police leaders who are able to withstand such pressures are particularly rare and they are usually sidelined to non-executive functions to enable the political leadership to do as they like, with a subservient force at their command. Laws are needed to prevent politicians from becoming the actual powers running the police forces.

The people who have been greatly angered by the happenings of 26 November should join mass protests and raise their voice in favour of police reforms that make the police force accountable to the law alone rather than the political party in power. The role of the politicians should be confined to laying down policy and not to administering or enforcing. The role of the politicians should be to monitor the performance of the police and ensure that the rule of law is always honoured and that they serve the people and not trouble them.

After the NSG had successfully carried out its operations and rescued whoever was alive in the Taj and Oberoi hotels, there was a massive outpouring of people's anger. Since this time the upper middle class was hit, opinion makers who belong mainly to this class, came out strongly for police reforms. Activists have been harping on such reforms for the past twenty years but nothing concrete emerged from their efforts despite a Supreme Court ruling in Prakash Singh's case.

Prakash Singh, a former DG of the Assam and UP police and a former DG of the BSF, had approached the Supreme Court with a PIL demanding police reforms, back in 1996. He succeeded in getting a favourable ruling but only ten years later, from a Supreme Court bench headed by the then Chief Justice Y.K. Sabharwal, even though the states were very reluctant to introduce the required legislation. A few small states did comply, but almost all the bigger states dragged their feet because they feared that their ability to manipulate the police would be lost. Their excuse – the police will slip out of political control and become a law unto itself! Actually the police can never be independent in any form of government, particularly in a democracy. It should be accountable to the law and to the people through its elected representatives but that does not mean that the elected representatives misuse their power over the police to feather their own nests, or to make the law stand on its head, which is what is happening at present.

Among many others who protested against the inaction and ineptitude of our politicians, a group of citizens has got together to address the main lacunae in the government's response to the terror strike. The group has called itself 'Citizens Take Charge'. It is headed by B.G. Deshmukh, former cabinet secretary to the Government of India, D.M. Sukhtankar, former chief secretary to the Government of Maharashtra, Justice B.N. Srikrishna, formerly of the Supreme Court of India and others, including this writer. The group intends to bring all other protesting groups together on one platform to address not only the sensitive problem of police reforms but also the inadequacies in the disaster management planning and responses by government and municipal agencies.

It is important for people to understand that they have to work within the system and attempt to correct it. They can only do this if they are able to make politicians answerable after election results are announced. Because the middle classes have direct access to important politicians and bureaucrats, they do not feel the necessity of joining the mainstream political process which is affected through the electoral route. The poor, on the other hand, do not have any other clout except their votes and this they exercise very religiously at the time of elections. The middle classes have now realized that they too have to register and vote in order to send better people to the legislatures. Otherwise, rogue elements including some convicted for crime find their way into legislatures where laws are enacted, and later broken with the blessings of the same lawmakers and enforcers. If the politicians know that a sizable middle-class vote will ensure the defeat of criminal and selfish elements, political parties will think twice before nominating them as their candidates. Therefore, one of the three main areas of 'Citizens Take Charge' includes mobilizing the middle classes to vote, which in turn would make our politicians more accountable and ensure better governance.

Disaster management is another important area that needs attention. Disasters can strike through the vagaries of nature, like the floods in Mumbai in 2005, or through man-made disasters like the one that struck us on 26 November. Disaster management drills are prescribed but hardly ever practised and in times of crisis, it takes ages before they are put into operation. It is necessary to organize citizens in a holistic manner, to take charge of their own needs and alert the fire services, the Red Cross, hospitals and other disaster management components that are located in their residential areas. Having citizens groups in every area of this city, who are ready to go into action during times of crisis, will galvanize the disaster management teams and agencies located in their respective areas. Otherwise, there will be numerous headless chickens running around not knowing where to go and what exactly they should do, similar to the chaos we observed in hospitals on 26 November.

This also brings us to the need of a single authority to coordinate all activities, like the first police response, induction of NSG and summoning of disaster management teams. It was Mayor Rudy Guiliani, who took charge as the single authority in New York after the 9/11 plane crashed in the World Trade Center. He was assisted by his police chief and the fire brigade head and all other supplementary services. On 26 November in Mumbai there was no such leader and every agency worked on its own, sometimes at cross-purposes. In our city and in our system, the police commissioner is the best placed to assume this leadership role. He should be seen, heard and obeyed. In Punjab, during the two Black Thunder operations conducted by the NSG in the Golden Temple, the DGP was in charge and every government agency, including the NSG, reported to him. Television interviews and press briefings were conducted by the DGP himself and disseminated all over the world, to everybody's satisfaction. In Mumbai, during this terror attack, there did not appear to be a single authority. The NSG chief, his director of operations, the admiral commanding the Western Naval fleet, his commandos and even the fire brigade, all gave their private interviews to the electronic media, thereby causing much confusion about the facts.

When I took this issue up with the chief minister personally, he told me that he would appoint the secretary, rehabilitation, to be the point man next time out. This is a most unfortunate choice because it has to be a uniformed officer in our context and preferably, as I said, the police chief of Mumbai. When the Army was called out in Mumbai in 1982 during the police revolt and then again in 1984 during the communal riots, the Army contingents reported to the police commissioner and he was in charge throughout, even though Army operations were independently conducted under their own command. The police commissioner did not interfere in operations but the coordination and the overall responsibility was his and his alone. Nothing was done without his knowledge or consent.

Union Minister A.R. Antulay advocated the unfortunate theory that Hemant Karkare, the ATS chief who lost his life in this operation, could have been the victim of a conspiracy put together by Hindutva elements, whose involvement in the Malegaon blasts had been discovered by Karkare, during the ATS investigations. This was a patently communal and extremely stupid allegation to make and embarrassed the government no end. There is no need to advance any argument to disprove this theory of the minister for the simple reason that it doesn't require even a child to understand that a conspiracy between the Lashkar-e-Toiba and the VHP/Bajrang Dal was/is impossible.

The fact remains, however, that two senior IPS officers and one senior inspector, known widely in the city as an encounter specialist and responsible for the elimination of several gangsters, jumped into the same vehicle and were brought down by the two terrorists who had attacked innocent commuters first at CST and then later on the streets near Cama Hospital and Metro Cinema. Hemant Karkare was the chief of the anti-terror squad and when he learnt that terrorists were on a rampage, it was incumbent on him to go and find out what was afoot. The encounter specialist was attached to the crime branch and had been ordered by his boss to proceed for action. Ashok Kamte, who was the additional commissioner in charge of the Eastern Suburbs, need not have gotten involved but he had always been a daredevil. He was the son of a retired military officer and the grandson of the old Bombay State's first Indian police chief. They all met purely by chance and if they jumped into one jeep together, it was not for any particular reason except perhaps, the excitement of the chase. All theories about their folly in going together are invalid and misconstrued. It just so happened and could happen again unless one central authority directs the movements of senior officers and assigns specific duties and geographical areas to them, which sadly, did not happen on that fateful night.

People have come out in praise of the brave men who laid down their lives and those who acted against the terrorists. Individual IPS officers like Hemant Karkare and Ashok Kamte, who died in action, as well as the Additional Commissioner Sadanand Date and DCP Nangre Patil showed immense personal leadership to lead from the front. Sadanand Date fired at and prevented the terrorists from leaving Cama Hospital for more than half an hour. He was injured at Cama Hospital when the two terrorists threw a grenade from the roof of the hospital. The grenade burst and its splinters injured him all over his body; one splinter is still embedded behind the retina of his eye. Date is one of the finest officers I have come across in my entire career. Low-key and unassuming, he is a man who does his duty without flinching. It is hoped that the government suitably recognizes his role in this entire event.

At the same time the authorities should be careful of officers and men who have exaggerated their individual roles just to claim rewards. This is not an uncommon police practice in Mumbai and other places; the tendency should be discouraged so that those who have actually risked their lives do not turn cynical.

When accused of failing to collect intelligence, the IB and RAW, the two main agencies concerned, resorted to leaks to the media to extricate themselves from the possible ignominy. They have no other option except leaks to defend themselves since they are not permitted to go public and individual officers are advised neither to be seen nor heard. But these very interesting leaks tell us that the interception of conversations between LeT masterminds in Pakistan indicated the possibility of a terror attack via the sea route, in the city of Mumbai. Furthermore, the Taj hotel had been mentioned as a possible target. We do not know how this important information was disseminated by the agencies and to what levels it percolated, but Ratan Tata, the chairman of Indian Hotels which controls the Taj, admitted that the hotel management had been alerted a month earlier. In fact, the hotel had beefed up its security and only relaxed it a week before 26 November because hotels tend to place the comfort and hospitality of guests as a priority over security. Ratan Tata has changed his mind after this incident and called an Israeli security firm of repute to advise the Taj on how to avoid further attacks of this type.

It has also been reported that the coastal route had been anticipated and Admiral Sureesh Mehta, chief of Naval Staff, admitted that the Navy was informed but had not received 'actionable intelligence'; the coordinates of the ship suspected to be bringing the terrorists showed that the vessel was in Pakistani waters – beyond the jurisdiction of the Indian Navy.

A politician in the know of inside information, who I met in Delhi soon after the attack, told me that the Indian Coast Guard had intercepted the Kuber, the Indian fishing vessel hijacked by the terrorists. However, they did not search the boat because an identity plaque was flashed showing that the vessel belonged to Indian owners. We really do not know who to believe and what to believe. But we do know that coastal security has been severely neglected and was taken rather lightly even after intelligence was passed on to the Indian Navy and perhaps, also to the Coast Guard and the Mumbai police.

Some fishermen and residents of the fishermen colony at Cuffe Parade, opposite the Badhwar Park where railway officials reside, saw the terrorists getting down from a dinghy and questioned them. They did not pass on this information to the police despite the suspicious nature of their landing, in a rubberized and inflatable boat not normally used by fishermen or tourists, and despite the outsized backpacks that the terrorists were carrying. Obviously the fishermen had not been alerted about a possible landing. Moreover, the police themselves, who are present in these areas bordering the coasts, had not been alerted about a possible threat from the sea route. Somewhere along the line, this crucial intelligence had not been disseminated. It could have been done without causing any panic, if there was some understanding of the type of threat that loomed over the city. A thorough research into the lapses and lacunae in the intelligence gathering and dissemination system is imperative in order to plug all the loopholes. There should be only one authority responsible for the collection and dissemination of all such intelligence. That authority should also monitor the progress of the passage of information, to ensure that the people who have to act have received requisite warnings.

I do not know the exact role of the national security adviser (NSA) in this entire episode. When the attack on Parliament House was mounted, we had blamed the then NSA, Brajesh Mishra, of piling too much on his platter, with the result that he did not have time to attend to internal security. At the time, Brajesh Mishra was also principal secretary to the prime minister and those duties occupied most of his time. Similarly, M.K. Narayanan or MK, as I call him, bit off more than he could chew. After J.N. Dixit died, MK took over external security and according to the same Delhi politician friend of mine, spent nearly 250 days out of the country in the year 2008 alone. He was involved very intimately in the nuclear deal negotiations and then with the border dispute with China. He did not have enough time to devote to internal security issues which were actually his area of expertise.

I know MK personally. I had worked very closely with him and P. Chidambaram in the home ministry as special secretary and later in Punjab where I served, first as the DGP and then as adviser to the governor. MK has his eyes and ears to the ground and is very astute when it comes to political instincts. His judgements have always been correct as they are based on ground observations and grass-root sentiments. It is obvious that he slipped up on this one particular occasion because he had too much on his plate. He is not young anymore and should divert some of his powers and responsibilities to younger people who need to be groomed.

A professional police force needs good police leaders, men whose integrity and competence are established. There is no dearth of such officers in the IPS but independent minded officials are often sidelined in the interest of expediency. Unfortunately, politicians prefer those who will do their will and not those who wish to serve the people and uphold the rule of law. Police reforms will start with the selection of good police leaders and that should be the main demand of the public.

After these good leaders are selected in a transparent manner through the medium of the Security Commission, advocated by the National Police Commission of 1979, these leaders should be given operational independence. Only then will we get a professional police similar to what exists in other developed countries of the world. Ultimately, it is for the people to demand good service and force their government to introduce police reforms that are conducive to good service.

'Shivraj Patil delayed the NSG flight by 45 minutes.'

Why India will be Hit Again

Harinder Baweja

The story of MV Kuber – the shipping trawler in which the heavily armed terrorists travelled from Karachi to Mumbai – tells the story of India's security apparatus in so many ways. It was one of the estimated 50,000 trawlers registered in Maharashtra and Gujarat – an awesome number, the Navy chief Admiral Sureesh Mehta now tells us. Yet, it was only one of those 50,000 trawlers that came back to shore – Porbandar in this case – on 13 November 2008 and sailed out again soon after. Its captain, Amar Sinh Solanki was a happy man that day. He had been out on the high seas for a fortnight – as most fishing trawlers are wont to do – and had come back with 1,000 kilogrammes of fish. Enough for the captain, or *tandel* as captains are referred to, to rest a few days with his family.

But quite unlike all the other 50,000 trawlers, Kuber set sail again on 14 November. This should have alerted the coastal authorities' antenna but Kuber sailed on. When Solanki set sail aboard Kuber on 14 November, he was not alone. Another trawler, Maa, with Jeevabhai Hardasbhai as its *tandel* too sailed out of Porbandar and the two navigated the waters side by side for two days and kept in touch over VHF radio sets for at least 'seven sunsets'. Investigators who have spoken to Hardasbhai know that he had harboured Maa on a safe shore due to choppy weather, nine days after leaving Porbandar and are now trying to find out if Kuber merely strayed into Pakistani waters or whether Solanki – whose dead body was found in the engine room – deliberately steered the vessel into Pakistan.

Solanki, in all probability, steered the trawler deeper into Pakistani territory because the GPS (now being examined by investigators) has two directions logged into it: Mumbai to Karachi and Karachi to Mumbai. Investigators reveal that Kuber travelled along the coast in its onward journey and returned via the high seas. But this is hindsight. The question that the internal security network needs to ask is: Why was there no alert when Kuber went missing. Neither Maa's *tandel*, nor Solanki himself called for help.

Unknown to Indian authorities, Kuber had been hijacked by the Lashkar-e-Toiba on 22 November 2008. According to the dossier of evidence given to Pakistan by the MEA, 'the terrorists set sail from Karachi in a small boat at approximately 0800 hours on 22 November 2008. After travelling for about forty minutes, they were shifted to a larger boat, *Al-Husseini*, which according to Ajmal Amir Kasab belongs to Zaki-ur-Rehman Lakhvi alias Chacha. There were already seven LeT members on board. The terrorists spent the entire day on board the *Al-Husseini* and the next day, on 23 November, at about 1500 hours, Kasab noticed another boat docked next to *Al-Husseini*. This was an Indian registered fishing vessel called Kuber which had five crew members. Four crew members were shifted to *Al-Husseini* and were later killed by the LeT. The captain of the trawler, Amar Sinh Solanki was allowed to remain on board the Kuber and it was he who navigated Kuber for approximately 550 nautical miles to Mumbai.'

But again, this is all on hindsight.

Kuber went missing without detection and kept sailing the high seas and making its journey towards Mumbai with ten heavily armed terrorists as its passengers, ironically around the same time that the RAW had specific intelligence warning of the possibility of a sea attack. Enough advance information was in fact available and if the handlers of intelligence in RAW, IB, the Navy and the Coast Guard had cared to analyze it, they could well have joined the dots to even avert 26/11.

An internal probe conducted by P. Chidambaram, the new occupant as the home minister in South Block, reveals frightening truths of the disarray that the internal security apparatus is in. The investigation into the intelligence failures that preceded the Mumbai attacks reveals particularly that there was ample actionable evidence available and worse, that the specific information that was available was neither properly analyzed nor acted upon with the seriousness it ought to have, given the fact that India has earned the sobriquet of being a soft State, attacked as it is repeatedly.

What was this 'specific' information available to the different intelligence agencies? RAW, India's external intelligence agency, it is now known, had provided several intercepts gleaned from signals intelligence in the three months preceding 26/11. On 18 September 2008, RAW intercepted a satellite phone conversation between a Lashkar man and an unknown person. The contents of the conversation were fairly bang on – the Lashkar operative said that an operation to target a hotel at Mumbai's Gateway of India was being planned and that the sea route would be used.

Again, on 24 September, RAW intercepted another satellite phone conversation. This time, the LeT operative identified the hotels that were being considered for the attack. The hotels named were the Taj, the Marriott, the Sea Rock and Land's End. If the handlers of intelligence had put their heads together to analyze the intercept, it would have endorsed the information gleaned from the 18 September alert that had mentioned that the sea route would be used. All these hotels have one thing in common – they are all sea facing.

But this is not all. On 19 November, RAW picked up some more chatter on satellite phones and this time a voice said, 'We will reach Bombay between nine and eleven.' RAW identified the exact coordinates of the call and discovered that it came from the sea near Mumbai, 40 km west of Jhol. This important piece of information was forwarded by RAW to the IB, who in turn forwarded it to the Indian Navy. The information kept getting kicked like a football from one agency to another. Neither asked the other if any follow-up action had been taken. The Navy did go out to sea to comb the exact coordinates that had been given to them but did so for only one day and then forgot about it. All this while, Kuber sailed the seas and unknown to either RAW, the Navy or the Coast Guard, inched closer to its destination. Alarmingly, they were only half an hour off from the promised time of arrival.

According to the MEA dossier, the ten terrorists reached the locality of Badhwar Park (Cuffe Parade) in South Mumbai at about 8.30 p.m. For all the time that the Navy and the Coast Guard should have been searching for the 'Lashkar' ship, the ten terrorists were aboard Kuber, as per the plan masterminded by their handlers in Pakistan, and were inching closer to their target, their individual pack bags securely in place. Each bag contained a Kalashnikov, ammunition, 9mm pistols, hand grenades and dry fruits that would come in handy for the long battle that was soon to begin. And as they approached Mumbai, Kasab and his nine accomplices performed watch duties aboard the trawler. Log sheets maintained by them – which have now been seized – show that Kuber reached a point 4 nautical miles off Mumbai at 4 p.m. on 26 November 2008. Here, as soon as it was dark, Ismail Khan – the team leader who was soon to pair up with Kasab and direct the shooting at Mumbai's CST – contacted the handler in Pakistan, who directed them to kill Solanki, the captain of Kuber. After killing Solanki, the dossier says, 'the terrorists along with their weapons and IEDs boarded the inflatable dinghy. They traversed the last 4 nautical miles to Mumbai in about an hour and fifteen minutes, reaching the locality of Badhwar Park at 2030 hours.'

Even at this precise time, the intelligence agencies could perhaps have been forewarned of the impending attack. First, let me quote from Prime Minister Manmohan Singh's speech, from his inaugural remarks to the conference of chief ministers on internal security on 6 January 2009. In a forthright address, he said: 'It is important at this juncture to demonstrate our combined will, and for that we are effectively galvanizing the internal security system to deal with future terrorist attacks. Technology is empowering non-state actors across the globe and it is necessary for us to come up with a comprehensive strategy that combines the best of technological and human capabilities within the country to defeat terrorism in all its manifestations ...

'The main message is that we need to break down barriers to information-sharing between the various agencies. What I would add is that we need better intelligence and perhaps, more importantly, sophisticated assessment and analysis of the intelligence that is available. Complaints are often heard that the intelligence provided by the agencies is not actionable. All intelligence produced is actionable, though it may not always be specific. It depends on the capability and ingenuity of those who assess the information to further develop and convert the fragmentary pieces of intelligence into a complete whole and for those who have to act on it to possibly pursue each and every lead ...'

If the prime minister chose to pointedly focus on the crucial issue of 'information-sharing between various agencies', it was with a specific reason, a reason he could not openly share. He knew that vital and critical intelligence had simply been ignored. It had simply lain unattended in various files in the offices of different premier intelligence agencies. He is aware that if all the intelligence that came in two months before the Mumbai terror attack on 26/11 had been put through a 'sophisticated assessment and analysis', senior officers could well have been able to join the dots and zero in on the fact that terrorists were going to use the sea route to come into Mumbai and attack five-star hotels. Incredibly, this author has learnt through the highest quarters in Delhi that the mobile numbers that were used by the Mumbai terrorists were available with the IB five days before 26/11.

Highly placed sources shared the contents of a 'secret' note that contains thirty-five mobile numbers. Of the thirty-five SIM cards, thirty-two had been purchased from Kolkata and three from Delhi, by overground workers (OGWs) of the LeT and sent to Pakistan occupied Kashmir by mid-November. The precise contents of the secret note could not have been more direct. It reads, 'The numbers given below have been acquired from Kolkata by overground workers and have been sent through Pakistan-trained militants based in Kashmir to PoK. These numbers are likely to emerge in other parts of the country. These numbers need to be monitored ... ' The note contains more: 'These numbers need to be monitored and the information taken from these numbers regarding the contents of the conversation, current locations of the call detail records are required for further developing the information. The monitoring is possible at Kolkata.'

This crucial and stunning piece of information, as revealed by highly placed sources, was received by the IB on 21 November, at least five full days before Ajmal Amir Kasab and his nine accomplices landed at Mumbai. The prime minister and home minister are aware that for all the five crucial days that the numbers were available, they were not being monitored. The lapse is all the more critical because at least three of the thirty-two numbers contained in the secret note were exactly the same cell numbers that the terrorists used to keep in touch with their handlers in Pakistan. It is possible that the terrorists only activated their mobile numbers after reaching Mumbai but that does not excuse the fact that the numbers were not put under surveillance despite the knowledge that they had been sent to trained militants in PoK. But the agencies had failed in monitoring the vital numbers, just as they had failed to connect RAW's intercepts.

If the intelligence was being analyzed and not ignored and if the secret note the IB received on 21 November had been connected with RAW's intercepts, and the numbers had been put under surveillance, an alert intelligence apparatus may have been able to connect the activation of the Kolkata numbers with the arrival of terrorists in Mumbai. Were the phones activated at 4 p.m. or at 8.30 p.m.? The answer to this question was not known, at least on the day of the attack.

Sources in the PMO reveal that the numbers were not being monitored. It is only after Ajmal Kasab and his accomplice Ismail Khan had killed 58 passengers and injured 104 at CST, after ATS chief Hemant Karkare had been shot dead along with two other senior officers; after the remaining four pairs had lodged themselves at their intended targets (Nariman House and the Taj and Oberoi hotels) that someone in the IB woke up to the fact that it had received a list of phone numbers. Quick calls were then made to Kolkata, the service providers alerted and the bloodcurdling truth soon hit home – three of the thirty-five numbers that ought to have been monitored, were being used by the terrorists.

It was only after this that the Mumbai police was alerted and the process of recording the conversations began. The dossier of evidence provided to Pakistan emphasizes the fact that the terrorists were using mobile phones to stay in touch with their handlers in Pakistan. It however, does not go into the details of which numbers the terrorists were using or how they were procured. The dossier says, 'Even while the terrorists had occupied the target buildings and the security forces were engaging them, the terrorists were in contact with their controllers/handlers over mobile telephones. They also used mobile telephones belonging to hostages/victims. Shortly after the attack on Taj hotel, Indian agencies were able to intercept mobile telephone calls made from and to the hotel. The controllers/handlers used the virtual number to contact a mobile telephone with one of the terrorists (obviously one of thirty-five numbers). This conversation was intercepted and thereafter, all calls made through the virtual number (being used by the handlers) were also intercepted and recorded.'

The dossier also contains excerpts from these recordings. The intercepted conversations are listed as per the location of the terrorists and also have a timeline. The timing therefore also reveals that the entire procedure of recording the conversations started not on 26 November, the day of the attack, but in the early hours of 27 November. One of the first conversations revealed that the terrorists had left behind their satellite phone on the Kuber by mistake and also failed to sink the boat before jumping into the dinghy.

The terrorists were not the only ones who had made a mistake. Indian intelligence agencies had committed grave mistakes. The casual attitude with which information is gathered but not analyzed and acted on is what makes India a soft state. Another reason why, in the same address to the chief ministers, the prime minister stressed the need for 'zero tolerance' saying we are 'effectively galvanizing the internal security system to deal with future terrorist attacks. Technology is empowering non-state actors across the globe and it is necessary for us to come up with a comprehensive strategy that combines the best of technological and human capabilities within the country to defeat terrorism in all its manifestations'.

Covert operations are key to gathering advance information and keeping pace – if not staying at least one step ahead – with what terrorist groups are planning. In this case, in a superb covert operation, Indian forces had managed to penetrate the ranks of the LeT and plant thirty-five Indian SIM cards among them. In other words, the SIM cards used by the Mumbai terrorists were like Trojan horses in the LeT ranks. But in a terrible communication and execution bungle the scrupulous follow-up monitoring of the SIMs that should have taken place was not done. And now ironically, despite the gravity of the Mumbai attack and the prime minister's call for information sharing between various agencies, the agencies are once again engaged in a blame game, with the IB blaming the Jammu and Kashmir (J&K) police for having provided the SIM cards in the first place!

The J&K police is hardly to blame since it passed on the details of the mobile numbers to the IB. Having been shown up and embarrassingly caught for not monitoring the numbers, the rivalry has reached tragic proportions. Mukhtar Ahmed, the J&K police constable who travelled from Srinagar to Kolkata to procure the SIM cards (used to infiltrate the LeT) has been arrested and jailed. In a knee-jerk reaction, the agencies have also temporarily deactivated all the mobile numbers instead of putting them under surveillance – a move that could have perhaps yielded further intelligence!

The government has launched a massive diplomatic effort against Pakistan through the credible evidence it has succeeded in getting. A similar offensive is needed to ensure that the different intelligence agencies work in tandem and not at cross-purposes. Prime Minister Manmohan Singh emphasized precisely this when he said, 'The information available from diverse sources, thereafter needs to be properly channelized to reach a common point such as the recently revitalized Multi-Agency Centre (MAC) in Delhi for collation and analysis. It will, hence, be necessary to establish centres locally, at the state and lower levels across the country, to collate all the available information which might have a bearing on a potential terrorist situation.'

In fact, if there is one important lesson post 26/11, it is this – that the diverse agencies work in a coordinated manner to process information. Advance information will be key in preventing future attacks.

Ironically, enough intelligence was available for the 26/11 attack, an attack that is referred to as India's 9/11. Even the Taj hotel had been identified as a definite target. Ratan Tata only confirmed this when he told live television that yes, he had been alerted and they had also increased security at the hotel. A senior IB officer confirmed to this author that RAW's intelligence alert which came on 19 November – a week before terror struck Mumbai – was sent to the Navy but Admiral Mehta while admitting that there was some information, still presses the point that the input was not 'actionable'. Political heads rolled after 26/11 when Home Minister Shivraj Patil and Maharashtra Chief Minister Vilasrao Deshmukh were claimed as victims but critical intelligence lapses only led to an offer of resignation by the National Security Adviser M.K. Narayanan. The Navy and the Coast Guard and indeed the intelligence agencies appear to have gotten away with mere admonishment for not monitoring vital numbers and for not proactively patrolling the high seas when they had received information, including the coordinates of the 'Lashkar ship'.

Kuber's story *does* tell the story of our internal security apparatus in so many ways.

The possibility of a threat from the seas, far from being unknown or unexpected, has been a matter of government record at the highest level since 2006. That year, Shivraj Patil had categorically said, 'We understand they (the terrorists) have been collecting information regarding location of various refineries on or near the Indian coastline ... Some LeT operatives are also being trained specifically for sabotage of oil installations. There are plans to occupy some uninhabited islands off the country's coastline to use them as bases for launching operations on the Indian coast ... ' In November 2008, literally a few days before the attack, he again reiterated the threat when he told director generals of police, 'To control terrorism in the hinterland, we have to see that infiltration of terrorists from other countries does not take place through the sea routes and through the borders between India and friendly countries. The coastlines also have to be guarded through Navy, Coast Guard and coastal police.' Similarly, Defence Minister A.K. Antony informed the Lok Sabha in March 2007 that 'Pakistan-based terrorist groups, particularly LeT, have been exploring possibilities of induction of manpower and terrorist hardware through the sea route ... ' Even, M.K. Narayanan, whose primary duty it is to strengthen and streamline security was aware of the threat. He is ducking television cameras following reports that he had offered to resign but only recently he had told the International Institute of Strategic Studies that the sea route in particular was becoming the chosen route. On 12 March 2008 the home ministry had briefed the senior staff of ISRO, Bhabha Atomic Energy Centre, Reliance and others who have coastal assets of the threat of a sea attack.

Yet, Kuber sailed on.

Unknown to either the Navy or the Coast Guard, Kuber got hijacked on 22 November and Solanki, its *tandel*, helped the heavily armed men steer their way almost up to Mumbai – actually only 4 nautical miles short of the country's financial nerve centre. Once they alighted at Cuffe Parade's Badhwar Park, the group broke up into pairs and went about their business. They had made it past several layers of security, just as their counterparts have through successive attacks.

India was hit with ferocity on 26 November 2008. The country's Parliament was stormed on 13 December 2001. Unit after unit of Pakistan's Northern Light Infantry infiltrated the heights of Kargil in 1999. Srinagar's assembly faced a determined suicide attack in 2000, few months after it released Maulana Masood Azhar in Kandahar. The hijacking of flight IC 814 from Kathmandu to Kandahar was perhaps the worst example of national intelligence failure and yet, attack after attack has only been met with a lot of empty rhetoric.

Committees have been set up and pledges to refurbish the security apparatus have been made in earnest, but the frightening postscript is simply this – we will be hit again.

26/11 was the seventh attack in the year 2008 alone. The new year 2009 began with a fierce encounter between the Army and the Lashkar in Poonch in J&K, an encounter which the Army was forced to call off after eight days when it realized that the terrorists, instead of being cornered in the cordon it had thrown around the area, had actually escaped. India will be hit again. For those who find this alarming, examine this:

- A comprehensive security review was ordered after close to 600 soldiers died securing the heights of Kargil. A task force on border management had then, in the year 2000 warned, 'The long coastline with its inadequate policing makes it easy to land arms and explosives at isolated spots on the coast.' In January 2005 a coastal security scheme was formulated for enhancing security. The home ministry's own website says, 'The scheme envisages setting up of coastal police stations, outposts and check-posts in the coastal areas for strengthening surveillance and patrolling of the coastal areas. The coastal police stations will be equipped with vehicles, vessels and equipment for mobility on coast and in waters close to the coast.' The scheme was approved in January 2005 for complete implementation in five years from the year 2005-06 with an approved outlay of Rs 550 crore. Till date, only Rs 13 crore have been released. Maharashtra specifically only received Rs 2 crore of the Rs 40 crore outlay approved for the state. A home ministry official admits that there are negligible patrol stations functioning. Close to four years after the approval of the scheme, even the IB, which was to get nine patrol boats, is waiting for the first one to arrive.
- In 2001, the Girish Saxena Committee submitted a report on the country's intelligence apparatus. The report recommended an overhaul of technical, imaging, signal and, electronic counter-intelligence capabilities. The recommendations were accepted by a Group of Ministers (GoM) but in the seven years since they gave the report their stamp of approval, it has never been implemented beyond a few symbolic changes. Among other suggestions it made was a proposal for the immediate

recruitment of an additional 3,000 cadres to the IB but, by 2008, only 1,400 additional posts had been sanctioned.

- The Saxena Committee had called for a Multi-Agency Centre (MAC) and a Joint Task Force on Intelligence (JTFI) to be set up under the IB. The MAC was to collect and coordinate terrorism-related information and the JTFI was to share the information with state governments. Both are functional but are under-staffed and under-equipped. Prime Minister Manmohan Singh released funds for MAC only after the bomb attack in Delhi in September 2008, seven years after the committee first recommended that it be set up.
- Former Prime Minister I.K. Gujral, as part of his Gujral Doctrine (of India extending a hand of friendship to Pakistan as the bigger brother) halted all covert operations in Pakistan.
- In 2001, senior bureaucrat N.N. Vohra – currently governor, Jammu and Kashmir – took months crafting a report on internal security. His recommendations have obviously been gathering dust, for Vohra had indicted the home ministry saying it needed to be completely restructured as 'it has lost the capability to respond to any internal security challenge'.
- It was only in August 2007 that the home ministry even included the police-population ratio in its report to Parliament. According to Ajai Sahni, executive director, Institute for Conflict Management, 'After reeling under terrorism for at least two decades, the home minister for the first time demonstrated awareness of the fact that the country was severely under-policed and had meagre intelligence cover to deal with terrorism. The reality is, India's entire justice system, from the *thana* to the Supreme Court, appears to be in a state of terminal sickness. This, and not the minutiae of the latest terrorist attack, is the critical issue confronting the country.'
- In another appalling revelation, senior NSG officers who travelled from Delhi to Mumbai now concede that their flight to Mumbai was delayed by forty-five minutes because they were waiting for the then home minister, Shivraj Patil, to reach the airport. That's how seriously the home minister took the attack and why the Congress party chose not to replace Patil despite terrorism having raised its head time and again at different locations – Allahabad, Lucknow, Faizabad, Delhi, Jaipur, Guwahati, Ahmedabad – is a chapter in itself.

Kuber managed to sail because India's counter terrorism policy is clearly only on paper. This is endorsed by some of the best security analysts. According to C.D. Sahay, former director, RAW, 'There appears to have been enough intelligence to avoid Mumbai. You can't expect the Lashkar patron, Hafiz Sayeed to pick up the sat phone and give precise information with names of those who were being sent.' According to him, 'The tendency is to only push intelligence reports like babus push papers. Why have only political heads rolled? Why are the officials being protected? The culture will not change until key officials are held accountable.'

The threat, as Mumbai and the blasts in Delhi, Hyderabad and Ahmedabad have shown, is grave but how prepared are our security managers? Ask Ajai Sahni and he says, 'We are not in for big trouble, we are already in big trouble. The only way to prevent terrorism is through policing and intelligence but the system is so rotten, it will take five years to refurbish.' Ask him then of the possibility of being hit again, of another Mumbai and he says, 'For the next decade, yes. Even if you start the responses today, it is going to take you four to five years to get to steam.' C.D. Sahay says, 'If the government keeps trying to cover up, yes. It is time for accountability and for case officers being put on intelligence inputs so they are analyzed up to the last detail.' Vikram Sood, also a former director, RAW, puts it simply, 'Our greatest responsibility is the lack of a response mechanism. Security does not just consist of deploying armed guards outside the doors of our politicians.'

Mumbai from 1993 to 2008 is proof of India's vulnerability and its inability to learn even from hindsight. On 23 November, three days before the mayhem in Mumbai, the prime minister, while addressing the director generals of police had said, 'We cannot afford to be hit again.' It is time to implement the reports authored by some of the best security experts because even then it will take at least five years before an Indian prime minister can promise that we will not be hit again.

Apart from the lucid details of Kuber's journey from Pakistani waters, the internal security apparatus can also be judged through another instance. Funds for the MAC were released only seven years after it was first set up and it is only now that it has been empowered by an executive order under the Constitution. It is only now that it will begin in earnest, a task that had been mandated seven years ago. It is only now that P. Chidambaram has promised that no agency will be allowed to pass the buck.

P. Chidambaram knows what he is talking about and he has been candid enough in admitting that the intelligence pointing to the Mumbai attack was as specific as it can get. He said in an interview published in the *Indian Express*, 'You will not get an invitation card which says you are cordially invited to come and witness a sea side incursion into India.' He knows the problem areas are grave – the giver and the receiver of the information on Mumbai were neither talking to each other, nor giving any information. Clearly, even in the case of the SIM cards, intelligence could not have been more actionable but there are turf wars and egos that dominate the intelligence apparatus. MAC will now be asking questions and its officers are going to be held accountable even for not asking the right questions.

The humiliation in Mumbai – ten terrorists holding the country to ransom for sixty hours – has come as the much needed and long overdue wake-up call. Only three days before 26/11, Manmohan Singh had said that we cannot afford to be hit again. Equally true is the analysis that it will take at least five years of continuous work and accountability, for that truth to become a reality.

About the Authors

Ashish Khetan is a journalist who has done several cutting-edge investigative stories for the newsmagazine *Tehelka* before moving to the Hindi news channel, Aaj Tak. His daring exposé of the collusive nexus between the Gujarat government and the Hindu right-wing perpetrators of the Gujarat riots of 2002, broke new ground in investigative journalism in 2007. He has personally interviewed the policemen involved and key eyewitnesses for his account of the terror attacks in Mumbai in November 2008.

Bachi Karkaria has created and edited some of the Times Group's most successful publications. 'Erratica', her satirical column in the *Sunday Times* has a huge following, as does 'Giving Gyan', a relationships advice column in the group's *Mumbai Mirror*. Passionate about cities, she pioneered in-depth writing on urban issues in India. Her other specialization is AIDS. She is the first Indian on the board of the World Editors Forum. Her books include *Dare to Dream*, a bestseller biography of M.S. Oberoi, *Mumbai Masti* with Krsna Mehta, and *The Cake That Walked*, on Flurys, Kolkata's iconic tea room.

Chris Khetan is a media professional who has worked with radio, television, print and the web medium. She has presented news and music-related shows on radio and television. She is also known for her writings on human-interest issues, society, travel and food. Currently she is working with Tata Services where she writes for their publications – both print and web.

George Koshy is currently working with CNN-IBN as a principal correspondent. A freelance writer and poet, Koshy has worked with the *Asian Age*. A few of his 'remembered' stories as a journalist are the impact of the bird flu virus when it struck rural Maharashtra, the effect of the Narmada dam on the embankments of remote villages in Madhya Pradesh and Gujarat, as well as an exclusive interview of Sir Richard Branson, chairman of Virgin Group.

Harinder Baweja is editor, News and Investigations with *Tehelka* newsmagazine. She was earlier associate editor of *India Today* in Delhi. A current affairs reporter, she has written extensively on Punjab, Kashmir, Pakistan and Afghanistan. She was also in Iraq in mid-2003, reporting on the US invasion. Baweja has been writing on terrorism and defence for the last two decades and is also the author of a book titled, *Kargil: The Untold Story.*

Harsh Joshi is a Mumbai-based Dow Jones Newswires reporter. He went to the sites of the attack on the night of 26 November and also spoke to various eyewitnesses over the next three days.

Julio Francis Riberio is the former police commissioner of Mumbai and director general of police, Punjab. While in Punjab, he successfully dealt with Khalistani terrorism that had ravaged the state for a decade. He has also served as Ambassador of India to Romania after his retirement.

Rahul Shivshankar is a senior news editor and anchor with the news channel Times Now. He has previously worked with TV Today and he was the leader writer with the *Times of India*. He reported on the 26/11 terrorist attacks on Mumbai and was witness to events at the Chabad House.